The *Fin de Siècle* Imagination in Australia, 1890–1914

The *Fin de Siècle* Imagination in Australia, 1890–1914

Mark Hearn

BLOOMSBURY ACADEMIC
LONDON • NEW YORK • OXFORD • NEW DELHI • SYDNEY

BLOOMSBURY ACADEMIC
Bloomsbury Publishing Plc
50 Bedford Square, London, WC1B 3DP, UK
1385 Broadway, New York, NY 10018, USA
29 Earlsfort Terrace, Dublin 2, Ireland

BLOOMSBURY, BLOOMSBURY ACADEMIC and the Diana logo are trademarks of
Bloomsbury Publishing Plc

First published in Great Britain 2022
This paperback edition published 2024

Copyright © Mark Hearn, 2022

Mark Hearn has asserted his right under the Copyright, Designs and Patents Act, 1988, to
be identified as Author of this work.

For legal purposes the Acknowledgements on p. vii constitute an extension of this
copyright page.

Cover image © Charles Conder, *While Daylight Lingers* (detail), 1890. Oil on canvas,
35.7 × 56.0 cm. National Gallery of Victoria, Melbourne. Bequest of Mrs Mary Helen Keep,
1944. Photo: National Gallery of Victoria, Melbourne.

All rights reserved. No part of this publication may be reproduced or transmitted in any
form or by any means, electronic or mechanical, including photocopying, recording,
or any information storage or retrieval system, without prior permission in writing
from the publishers.

Bloomsbury Publishing Plc does not have any control over, or responsibility for, any third-
party websites referred to or in this book. All internet addresses given in this book were
correct at the time of going to press. The author and publisher regret any inconvenience
caused if addresses have changed or sites have ceased to exist, but can accept no
responsibility for any such changes.

A catalogue record for this book is available from the British Library.

Library of Congress Cataloging-in-Publication Data
Names: Hearn, Mark, 1959- author.
Title: The fin de siècle imagination in Australia, 1890-1914 / Mark Hearn.
Description: London; New York: Bloomsbury Academic, 2022. | Includes
bibliographical references and index.
Identifiers: LCCN 2022000822 (print) | LCCN 2022000823 (ebook) |
ISBN 9781350291393 (hardback) | ISBN 9781350291423 (paperback) |
ISBN 9781350291409 (pdf) | ISBN 9781350291416 (epub)
Subjects: LCSH: Australia–Biography. | Australia–History–1788-1900. |
Australia–Civilization–19th century. | Australia–Civilization–20th century.
Classification: LCC DU115.2.A2 H43 2022 (print) | LCC DU115.2.A2 (ebook) |
DDC 994.03/0922 [B]–dc23/eng/20220427
LC record available at https://lccn.loc.gov/2022000822
LC ebook record available at https://lccn.loc.gov/2022000823

ISBN: HB: 978-1-3502-9139-3
PB: 978-1-3502-9142-3
ePDF: 978-1-3502-9140-9
eBook: 978-1-3502-9141-6

Typeset by Deanta Global Publishing Services, Chennai, India

To find out more about our authors and books visit www.bloomsbury.com and
sign up for our newsletters.

Contents

List of figures	vi
Acknowledgements	vii

Introduction: Ends and beginnings: Life and mind at the Australian *fin de siècle*		1
1	The bush undertaker: Henry Lawson and the stragglers of the second industrial revolution	15
2	Rose Summerfield imagines a New Woman	43
3	The wanderer: Christopher Brennan's two lives in *fin de siècle* Sydney	63
4	'A modern Eve': Vida Goldstein stands for Parliament	87
5	'Some disquieting symptoms': Alfred Deakin's nervous breakdown	109
6	David Unaipon, 'the super-aborigine'	135
7	John Dwyer's family stories	155
Conclusion: *Fin de siècle afterlife*		177

Notes	187
Bibliography	223
Index	232

Figures

1	Norman Lindsay	2
2	In *While Daylight Lingers* (1890) Charles Conder exposed the isolation of human presence in the stark Australian landscape	10
3	The bush symbolized as fatal temptress found a vivid expression in the Australian *fin de siècle* imagination	20
4	Henry Lawson arrived in a town where economic pressures were bearing down on the working population, their families and the unemployed	28
5	Ferry punt and paddle steamers on the Darling River unloading wool at Bourke, *c.* 1892	30
6	A New Woman: Katherine Mannington Caffyn	46
7	'This is our moment – there's none other'	60
8	A wanderer 'on the way to himself'	66
9	*The Australian Magazine* flirted with the spirit of the transformative quest of Symbolism	74
10	Goldstein's 1903 election campaign reflected the gender and racial tensions concentrated at the *fin de siècle*	96
11	Goldstein defied the claim that the Victorian people 'are not yet anxious for . . . equality of the sexes'	105
12	Alfred Deakin in London, 1907	112
13	Many Australians shared Deakin's fascination with France	117
14	The 'lone hand' responds to the call to arms	126
15	'Tired . . . exhausted'	131
16	A 'pleasure-loving' white race flourished in 'Australia Felix'	137
17	David Unaipon's 1909 patent for a shearing tool	140
18	Point McLeay's fiftieth anniversary, 1909	150
19	John Dwyer (left) and John Arthur Andrews unfurl the Active Service Brigade's banner	166
20	Annie and Daniel Dwyer	172
21	Unveiling of the Henry Lawson Memorial, 1931	186

Acknowledgements

I acknowledge the traditional Aboriginal and Torres Strait Islander owners and custodians of the land described in these pages, and pay my respects to their Elders past, present and future. I acknowledge the Ngarrindjeri people, the traditional owners of the country (*ruwi*) in the Lower Murray, Lakes and Coorong region of South Australia, and the community of Raukkan.

This book has gestated in a research project that commenced in the millennial *fin de siècle*, cultivated in research publications and stimulated by the great benefit of fellowship awards for which I would like to acknowledge my deep appreciation. In 2006 I was the C. H. Currey Memorial Fellow at the State Library of New South Wales, researching the *fin de siècle* imagination in Australia. In 2014–15 I was able to devote attention to the prime ministership of Alfred Deakin as an Australian Prime Ministers Centre fellow, Museum of Australian Democracy, Canberra. In 2018 a visiting scholarship at the Centre for Philosophical Studies in History, University of Oulu, Finland, facilitated research into the historical periodization of the *fin de siècle*. I have also been significantly sustained from the counsel and encouragement of colleagues who kindly took the time to read chapter drafts. I would like to warmly thank Frank Bongiorno, Toby Davidson, Tanya Evans, Kate Fullagar, Stephen Garton, Alison Holland, Marion Maddox and Ian Tregenza. I also thank the anonymous referees and the Bloomsbury editors Maddie Holder and Abigail Lane for their encouragement and support. I would also like to thank the Department of History and Archaeology at Macquarie University for providing research funding and time. Work and life would not have been bearable without Margaret and my family, to whom this book is lovingly dedicated.

Introduction

Ends and beginnings: Life and mind at the Australian *fin de siècle*

The *fin de siècle* imagination in Australia reflected powerful movements that emerged from the mid-nineteenth century, exerting a transformative influence on culture, economy and society across the globe. Socialism and alternative religious faiths, ideas and therapies impacting medicine and the sciences, ranging from social Darwinism to psychology, generated hopes of boundless opportunity and intensified anxieties about the future. Reflections on the end of the century found focus in the deployment of a term 'originally French but afterwards cosmopolitan', as in 1899 the *Sydney Morning Herald* traced the evolution of the meanings associated with the phrase *fin de siècle*. In the period from 1890 to 1914, Australians employed a heterogeneous, and at times contradictory, metaphor, which could symbolize the promise of progress and technological innovation or capture a fear of national decline.[1] The term reflected an unstable compound of time and technology, capital and culture.[2] The people of the *fin de siècle* were caught in the ambiguities of the 'double consciousness' of the period, as old forms and new forces clashed and sometimes uneasily merged in a fragile trajectory towards twentieth-century modernity – between mysticism and scientific rationality, the emergence of pluralist philosophy and nationalism in contest with cosmopolitan or transnational ideas and movements.[3] The rational, objective construction of the world contested with the subjective experience of it. A tension between ends and beginnings shadowed the *fin de siècle* imagination in Australia.

Tracing its subjects from the early 1890s to the advent of the First World War in 1914, *The Fin de Siècle Imagination in Australia* provides a new perspective on their experience: the writers and poets Henry Lawson and Christopher Brennan; the first-wave feminists Rose Summerfield and Vida Goldstein; working-class radical and theosophist John Dwyer and his wife Annie, witness to the cost of iconoclasm; the inventor and Indigenous rights advocate David Unaipon; and apparently presiding magisterially over national life, the Australian prime minister Alfred Deakin, one of the architects of the federation of the colonies as the Commonwealth of Australia in 1901. As described in the chapter outlines, their stories draw out key themes of the *fin de siècle*: the impact of the second industrial revolution; first-wave feminism and the New Woman; the emergence of working-class mobilization, radical politics and anarchism; the intellectual ferment and exploration of alternative spirituality and psychical research; the racialized, 'scientific' rationales such as eugenics confining the Indigenous; the construction of *fin de siècle* liberal governance and industrial modernity. French influence was abundant in Australia in the period, helping to shape culture and intellectual fashion.[4] Christopher Brennan and Alfred Deakin were fluent in the language and eagerly immersed in the literature and philosophical ideas emanating from *fin de siècle* France.

The emergent international styles of Symbolism and Art Nouveau in literature and the plastic arts reflected the ambiguities of the Australian *fin de siècle*, invoked to challenge established forms of identity and perception while also enlisted, in Art Nouveau's whiplash line and flourishing natural forms, to signal that 'nature was taken possession of, and became a means for the urban wealthy of the Industrial Age to express their sense of abundance'.[5] Art Nouveau's 'cult of nature' was deployed in cultural journals like *Lone Hand* to celebrate an emerging young nation and white dominion over 'Australia Felix'.[6] Promoting

Figure 1 Norman Lindsay, cover illustration, *Lone Hand*, May 1907, National Library of Australia. Copyright A., C. and H. Glad.

a nascent national identity with French flair, Lone Hand was emblematic of the Australian *fin de siècle*, and its themes and illustrations resonate in several of the lives recounted here. Depictions of bush isolation, alternatively bleak or romanticized, provided a signature motif of the Australian *fin de siècle*: the bush undertaker and drover's wife of Henry Lawson stories, and Charles Conder's painting *While Daylight Lingers*. The illustration by the artist Norman Lindsay for the cover of the inaugural edition of *Lone Hand* in May 1907 celebrated a mythical white pioneer glorying in acquisitive individualism.[7] White Australians boasted of their national isolation and feared its consequences (Figure 1).

In *Vivid Faces*, a study of the Irish 'revolutionary generation' between the 1890s and 1923, R. F. Foster observed a growing recognition of the importance of life stories and mentalities in developing historical research of the revolutionary struggles of the period, in which individuals pursued both political change and cultural transformation.[8] In recent years the history of the *fin de siècle* and the New Woman has been enhanced by exploring the intersection between life experience, ideas and ideals, evident in Rachel Holmes's biographies of the energetic and outspoken spirit of the *fin de siècle* socialist and feminist Eleanor Marx and the radical suffragette Sylvia Pankhurst, and Sheila Rowbotham's biography of pioneering gay rights activist Edward Carpenter and her subsequent account of transnational radical and New Woman activists, *Rebel Crossings*.[9] In *Oscar Wilde and the Radical Politics of the Fin De Siècle*, Deaglan Ó Donghaile challenges representations of Wilde as politically disengaged, while Jessica M. Dandona uncovers the neglected story of French artist and designer Emile Gallé's passionate politics and nationalism.[10] These studies reflect the heterogeneous, and at times contradictory, impulses at work in the lives and minds of their subjects.

The biographical subjects of this book are representative of the engagement with the varied dynamics of the period and yet focus on a key theme of this book: how these apparently disparate lives were shaped by the intensification and acceleration of forces of culture, economy and technology that provided the transformative and distinctive nature of the *fin de siècle*. Reinhart Koselleck argued that from the Industrial Revolution the modern world 'unfolded under the sign of acceleration'.[11] Production, culture and time itself were transformed, releasing a future 'open and without boundaries'.[12] Tensions generated by accelerated openness characterized the *fin de siècle*. There was no identification of a 'New Woman' without a technological and communicative revolution that enabled faster and cheaper forms of print production, disseminating an identity that also attracted a hostile reaction. The innovations that sped large-scale industrialization also concentrated on urban workforces and stimulated the mobilizations of the working-class and radical politics. Intensification of racialized anxieties could not have occurred without the technological innovations in shipping – the transition from sail to steam – that enabled unprecedented population movement and allowed minds to focus upon the threat of that transfer. New military and naval technologies drew the sudden threat of imperial rivalry or racial invasion closer.

The nature of the Australian *fin de siècle* is revealed in the infiltration of these forces in the lives and minds of individual subjects. Henry Lawson was a sensitive witness to the accelerations of the late nineteenth-century pastoral industry and its impact on subjects compelled to conform to its demands on the frontier of late colonial society. Rose Summerfield's conception of the New Woman could not tolerate the inclusion of non-whites, from whom she recoiled in Sydney's streets, as they seemed to swarm from ships and in marketplaces. Alfred Deakin's liberal policy agenda was driven by a reaction to accelerating industrial modernity; his obsessive and diverse reading illuminates how Deakin turned to culture to make sense of the vibrant, strange and intimidating forces that confronted him and the nation that he led. Idealism was complicated by anxiety, resistance and plain contradiction. Many of these subjects extolled freedom and rights for some while denying those benefits to others – denials fashioned by racial fear, gender discrimination and class marginalization. This unresolved tension provides a key for exploring the historical specificity of the *fin de siècle* imagination in Australia, as subjects moving from colony to nation negotiated an unstable world of change brimming with novelty and opportunity, and imminent with powerfully imagined threats.

Historical research into the *fin de siècle* has significantly developed in recent decades, challenging assumptions of a narrow literary-cultural domain or a tight 1890s time frame. The authoritative survey *The Fin de Siècle World*, published in 2015, and other works have departed from privileging high culture to 'surveying a diversity of fields', as Mikulas Teich and Roy Porter describe in the project of the contributors to *Fin de Siècle and Its Legacy*.[13] In forty-five chapters *The Fin de Siècle World* spanned a wide range of topics, transnational connections and national settings across a 'loose periodization' from 1870 to 1914, although Australia was one of 'the topics and locales it was unable to include'. *The Fin de Siècle World*'s diversity reflected a 'third wave' of research, acknowledging that the dynamism of the *fin de siècle* was as much a result of global exchanges as local challenges to traditional norms.[14] Christopher Bayly argued that the distinctive characteristics of the *fin de siècle* were generated by the 'great acceleration' in the period 1890–1914 of economic, technological and cultural forces that swept the globe.[15] There has been less specific research development on the subject of the *fin de siècle* in Australian historiography, although a range of works have addressed important aspects of the culture and politics, gender relations and racial anxieties of the period.[16] It has been argued that the term *fin de siècle* distracts attention from 'the extent to which 1890s Australia was preoccupied with the birth of the new century rather than the end of the old'.[17] As a device for repudiating illegitimate values or outmoded systems, the deployment of the term cleared a path of progress. In 1897 the Australian press celebrated Marconi's 'wonderful discovery' of 'telegraphing without wires . . . a fitting tribute to the enterprise of this *fin de siècle* age'.[18] *Fin de siècle* discourse helped Australians break with the past in order to imagine a modern future.[19] By focusing explicitly on individuals negotiating the historical condition and perspectives of the *fin de siècle*, *The fin de siècle Imagination in Australia* offers a new perspective on historical interpretations of the nature of the emerging Australian nation and the global transformations that formed it.

Australia was a site upon which *fin de siècle* hopes and fears could be projected. As the world turned to a new century, observers from other nations saw Australia as a form of experiment, observing the productive energy that also seemed to convey anxieties that troubled progress.[20] That Australia was either breaking with degeneracy or being overcome by it was a dilemma exercising

> the secret uneasiness of many English minds. It has for a long time been plain to the thoughtful that the immense capacities of Australia were not being developed, and that sooner or later the task which the Australians expressly decline will be taken in hand. . . . The few white people in Australia are face to face with the ever-growing strength and self-conscious intelligence of the giant peoples of the East.[21]

Yet Londoners were also assured in 1909 that Australia was a complacent 'working man's Paradise'. The leader of international Theosophy, Annie Besant, and a recent visitor to Britain's distant dominion, declared, 'the working classes have got everything that they are asking for here. . . . No need of agitation there.' Yet the boys cared more for football and girls for bonnets than 'the way in which their votes ought to be cast. They have all got the vote, and do not know what to do with it'.[22] Perhaps that was due to youth coddled by the encroaching reach of the state, as a study of Australia published in New York declared. 'The State trains teachers and manages the Schools. . . . The State regulates the hours of labor, fixes wages, and decides industrial disputes. All this cannot tend to strength and individuality of character, and necessitates the existence of a large official class.'[23] Troubled by a sense of remoteness, Australians seemed content to be enfolded in the arms of state-legislated 'protection' of race and economy. Following a visit to Australia in October 1906, the British Labour leader Ramsay MacDonald published *Labour and the Empire*, in which he observed that 'the cry of White Australia' and the tariff protection of industry were 'fixing itself like a million-rooted parasite in every fibre of the national life'.[24] MacDonald travelled 'a land of vastness and of solitary and mournful men'. In the 'dense scrub' there was a 'funereal solemnity brooding over those dark masses of deep green which enters one's soul like a chilling mist'. In Sydney and Melbourne, MacDonald found that 'the greed of commerce fills the lives of men'.[25] *Labour and the Empire* was a product of the 'global phenomenon' of the *fin de siècle*: a manifestation of the 'widely diffused cultural artefacts' generated in the period, reflecting an emerging consciousness of 'sense-making whereby countries and cultures reflect on each other's experiences, past and present, and then reflect on each other's reflections'.[26] In the period the Australian press was fascinated with reproducing reports of 'As Others See Us'. In the eyes of others, Australia was observed as an other of the self and how the white European subject might break down from the strain of pioneering a remote settler society beset by strangers and a strange environment.

Australians helped to shape the global *fin de siècle*. Vida Goldstein engaged in the international development of first-wave feminism in the United States, working alongside the pioneering American feminist Susan B. Anthony at the International Woman Suffrage Conference in Washington in 1902. Christopher Brennan exchanged correspondence and his work with the leading French Symbolist Stéphane Mallarmé, who described his 'dreamlike affinity' with the Australian poet. Alfred Deakin was a key agent of the 'New Imperialism', promoting John Seeley's conception of 'Greater Britain', communities of common race and interest, as new rivals, such as Germany and Japan, emerged to challenge Britain's imperial hegemony and the racial unity of the empire's 'white dominions' and the mother country.[27] Deakin advocated imperial federation through closer trade ties with Britain. In 1907 Deakin emerged as an influential advocate in Britain of adopting schemes to enhance military preparedness, including compulsory military training. Deakin was also a fervent advocate of a 'White Australia', and in 1901 he introduced legislation, in the first session of the new Commonwealth Parliament, that provided a model of institutionalized resistance to non-white immigration, influencing the terms of the Aliens Act passed by the British Parliament in 1905.[28] Federation provided its own stimulus to the impact of the *fin de siècle*, evident in initiatives of progressive reform, such as the granting of voting rights to women in 1902 – an innovation which attracted worldwide attention – and in responses against trade, racial and potential military threats.[29] Deakin sought to harness the powers of the state to protect Australians through a 'mingling of xenophobia and idealism'.[30] Federation also provided a fulfilment of the globally imagined ascendancy of the white man by denying any recognition of the Indigenous in the new Commonwealth and its Constitution.[31] Denial stimulated demands for Indigenous recognition, as championed by David Unaipon.

In Australia the impact of global industrial modernity unfolded, and the consequences of this extraordinary development emerged. In the last decades of the nineteenth century, and the first decade of the twentieth century, a '*fin de siècle* industrial transformation' generated a 'second industrial revolution', propelled by a surge in technological innovation. 'The new technologies brought into being a new type of industrial enterprise . . . and a new system of global capitalism', based in unprecedentedly powerful corporations and trusts, such as US Steel and Standard Oil.[32] The opportunities for these corporations to reach product markets and energy resources around the globe were facilitated by the advent of the steamship – and the power of nation states and empires to open new markets and resource access through colonial conquest. Christopher Bayly stressed that while 'rapidly developing connections . . . created . . . complex forms of global economic activity', these connections could also intensify antagonism between nations and increased racial anxieties in settler societies such as Australia.[33] British 'white men's countries' 'rested on the premise that multiracial democracy was an impossibility', a fear aroused as the mass migration of non-white peoples at the turn of the century seemed to threaten white European identity in the distant reaches of the empire.[34] As a consequence of globalization in the period, 'there was simply no escaping one another; the world had become one large community with a shared destiny'.[35] William Thomson's (Lord Kelvin) research breakthroughs transmitted electricity from science into global culture, enabling the laying of undersea telegraph cables – first across the Atlantic in 1866, then binding the world in a system of intercontinental communication through cable news networks and the rapid transfer of knowledge that exposed hungry minds to the intensifying ideas, fantasies and anxieties of the *fin de siècle*.[36] The 'vitality and multiplicity' of the 'creative energy' unleashed at the *fin de siècle* becomes, Gail Marshall argues, 'the most effective statement against our understanding of this period as the end of anything'.[37]

It was not always easy to discern beginnings from ends. *Fin de siècle* quests were often enervating and unquenchable; the process of narrating an identity is 'an unstable ordering of multiple possibilities' which readily evaporated into ennui and failure.[38] In contrast to observations of the 'creative energy' unleashed at the *fin de siècle*, John Jervis has argued that *fin de siècle* decadence reflected an 'energy crisis', a fear of 'self-destructive extravagance leading to degeneration', fuelling the sombre forecasts of Max Nordau in *Degeneration* (1895), as he observed the dissolute *fin de siècle* 'dusk of nations'. Jervis argues that decadence 'testifies to the lateness of the modern . . . over-ripe, rotten'. Perceptions of lateness and degeneration reflect a dissipation of energy, a sense that the effort expended on creativity and activism has failed to achieve the aspired breakthrough. The *fin de siècle* witnessed a number of programmes and policies, scientific and technological innovations designed to more efficiently harness energy for productive purposes and accelerate progress and modernity; acceleration seemed an end in itself, regardless of consequence. Alfred Deakin's 1905–8 government provided an intersection for the direction of these urgent productive energies, and Deakin himself was identified as a highly efficient and dedicated agent of this transfer – although he was also identified as a nervously intense personality whose capacity to govern almost irretrievably broke down in 1907 and thereafter never quite recovered.

The capacity of the body to function under stress was a crucial dilemma of the *fin de siècle*. Andreas Killen has observed that the economic and social accelerations of the period were reconfiguring 'the physical and social geography of the late nineteenth-century world. It was also not lost on observers that similar transformations were occurring at the level of the body', heightening productive output or triggering exhaustion and nervous breakdown.[39] Deakin and the writer Henry Lawson felt compelled to conduct a surveillance of this internalized struggle. The question of who controlled the body was also key: Shearer West argued that 'one of the strongest focal points of early feminism was the idea that women should be in control of their own bodies'.[40] The feminists Rose Summerfield and Vida Goldstein contested for this control in the public sphere, as disruptive agents of reform. They drew upon the transnational discourse of the New Woman and progressive politics to shape their mobilizations, although like the subjects of Sheila Rowbotham's studies of radical and New Women activists in the period, 'they found that their lived experience jostled against their hopes and quests'.[41] Many working-class women were driven from participation in the public sphere by the demands on mind and body of work and the home. Annie Dwyer, the wife of the theosophist and working-class radical John Dwyer, was confronted with the family consequences of his dreamy proselytizing as she was left to manage the physical grind of running boarding houses. The inventor David Unaipon endured surveillance and control of his body in public space, even as he emerged as a narrator of his life, ideas and the rights of the Indigenous.

Unaipon craved an immersion in the accelerations of *fin de siècle* industrial modernity by mastering the energy of perpetual motion and harnessing electricity to hurl as a weapon of the future.

* * *

The chapters of this book explore how the subject narrates experience and constructs identity, and is shaped by the narrative currents around them. Patrick Joyce has observed 'the centrality of narrative to social life': 'stories guide action . . . people construct identities (however multiple and changing) by locating themselves or being located within a repertoire of emplotted stories.'[42] The subjects of this study were skilled narrators, able to link compelling stories of their lives with their ideals. A diverse emplotment seemed intensely available at the *fin de siècle*, as the ferment of the 'new' opened the possibility of breaking with traditional religious and political forms, gender constraints and established forms of identity: 'the new woman, the new imperialism, the new realism, the new drama, and the new journalism, all arriving alongside "new" human sciences like psychology, psychical research, sexology and eugenics.'[43]

The *fin de siècle* emerged as colonial progress was destabilized in the late 1880s and early 1890s. Australia was gripped by economic depression, drought and bushfire conditions that heightened personal struggle and disquiet over the future, and which found cultural expression in the works of artists and writers. The Heidelberg School of Australian impressionism that emerged in the late 1880s, and which included the artists Tom Roberts, Arthur Streeton and Charles Conder, captured a sense of emerging Australian identity and romanticized the harsh conditions of Australian bush life, depicted in their *plein air* paintings executed on the fringe of Melbourne. Symbolist and Art Nouveau motifs emerged in their work, notably Conder's *Hot Wind* and *Mirage*, both painted in 1889, as the devastating impact of drought and bushfire intensified.[44] In *While Daylight Lingers* (1890), Conder exposed the isolation of human presence in an almost abstract rendering of the stark Australian landscape.[45] These works are emblematic of diverse connections between creative forces and anxieties that characterized the *fin de siècle* in Australia. Conder's links with Australian contemporaries are observed in several chapters, and the conclusion reflects on the meanings applied to Conder's life and work in the afterlife of the Australian *fin de siècle* (Figure 2).

In the period 1892–4, the fraught conditions of economy and environment found expression in the work of the writer Henry Lawson, drawn from the colonial capital, Sydney, to capture the alienation of rural life. 'I am the rassaraction', Lawson's inebriated bush undertaker prayed over the withered remains of a mate

Figure 2 In *While Daylight Lingers* (1890) Charles Conder exposed the isolation of human presence in the stark Australian landscape. National Gallery of Victoria.

who died alone on a bush track.[46] Lawson provided an extraordinary witness to the impact of an intensifying global industrial revolution on those labouring in the operations of the pastoral industry in the Bourke district of north-western New South Wales. Lawson interpreted this impact through the lens of *fin de siècle* influences that filtered into his perceptions and his writing. Lawson's work exhibited a profound apprehension of the punishing effects of work and alienation on the mind and body of the 'stragglers' he observed, and who were often reduced to a residue of processed refuse: 'nothing matters', the old bush undertaker of Lawson's eponymous story muttered over the grave.

Henry Lawson's Bourke experience has come to form the centre of the legend built around his life: the radical and feminist Rose Summerfield's agitation in Bourke on behalf of women workers dissolved into the oblivion of the archive. Rose Summerfield pursued a quest for transformation in the 1890s through the force of her agitation for the causes of women's suffrage and justice for workers; the technological, industrial and discursive conditions of the *fin de siècle* provided her opportunity. Unable to control the space in which she and other workers functioned, Summerfield imagined another sphere of the new world that seemed to offer a promise of the transformation she imagined: the dream of a New Australia, in William Lane's socialist colony in Paraguay, for which she set out in 1899, even as it was already too late to embrace that failing experiment.

Gail Marshall observes that 'there is some debate as to the extent to which the New Woman existed beyond the pages of the novels, short stories and newspapers of which she was an integral part'.⁴⁷ Rose Summerfield and the feminist and political progressive Vida Goldstein embodied the idea of the New Woman, even as doing so rendered them targets for the hostility and derision directed at that disruptive identity. In 1895 Rose Summerfield defended the New Woman against the 'contempt and sneers' of the press.⁴⁸ Anxieties over biological degeneration saw the term invoked in a gendered discourse to repel this apparent threat and enforce the domestic subjection of women, and particularly to compel young women to accept their childbearing function. The Sydney *Evening News* warned that the '*fin de siècle* New Woman is all wrong from start to finish, and a national disaster'.⁴⁹

Fears over the impact of the New Woman re-emerged during the federal election in December 1903, the first in which women could vote and stand for office. Vida Goldstein defied confinement to the traditional roles allocated to women by standing as a candidate for the Australian Commonwealth Senate. A ditty circulated in the press in Victoria in 1903 about an identity whose troubling ambiguity was signalled with the insertion of a question mark in the title: the 'New (?) Woman', 'always hurrying and humming', had a 'heaven-born ambition to reform the world's condition', with 'a great variety of remedies at hand'.⁵⁰ The diverse variety of women's rights and social reforms that Goldstein advocated reflected the opportunities for social change that seemed to become available at the *fin de siècle*. Vida Goldstein found her vibrant energies hemmed by the intensifications of gendered industrialized work and machine party politics that increasingly defined post-Federation Australia.

Symbolism provided the poet Christopher Brennan with a metaphor of transcendence, as he attempted to recast his life and pursue his literary and intellectual ambitions. Denied a position at the University of Sydney despite academic brilliance, and unable to make a public mark as a leading scholar and poet, Brennan felt suspended in 'two lives', as he observed in 1904: 'The imperfection is in ourselves; the imperfection of a divided consciousness, a divided life; war within us and war upon the earth.' Brennan made this observation in his lecture series, 'Symbolism in Nineteenth Century Literature'.⁵¹ Providing an original and wide-ranging exploration of literary symbolism and Brennan's engagement with the *fin de siècle* imagination, the lectures have received relatively little attention in commentaries on his life and work. Two years earlier, Brennan had published his 'Wanderer' poems, a cycle that reflected the end of his quest to seek transformation through his literary project. Edward Said argued that 'lateness is being at the end, fully conscious, full of memory, and also very (even preternaturally) aware of the present'.⁵² It was an awareness of being held in 'a limbo of defeated glory', suspended in an exhausted present full of memory, which lent Brennan's 'Wanderer' poems their expressive power.⁵³

Serving three terms as prime minister of Australia between 1901 and 1910, Alfred Deakin's private writings were expressions of a spiritual search, and often preoccupied with the ethics of living in the world, and hence provide access to 'the connections between the private man and the public world of events and actions'.⁵⁴ This quandary found traumatic focus in the physical and emotional breakdown Deakin experienced in mid-1907: the tensions of the public and private spheres collided. Deakin's prodigious reading reflected his enthusiasm for a welter of new ideas and alternative spiritualism as he struggled to revive and lead himself, and the nation, to meet the challenges posed by early twentieth-century modernity, particularly in response to threats of war, and international trade competition. Deakin's negotiation of the imaginative and material conditions of the *fin de siècle* world is brought into focus by exploring the crisis that threatened to unravel self and career.

At the *fin de siècle* technology and industry shaped cultural response. The Aboriginal activist and inventor David Unaipon wanted to be part of the dynamics generated by the second industrial revolution of the late nineteenth and early twentieth centuries, as he worked to create a device to harness the force of perpetual motion. A devout Protestant Christian, Unaipon absorbed and interpreted the tension between tradition and innovation, as he was assessed by the standards of established prejudice and new conceptions of race that emerged at the *fin de siècle*: pseudo-scientific discourses of eugenics and race increasingly classified the lives of Unaipon and Indigenous Australians; in reflecting on Unaipon's life and activism, it is regretfully necessary to refer to prejudicial opinions and language imposed on the Indigenous in the period. Most research on Unaipon focuses on the publication of *Legendary Tales of the Australian Aborigines* and the interwar period.⁵⁵ It was in the years 1907–14 that Unaipon was the subject of sustained press attention as the 'Aboriginal genius', as his many public speeches ranged across science and Christian religion, Aboriginal culture and mysticism, and Indigenous activism. Little of his ideas and activism in the pre-1914 period has been explored in depth, nor how Unaipon adapted Darwinism and eugenics in service to his world view and defence of the rights and identity of the Indigenous. Tim Rowse has identified a need to acknowledge the 'heterogeneity' of Indigenous historical experience of settler colonialism, suspicious of assumptions of white 'elimination' of the Indigenous and histories in which 'every instance of Indigenous agency is under suspicion of being "state-conceded"'.⁵⁶

David Unaipon's self-generated agency emerged at a moment when his race was denied a place in the new nation and when the control of his people by the state reflected a tension between protection and an anticipation of imminent Aboriginal demise.

Unaipon's adaptation of evolutionary theory demonstrates how science shaded into 'scientific ideology' at the *fin de siècle* and as expressed in the works of T. H. Huxley, Herbert Spencer, Francis Galton and Edwin Ray Lankester, Darwinists who helped to define a wide range of anxieties and social problems through a filter of scientific terminology. Sally Ledger and Roger Luckhurst argued that 'one of the most marked features of the *fin de siècle* is the authority given to science. Notions of developmental progress or degenerative and entropic decline insistently inform discussions of the individual, the city, and the nation-state.'[57] David Unaipon's narratives and Alfred Deakin's reading, and Deakin's 'survival of the fittest' anxieties expressed in statements on trade and defence policy, reflected these influences.

John Dwyer's restless immersion in new ideas, from Theosophy and the occult to radical Socialism and Darwinism, was driven by a quest for personal and social transformation.[58] Dwyer shared this impatient urge with radicals and writers, including Henry Lawson and Rose Summerfield, who exchanged ideas and experience in the area around Sydney's lower Castlereagh Street, a working-class district in the south of the city. Dwyer hoped that assimilation of *fin de siècle* ideas, and their projection into social reality, might 'change the face of the world', as he recorded in one of his occult manuscripts, relieving his alienated spirit and transforming the impoverished material circumstances he endured in Sydney from the 1890s and into the new century, as he experienced chronic unemployment and his family endured poverty. Dwyer's hybrid belief system reflected the double consciousness of the period. Matthew Beaumont has identified an 'elective affinity' between the apparent 'ideological contradictions' of *fin de siècle* socialism and occultism. 'The occult can be shaped by the hope of active social transformation as well as the despondent dream of passively escaping society altogether.'[59] Dwyer's activism and embrace of imaginative ferment were forms of cultural acceleration that yielded only exhaustion. By the years immediately preceding the outbreak of the First World War in 1914, Dwyer's story provides a rare account of the consequences of iconoclastic activism, producing a reaction within the family that reflected the personal cost of the pursuit of transformation. Dwyer's activism exacerbated the economic hardship of his family and alienated him from the traditional religious faith shared by his wife and children. Annie Dwyer struggled to exercise control over the terms of her life and could do little to alleviate the suffering of their son Daniel, stricken with tuberculosis, the 'white plague' of the *fin de siècle* world.

The conclusion reflects on the post-1914 fate of its subjects and the impact of the First World War on their lives and ideals. The global conflict divided Australian society and simplified notions of identity and belief: nation and empire defined the terms of causes embraced and forms of public self-expression. With little in common as pre-war literary identities, Christopher Brennan and Henry Lawson were idealized as champions of patriotic loyalty. The political priorities of war rode over John Dwyer's radicalism, effectively silencing him. Vida Goldstein stood against the tide of militarism and endured vilification and derision. Regardless of posture, by war's end almost all the subjects of this study were physically and creatively spent. Only David Unaipon found renewal in the legends of his own people, yet he was unable to control these stories in a public sphere from which his people were excluded.

By developing an understanding of the depth of the transnational exchange of ideas, social movements and the globalization of culture and production that characterized the period, this book enhances the international historical debate on the nature of the *fin de siècle*. The themes of this book remain relevant in a new era of intensive globalization. Historians have recognized that the tensions and anxieties of the *fin de siècle* have resonated in recent decades. Perhaps this is because, as Shearer West has argued, that while the First World War seem to terminate the period, it 'did not resolve the political, social and cultural tensions of the *fin de siècle*, which continue to haunt us as we approach the millennial year 2000'.[60] In the millennium marking the turn to the twenty-first century, the hopes and fears of the *fin de siècle* and its accelerations of 'science, technology, population, radical belief systems' re-emerged. A condition of 'millennium fatalism' was characterized by 'the sceptre of finality, of apocalypse'.[61]

'To make an end', the modernist poet T. S. Eliot observed, 'is to make a beginning'.[62] Reconsidering the transitional moment that prefigured twentieth-century modernity involves rethinking ends and beginnings. The Australian subjects of the *fin de siècle* pursued dreams of renewal. In Australia the *fin de siècle* imagination reflected the international and local transmission of ideas, and the accelerating forces transforming economy and environment. *The Fin de Siècle Imagination in Australia* describes how that energy shaped the lives of historical subjects, and both fed and challenged the assumptions that constituted the modern nation that emerged from the turbulence at the turn of the century. In search of this history the end, as represented by Henry Lawson in the death of the subject, is where we begin.

1

The bush undertaker

Henry Lawson and the stragglers of the second industrial revolution

The whole of the back country has been swarming with idle men ever since the completion of last season's shearing. These men have been hanging on in a state of semi-starvation, their only hope of obtaining employment lying in the return of the busy season. The shearing season has come, and with it also death to their hopes.[1]
I am the rassaraction.[2]

The death of hope, the end of life itself; the district around Bourke provided a macabre variety of extinction in 1892. The body of Henty Anderson was found in a small water tank near Louth. 'It is believed he was overcome by the terrific heat . . . and fell off the water cart, which he was filling from the tank, the water in which was only 2ft 6in deep.'[3] The remains of George Blair were discovered 4 miles from Temora. 'It appears the unfortunate man was riding an unmanageable horse, which ran him against a tree, smashing the frontal and nasal bones, and causing concussion of the brain; death being instantaneous. A verdict of accidental death was returned.'[4] A 'shocking' fate befell Thomas Frost, run over by a contractor's engine on the Cobar line. 'It appears that Frost went to sleep, his head being on the rails and one arm serving as a pillow. The engine cut the upper portion of his skull clean off and severed the arm. The head was terribly disfigured. Death must have been instantaneous. A verdict of accidental death was returned.'[5]

It is believed, it appears; perishing in isolation, no one quite knew what happened to these men. Sometimes the evidence of the body was plain enough. From Bourke came news in November 1892 of 'a most determined suicide'.

A teamster named Hill on Sunday, when near Dry Lake, noticed a man under some trees off the road. Thinking from the man's position that something was wrong, Hill went over, and discovered that apparently a suicide had been accomplished by cutting the throat from ear to ear with a razor. From papers in the man's swag, deceased's name appears to have been Patrick Murphy. In his teeth was tightly clenched the stem of a pipe, and, from appearances, it is probable the deceased was standing when he committed the deed. He had Queensland union tickets on him, which give his address as North Bargorah.[6]

An identity solely based in a right to unionize and whose pursuit of work had succumbed to despair by the mordantly appropriate Dry Lake. In June 1892 *The Sydney Mail* observed how the Bourke plains had been described as both 'sea' and 'barren waste' on white explorers' maps in the early nineteenth century, figurations shaped by bewildered confrontations with flood and drought. Since the township was established in the 1860s, it was the absence of water, save for the sluggish shallow flow of the Darling and Warrego Rivers, which clarified the stark nature of this vast space of red dust, scrabbled scrub and gum trees whose bleached branches teetered leaves in small crowns over their sparse shadows. 'Eighteen month's drought is a common thing here, and it has been dry for six months now.'[7] In the arid reaches of north-western New South Wales, Europeans readily perished from the brutal beating of the summer heat or the contrary nature of the livestock with which they were compelled to labour. Work, primarily on pastoral stations devoted to the export trade of wool, provided a common thread of the deaths recorded around Bourke: the need to perform tasks whatever the risks or conditions, the pressure to find a job or make a living, or the desire to be finally free of work's burden. Driven by global economic turmoil that triggered collapsing commodity prices, and spectacular bank failures that would within months be replicated in Australia, the colonial economy was tipping into depression in 1892.[8]

Isolation had been compounded by appropriation. Murdered, decimated by disease and dispersed from tribal lands since Thomas Mitchell's expedition had reached the Darling River in 1835, the radically reduced Indigenous population had been expelled to the margins of white settlement, contained in atomized pools of pastoral labour, denied wages and sustained with meagre rations. In 1892 the Aborigines Protection Board registered the Indigenous population in the Bourke township at 29. By that year, the European population of Bourke had risen over a twenty-year period from 500 to 3,500.[9] The scored space of dispossession, the apparent emptiness of the Bourke plains, was deceptive: by 1892 the 'second industrial revolution' of the mid to late nineteenth century left few parts of the earth 'untouched by Western expansion', reflected in a 'great acceleration' of global trade and unprecedentedly powerful corporations, technological innovation and intensifying systems of production. Andreas Killen observes that the acceleration 'that marked the *fin de siècle* included a process of increasing standardization' of the spaces in which bodies laboured, provoking 'new possibilities of heightened output but also of its inverse, pathological exhaustion or nervous breakdown'.[10]

Across the Bourke district a scattered swarm of unemployed pastoral workers dissipated their energies in pursuit of a mirage of work. By 1892, the pressure to be useful and sustain the well-being of the self, or a family, compelled men to risk dying of thirst as they tramped the tracks of the Bourke plains. Men crowded the gates at pastoral stations, desperate for a 'start' and renewing a respected function in production and progress. In Australian discourse Bourke is associated with remoteness, 'the outback', a sense of freedom from the confinements of urban life – descriptions that masked a vast system of enclosure, in which the human body was allocated productive functions or discarded as surplus. Privatized, mapped and fenced, penetrated by the grids of telegraph and railway, the domain of which Bourke formed a centre was absorbed into the 'single organism' of production and sensitive to 'power shifts anywhere on the globe'.[11]

Reflecting on the spatial dynamics of the nineteenth century, Jürgen Osterhammel observed that core spaces, such as cities, 'radiate out and draw in'; 'peripheries are the weaker poles in asymmetrical relations with cores', where 'people and power, creativity, and symbolic capital are concentrated together'. Yet 'new things keep appearing on peripheries', in a space of 'boundless possibility'.[12] In September 1892 the railway transferred an emissary of *fin de siècle* modernity, that turbulent combine of technology and industry, culture and innovation, from centre to periphery, an intervention that stirred something new into being. In the period 1892–4 a young Henry Lawson provided a profoundly creative response to an extraordinary opportunity: as witness to the impact of the second industrial revolution and interpreting it through the lens of *fin de siècle* influences that filtered into his perceptions and his work. Gifting five pounds to Henry Lawson and putting him on the train from Sydney to Bourke proved an efficient means of generating *fin de siècle* culture. Shrewdly, and perhaps cruelly, in making his investment in future copy the editor of the *Bulletin*, J. F. Archibald, had purchased only a one-way ticket on Lawson's behalf.[13]

By 1892 the 25-year-old Lawson had made a name for himself as a poet and writer of short 'sketches' that captured the character of colonial life; he was the scribe of the isolated, those who laboured in neglect or fell victim to a lonely death, their identities obscured or lost. The fate of workers like Henty Anderson and Patrick Murphy regularly tolled in the press in 1892 and shaded into Lawson's fiction. Lawson focused on the harsh conditions experienced by poor bush selectors, itinerant workers and the unemployed who milled Sydney before being dispatched into the rural hinterland of New South Wales by the Government Labour Bureau – ostensibly to find work, but also to reduce the unemployed's visibility and potential for disruption in the colonial capital.[14] Born in the rural town of Grenfell in central west New South Wales in 1867, Lawson's parents had separated while Henry was in his early teens. Lawson's partial deafness, a consequence of childhood illness, exacerbated a tendency to shyness and reticence. By 1880 Lawson was a habitué of a radical milieu in Sydney, where Louisa raised Henry as a single mother while struggling to establish her enterprises: Louisa Lawson was a feminist and publisher of the *Republican* and the *Dawn*, the latter inaugurated in 1888 to advocate women's issues and employing a number of women in her printing business.[15] Henry provided copy for the *Republican* and began to publish poems, including 'A Song of the Republic' (1887) and 'The Faces in the Street' (1888), which advocated republicanism and drew attention to the plight of the unemployed.[16] A number of Lawson's poems and stories appeared in the *Bulletin* from 1887, the provocative weekly journal established in 1880 and which under Archibald's editorship advocated nationalism and republicanism, and embraced 'the bush' as the genuine site of emerging Australian identity.[17] In 1891 Lawson briefly worked in Brisbane on the staff of the *Boomerang*, edited by the fiery labour journalist William Lane, although the journal's financial troubles soon left Lawson unemployed and forced to return to Sydney. Impoverished and inclined to drink, by 1892 Lawson was in need of income and inspiration.[18]

The outpouring of sketches, in fiction and non-fiction, that Lawson produced on the basis of his experience of Bourke and the north-west between September 1892 and March 1893 was focused on subjective domains – the body and the mind. Lawson's response to the conditions he experienced and observed in Bourke reflected one of the most intense contradictions that characterized the *fin de siècle*: the tension between 'the life of the spirit', the 'inner life' and the demands of participation in a culture that exalted 'competition and industrialization'.[19] By the late nineteenth century new technologies and the demands of work were seen to have a degenerating effect, reflecting 'the dark side of progress'.[20]

In his stories Lawson exhibited a skill for sketching an unsettling mix of the comic and the tragic, as he probed the inner life and the potential for empathetic connections between subject and reader. Two stories published in 1892 reflect

Lawson forming his imaginative response before he stepped from the train in Bourke. 'A Christmas in the Far West', or 'The Bush Undertaker', was published in November 1892. The setting was sourced from Lawson's trip to Mudgee in central west New South Wales earlier in the year. In its portrayal of bush life and in the subject of the story, inspiration for 'The Bush Undertaker', as the story has become known, might readily have been found in the country around Bourke and not least in the account of lonely death. The story unfolds a mordant comedy of corpses. Having made the shocking discovery of the 'blackened features' of a human body in 'a gully full of dead ringed-barked trees', an ageing, isolated and eccentric shepherd realizes – or imagines – that the remains are of an old friend, a shearer known only as 'Brummy'. On Christmas Day the unnamed shepherd buried Brummy and struggled for some appropriate words as he lowered the body into a makeshift grave. '"Brummy", he said at last, "nothin' matters now; nothin' didn't ever matter, nor don't."' Isolation had reduced the old shepherd to his own mangled dialect and a confusion of tense and time. Fashioning the mound with a spade, he muttered, 'I am the rassaraction', before covering his face with his hands.[21]

'The Drover's Wife' was published in the *Bulletin* in July 1892, as the colonial depression was collapsing the economic viability of small farms. The drover's wife suffered the consequences of financial collapse. Her husband was absent; droving, in service to another station owner, as the source of a basic income, so that the family could afford to abandon the selection and move into town. She had not heard from him for six months. Struggling to look after the farm and four small children, she was harassed by impoverished bushmen, 'villainous-looking' sundowners and 'gallows-faced' swagmen, and stalked by nature itself, preying on her few remaining livestock and her family. The story describes her struggle to kill a snake that slid beneath the hut and which might slither from one of many cracks in the boards. She is forced into a night-long vigil, aided by 'Alligator', the family dog. As dawn breaks, they combine in attack as the 'black brute, five feet long' emerges with the dog's stubborn grip on its neck. Alligator 'shakes the snake as tho' he felt the curse of Toil in common with mankind'.[22] Armed with a long stick the woman beats the snake to death and throws its bashed remains into the fire. Women endured the punishing consequences of work and capitalist alienation, and the predations of male aggression, of which the snake, 'the black brute', provided the most intensive symbolic representation in the story.

Alienated identities proliferated in Lawson's stories. The bush undertaker and Brummy are never identified by their true names; nor is the drover's wife, whose husband is not really a drover, although her identity is tied to his degraded status. Often in Lawson's stories from this period, no one is who they really are, reduced to 'types' by economic circumstance and isolation in landscapes stripped by ring-barking or by the gnawing of starved livestock on an exhausted selection. The 'bush' provides a stark setting for the exposure of his subject's alienation. 'Bush all round – bush with no horizon', so Lawson describes the setting of the drover's wife's threadbare hut.[23] In his Bourke stories the horizon resonated as metaphor of endless space and obligation. In 'On the Edge of a Plain' Lawson concludes by describing a favourite character, Mitchell, 'dolefully' pacing into the 'wide, hazy distance', in the renewed quest for a 'start'.[24] The search for work, or for the thin hope of transformation that might come through work, 'the curse of Toil', had no visible horizon. The hope of resurrection struggled with an instinct that nothing matters.

The bush as threatening landscape, representing the treacheries of nature and humankind, found vivid expression in the Australian *fin de siècle* imagination. In *Hot Wind* (1889) Lawson's contemporary, the artist Charles Conder (1868–1909), depicted an exotic goddess breathing fire-fuelled air from a brazier into

Figure 3 The bush symbolized as fatal temptress found a vivid expression in the Australian *fin de siècle* imagination. Charles Conder, *Mirage*, 1889. National Gallery of Victoria.

the parched landscape, while at the edge of the image a slightly sketched ensemble suggested pastoral life oblivious of the threat. The goddess is worshipped by the serpent of temptation; their bond is stressed by the sensuous lines of her prone body and the slackly loosened band that falls from her side to greet the poised snake. Conder's *Mirage*, from the same drought-stricken year, adapted Symbolist and Japanese influences to depict another femme fatale, bearing aloft a smoking torch as she idly pranced down a dry hillside. Conder borrowed 'a hallmark figure of Europe's *fin de siècle* culture' to represent women embodying 'a sexualised presence that commands the annihilation of the environment' (Figure 3).[25] Conder, like his fellow Heidelberg School artists, was accused by contemporary critics of disturbingly conjuring 'some fugitive effect which he sees, or professes to see, in nature', a dubious trait identified in Lawson's stories, accused in 1892 of morbidly fixating on a 'dismal' depiction of the bush.[26] Yet their work was also praised for celebrating bush life. Conder delicately dissolved horizon and sky in *While Daylight Lingers* (1890), populated by little more than shepherd, sheepdog and the dusty empurpled churn of the herd – a 'daring' work illustrating the 'strange beauty' of drought.[27] *While Daylight Lingers* might have provided an illustration appropriate for Lawson's 'The Bush Undertaker', lacking only a sketch of the shallow hump of a neglected grave.[28]

From the early 1890s Lawson has been cast as an embodiment of an 'Australian Legend' of bushworker struggle and mateship by both champions and detractors of the legend, praised for idealizing the bush and exposing its bleak deprivations.[29] In this masculine construction of Australian character women, it has been argued, 'frequently appear as idealized symbols of hope or are objectified into figures of defeat'.[30] Lawson has been represented as a socialist and a totem of 'radical nationalism'.[31] Christopher Lee has traced the permutations of Lawson's 'canonization' in the century since his death in 1922 and its implication in issues of race, place and identity in Australia. Lee also observed Lawson's useful malleability. 'The stature of Henry Lawson in the cultural history of Australia is due to the historical utility of his reputation for licencing various forms of social identity.'[32] Lawson's work reflects the diverse range of influences – the cultural and social, the economic and political – that he was subjected to in his life and which he incorporated into his sketches. Lawson's work was susceptible to appropriation because he absorbed so widely and richly from these influences while resisting the temptation to reduce experience to dogma. Lawson's texts mirror the ideas and tensions circulating in the public sphere, in the mainstream and labour press, in the lower Castlereagh Street milieu of radicalism and the *Republican* and *Dawn*, and in his daily experience of late nineteenth-century Sydney. Graeme Davison has observed the transfer of culture between city and bush in the 1890s, although Lawson's experience and his response to it reflected a more complex relationship.[33]

It is important to focus on Lawson's fiction and the often-overlooked non-fiction essays from the period 1892 to 1894. These publications reveal Lawson's absorption in the dynamic turbulence of politics, economy and labour exchanged between metropole and periphery in *fin de siècle* Australia.[34] This focus also challenges received interpretations of Lawson and unsettles his representative status as an embodiment of the Australian Legend or celebrating mateship, union solidarity and Australian bush identity – an interpretation of Lawson that may rely on assumptions based on reference to his later work, which tended to lapse into sentimental representations. A 1901 poem, 'The Shearers', exulted a defiant bushworker mateship that Lawson challenged and subverted in 1892–4.[35] In the early 1890s colonial urban life spilled its boundaries, as the economic crisis displaced its human surplus into the only space available. Lawson was part of this displacement, and although he was not responsible for the intensively masculine nature of that productive domain, he was rendered an instrument of it, transferred by railway technology as observer and novice shedhand during the shearing season at Toorale pastoral station near Bourke. It was into this unruly acceleration of capital and production that Henry Lawson was projected.

The second industrial revolution provided the technologies that triggered the pastoral industry's exponential expansion around Bourke, generating the largest pastoral production in the world by the late nineteenth century; the year 1892 represented the peak of Australian wool production in the period, before the impact of drought, depression and disinvestment.[36] The most extensive pastoral stations were the assets of expanding corporate entities. 'The largest number of sheep held by one owner in this colony' was M'Caughey and Co., which part-owned Toorale and Dunlop stations, together with Australian Sheep Farms Ltd. The two properties covered nearly two million hectares south-west of Bourke: 'the next in order is the Momba Pastoral Company, with over 330,000 [sheep]. There are nine firms or owners who each hold more than 200,000.'[37] Increasingly, efficient industrial presses baled the wool; river steamers delivered the fat jute bales to Port Bourke, emerging as one of world's busiest inland river ports. In 1892 E. Rich and Co., general merchants and forwarding and commissioning agents, dominated the trade in the movement of freight and people by steamer, installing three steam engines on the banks of the Darling River to provide the energy to lift the bales from the boats.[38]

In June 1892 an awestruck *Sydney Mail* recorded the scale of production in the Bourke district. The *Mail*, like its competitor the *Australian Town and Country Journal*, was published weekly and provided vivid portrayals of bush life, and dense reports and statistics of rural economy, celebrating the dynamic transfer of wealth from the inland periphery to the metropolitan port. 'Of the wool shipped E. Rich and Co. consigned over 50,000 bales, and some 30,000 bales came here by steamer. There is more wool and stock shipped here than any other provincial station in Australia.' The various enterprises conducted in Bourke by the appropriately named Rich and Co. covered 5 acres and generated an annual turnover of £100,000, or about £1,900 a week, at a time when the average wage was little more than £2 per week. Trade required rapid communication and distribution networks. 'The town is third for post and telegraph returns of any town in this colony outside of Sydney.'[39] The railway linked Bourke with the metropolis in 1885 and sped the bales to wool stores where they were sorted, auctioned and shipped by the new generation of steel-clad steamships to buyers in Britain, Europe and the United States.[40] The recently introduced Wolseley shearing machine, powered by electricity, made shearing faster and more efficient with a steady sweep of comb and cutter. The world's first mechanized shearing was conducted at Dunlop station in 1888. 'There is no cutting and hacking sheep, not much second cutting of the wool, and one misses that old familiar cry from all directions where hand shearing is carried on, of tar! tar! tar!'[41] Immense pastoral stations, such as Toorale and Dunlop stations, employed hundreds of men in the shearing season. These shearing sheds assumed the industrial scale of the factory, with piecework routines and regulated shifts of labour along an assembly-line operation to shear the half million sheep stocked on the two stations.[42] Shearing tallies increased as piecework encouraged faster, competitive shearing. Water supplies that sustained the stocking of vast flocks of sheep were provided by improved technology that enabled the sinking of over fifty wells to ever-greater depths around Bourke across 1892. The collaboration between government and private contractors drilling bores for water drawn from the abundant natural resource of the Great Artesian Basin had seen 'great strides . . . made in this direction during the last few years'.[43] Pent reserves of water flowed as fresh streams and swelled into shallow muddy lakes that panned the plain. In November 1892 the Petrolia Boring Company succeeded in drilling down 1,725 feet and tapping a supply of four million gallons of artesian water daily on Tobin and Son's Cuttabulla property, north of Bourke. 'The temperature of the water is 120 degrees, and the men have been compelled to stop work as the water blistered them.'[44]

Andreas Killen observed that '[a]mong the energy sources mobilized by late nineteenth-century society, human labour power remained vitally important, even as the new technologies of the era brought about significant changes in the nature of the work it performed'.[45] James Belich has observed how new technologies – steam, iron and rail – 'flowered' together with old technologies and physical labour in the white settler societies of the nineteenth century.[46] In the Bourke district new technology did not displace the need for physical labour, for bullock carriers and cameleers, shearers and shedhands, women labouring in homesteads and commercial laundries, at least for those lucky enough to access paid work. With an oversupply of labour, employers dictated terms. In March 1892 the employees of the Petrolia Boring Company worked 60 hours per week to pump scalding water. 'One of them asked the "boss" for a rise in his screw last week', reported *The Hummer*, the journal of the bush unions, 'and was told that if any change was made at all, it would be to lower it.'[47] The Pastoralists' Union (PU), representing the employers, declared before the 1892 shearing season commenced that shearers seeking a start would need to forward £1 deposit and references to the PU office, a demand the Amalgamated Shearer's Union declared 'derogatory to the principles of Unionism and Manhood', although a number of shearers conceded its terms.[48] Having suffered defeat at the hands of the employers and the state in the Great Strike of 1890, and faced with waves of non-unionized workers willing to take strikers' jobs, the bush unions felt unable to mobilize an effective resistance. The pastoral employers, and the owners of the Broken Hill mine in far west NSW, were determined to impose 'freedom of contract' – their right to determine pay rates and to choose to employ non-union labour. On the day of Henry Lawson's arrival in Bourke, the local *Western Herald* reported that a meeting of 'fully three hundred' citizens in Drew's Union Hall had condemned the NSW Government's arrest of the Broken Hill strike leaders.[49] The protracted industrial dispute dragged on for months across the middle of the year, evolving from lockout to strike. The Bourke branch of the Amalgamated Shearers' Union had raised over a thousand pounds for the miner's strike fund, subscribed by members.[50] By November the labour press bitterly recorded the strike's collapse and the debased humiliation of the strike leaders, 'shaved and put in prison garb like criminals'.[51]

Lawson arrived in Bourke in September 1892 just as the labour movement was developing new levels of organizational and communicative sophistication. The two main bush unions – the Amalgamated Shearers Union and the General Labourers' Union, representing shedhands or 'rouseabouts' – were discussing the merits of following the pattern of pastoral industry consolidation by amalgamating as one union, although the birth of the Australian Workers' Union would not occur until 1894.[52] The *Worker*, the journal of these unions, was born just as Lawson arrived in Bourke. Its predecessor, *The Hummer*, had been published in the country centre of Wagga, in southern New South Wales. The *Worker* was published from Sydney and reflected an increasingly complex and varied dialogue between core and periphery, and which also drew on the wider global realm of labour mobilization. With 10,000 copies distributed across the colony, a new space was opened up to express and contest working-class identity. From its inception the *Worker* reflected the heterogeneity of global *fin de siècle* experience and imagination, anxiety and aspiration, influences that resonated in Lawson's work.[53] 'The Brotherhood of man can only be brought about by mutual co-operation of the wealth-producers in every possible way', declared the editorial statement of the first edition in October 1892. An awareness of the global nature of industrial capitalism and labour mobilization was evident from the inauguration of the *Worker*: columns dedicated to reporting 'The World of Labour' featured on the front page. The terse technology of the cablegram, which compressed and accelerated knowledge, was set out in staccato broadcasts of a global mobilization – and the reaction against it – that stabbed down the front page:

> Labour federation in Germany takes in 65 organised trades with 2568 branches and 176,670 members.
>
> The big American transatlantic steam ship companies talk of Chinese labour on the boats at less than half American seamen's wages.
>
> Lancashire cotton kings have noticed another 5 per cent reduction in wages, and say that starvation and the military are both present to enforce the edict.[54]

Publication in periodicals such as the *Worker* and the *Bulletin* decisively shaped Lawson's work in the period 1892–4, particularly in the *Worker*, which published a wide range of his fiction and non-fiction pieces. It was in their weekly editions that he could find recognition and income. A small collection of his work, *Short Stories in Verse and Prose*, was published in 1894 by his mother's printery; it was extolled in the *Bulletin* as the product of a genuine 'voice of the bush'. Copies promoted and distributed through the *Worker* sold well, although bookshop sales were modest.[55] It was not until 1896 that his stories were published as a substantial literary and commercial product in a single volume, *While the Billy Boils*, by George Robertson and Co.[56] The stories published in these collections had been shaped by the prevailing conventions of press publication. The emerging labour press conformed to the requirements of the industrial nature of print production. Text was governed by the demands of generating news and entertainment, and over which the reader's eye skimmed: a few hundred words, perhaps a thousand, contained in one or two columns hemmed by broad blocks of display advertising. The *Worker* reflected the terms of the commercial culture in which it intervened.

It may be assumed that there was a common outlook in Lawson's work and the principal journals in which it was published in the period 1892–4. Lawson embraced the cause of labour and shared its racial anxieties: 'in all schemes for the furtherance of the universal brotherhood we must leave the Chinaman out of the question altogether.' On 'the woman question' he acknowledged women obliged to seek paid work while tending for families and 'a lazy or drunken husband' but shared trade union concern that women could be employed as a cheap alternative to male labour. Women should be allowed to work at trades 'as are suited to her', but only if 'the union standard of wages' was upheld.[57] Yet Lawson did not uncritically endorse the brotherhood codes of labour. Lawson's fiction and non-fiction sketches were often poised in tension with the *Worker* and the unions over conceptions of mateship and solidarity; and although it may be argued that Lawson fed *Bulletin* editor J. F. Archibald's 'half-glimpsed myth' of the 'Lone Hand' bushman ('Lone Hand' had been Archibald's originally preferred title for the *Bulletin*), Lawson did not share the *Bulletin*'s idealization of the bush as a more authentic form of Australian life.[58] Lawson's depictions of the alienation of shearing huts and the endless horizon of the bush track seem doubtful endorsements of romanticized mateship free of the bonds of family life.[59] Lawson's work reflected his disquiet with conventional forms of labour movement organization and political activism, and a resistance to mythologizing. Lawson imagined elemental, subjective alternatives to organized labour: he penned a portrait of a brutally anarchic 'leader of the future'.[60] He tested the patience of the *Worker*'s proprietors by empathizing with a pastoral station employer in his story 'Baldy Thompson'.[61] His work in 1892–4 more often challenged the terms of bush masculinity and union solidarity than embraced them. In his 1893 story 'Stragglers', Lawson focused not on mateship but on alienated 'exception': a strike breaker or, more harshly, a 'scab'.[62] In his article 'A Word in Season' Lawson urged his bush union readers: 'Remember that there are thousands of men in the city who are very nearly as good and true as you are; try to learn more about their lives.' Perhaps thinking of Louisa's struggles, he added: 'remember that the hardship of bush life at its worst is not a circumstance compared with what thousands of poor women in cities have to go through.'[63] By September 1892 Lawson was possessed of quick instinctive style, and a penetrating sympathy for his subjects, already at work in his mind on the train to Bourke.

'Draw a wire fence and a few ragged gums, and add some scattered sheep running away from the train.' Barely twenty words were all Lawson required to describe New South Wales 'from Bathurst on' as the train rattled west. The spare economy of his sketch matched the landscape and the private demarcations evident in the tracery of wire fencing paralleling the rails. The railway netted together what passed for community: Lawson observed a succession of railway towns, with railway hotels and railway stores, that periodically reinforced the monotonous repetition of the bush, blistering 'In a Dry Season', as Lawson styled his sketch of the drought-gripped colony, published in the *Bulletin* in November 1892. A dash of colour on the bush and physical settlement soon fixed on the effects on the body and spirit. He was drawn to the telling detail, the 'slop sac suits, red faces and old-fashioned, flat brimmed hats' that began to 'drop into the train on the other side of Bathurst'. Lawson was fascinated by the hats that adorned the travellers, 'with three inches of crape round the crown, which perhaps signifies death in the family, and perhaps it doesn't'. Death was economically observed. The bushman generally leaves the crape 'till the hat wears out, or another friend dies'. Lawson observed that 'this outward sign of bereavement usually has a jolly, red face beneath it. Death is about the only cheerful thing in the bush.'[64]

From the train Lawson caught sight of the first 'sundowner' of his journey: a solitary itinerant and presumably penniless refugee of work, tracking the line from one town to another. A swag bound round his body, a billy can for brewing tea in one hand and gripping a long stick in the other, Lawson described an almost clownish figure, 'in a tail-coat, turned yellow', a print shirt and moleskin trousers with calico knee patches, and a straw hat also covered in calico. Further along Lawson registered another disorderly reminder of the fragility of life, reduced to type: 'one or two square-cuts and stand-up collars struggle dismally through to the bitter end'. The city unemployed, persisting in redundant formality, 'with a letter from the Government bureau in his pocket, and nothing else', and misled about the proximity of the pastoral station and the remote prospect of work. 'God forgive our social system!'[65]

Somebody told Lawson to get away from the rail line: 'Yer wanter go out back, young man, if you wanter see the country.' Sufficiently disoriented, Lawson declined. 'You could go to the brink of eternity so far as Australia is concerned and yet meet an animated mummy of a swagman who will talk of going "out back"'. Lawson felt that 'The least "horrible spot in the bush, in a dry season, is where the bush isn't – where it has been cleared away and a green crop is trying to grow"'. Only an absolute transformation, utterly extinguishing the natural realm of north-western New South Wales, could sustain life. Transformation

Figure 4 Henry Lawson arrived in a town where economic pressures were bearing down on the working population, their families and the unemployed. Henry Lawson, Bourke 1892. State Library of New South Wales.

was under way, although in alien forms. Towards journey's end Lawson observed an unsettling tableau: 'a long line of camels moving out across the sunset.' Lawson arrived in the town just as agitation at the competition represented by Afghan cameleers drawing work away from European carriers reached a pitch of reaction. Lawson's sketch played on the hostile instincts of his readers and his own unease. 'There's something snaky about camels.' Then someone said, 'here's Bourke.'[66] (Figure 4).

'Where is Bourke? Right over there where the sun sets.'[67] In June 1892 a touring *Sydney Mail* 'Sketcher' described a town that appeared modest in scale: barely three and half miles in any direction from the centre. 'The growth of this trading station was . . . nothing more than traffic with those engaged directly or dependent upon the carrying, manufacturing, trading, and general trade incidental to, and growing out of, the station business around the large district of which this is the hub and centre of gravity.' Bourke controlled the trade of a 'vast stretch of country' extending nearly 200 miles west and north to the Queensland border, 50 miles south and 100 miles east. 'Sketcher' had expected this centre of gravity to be barely habitable. 'I had never stirred its dust before, and had inhaled the idea that the township itself was a dirty, smoky, ill-conceived and prairie-hut-built-kind of a place inhabited by a dirty, low-bred set of whites not much better than the reported reputation of the Chinese and Afghans that infested the plain.' Prosperity was 'wonderfully accelerated since the advent of the railway', clean streets, substantial public buildings and comfortable hotels; there was a hospital, a 'commodious' gaol and a mechanic's institute with 2,000 volumes in its library, 'and most of the current reviews and late papers'. Four banks were represented in a town with over 3,000 inhabitants and with property valued at least half a million pounds and possibly worth as much as one million. 'Sketcher' reassured the predominantly middle-class readership of the *Sydney Mail* with a narrative of wealth and security, largely untroubled by the accounts of falling pastoral profitability and labour unrest readers might find elsewhere in the *Mail's* encyclopaedic pages – although towards the end of his account 'Sketcher' briefly acknowledged 'the sad and poor state of the country' and that 'sheep are selling for as low as 9d and 1s each, and cattle will walk into your paddock and stay there for nothing'.[68]

Henry Lawson arrived in Bourke and found a different political economy to that identified by 'Sketcher': a town in which economic pressures were bearing down on the working population, their families and the unemployed. At the beginning of the year, 'hundreds' of Bourke residents had petitioned the NSW Government, humbly praying 'that you will not issue any further free railway passes to this district, as the local labor market is already overcrowded, there being some hundreds of men here unable to obtain employment'.[69] Still the unemployed poured into the district as the year drew on. In May, the Bourke branch of the General Labourers' Union addressed 'the coloured labour question' which it believed aggravated unemployment. The branch 'strongly protests against the proposed influx of coloured labour into these colonies, as such cannot fail to prove detrimental to the best interests of the Australian people'.[70] The importation of camels 'and their attendant Asiatics' was also opposed in Bourke; unless the government restricted their entry, the work available to white European carriers in the wool trade would collapse. Camels frightened horses, causing them to bolt; and 'the Afghans spend less in this county than the Chinese'.[71]

The predations of the pastoralists drew the ire of *The Hummer*. Several pastoral stations, including Toorale and Dunlop, were condemned for adopting the practice of engaging shearers through applications and deposits forwarded to the PU office. Bush unionists dreamt of a drastic upheaval of space. 'I reckon it's about time the vast area of country held by these gentry were burst up.'[72] The employers were sensitive to the threat of unrest. 'Shearing was started at Toorale station last Saturday', the *Sydney Mail* reported in July 1892.

Fully 300 men were on the ground when the roll was called, but no serious disturbance took place. Owing to the late shearing this year, caused through the drought, there are hundreds of men walking up and down the river unable to obtain employment. Many of them have come from Sydney in anticipation of getting work at the shearing sheds, and are now making their way back. It is useless for men looking for shearing through this district until rain falls. Toorale is about the only shed likely to shear, and they could have filled the board half a dozen times over.[73]

Through the intervention of the General Labourers' Union Lawson found work as a shedhand at Toorale in November 1892 (Figure 5).[74] As he wrote to his Aunt Emma in Sydney, since arriving in September he had only fitful work and income from house painting and a few published items, interspersed between sessions of steady drinking at the local pubs, including the Great Western, where he was staying. 'I must take to the bush as soon as I can.'[75] Lawson and his friend and fellow seasonal shedhand Jim Gordon crossed the Darling River by the Bourke punt on 24 November to begin the 40-mile tramp south-west to Toorale.[76]

Figure 5 Ferry punt and paddle steamers on the Darling River unloading wool at Bourke, *c.* 1892. Henry Lawson crossed the river by the punt to work as a shedhand at Toorale station in November. Museum of Applied Arts and Sciences, Tyrrell Collection. Gift of Australian Consolidated Press under the Taxation Incentives for the Arts Scheme, 1985. Photographer George Bell.

Bourke had already provided Lawson some inspiration in 1892, although the township was not represented as the site of solidarity or its public display in union meetings or parades; nor did Lawson find space for 'Sketcher's' bustling prosperity. Bourke provided a sparsely observed setting for the funeral of a stranger, whose name and life were unknown, even to his mourners. 'The Union Buries its Dead' was subtitled 'a sketch from life', and it bore a close resemblance to the published reports, particularly the *Western Herald*'s account of the death of 'James Tyson', who drowned after being kicked by the horse he was attempting to swim across the Darling River in November 1892. 'Tyson' had been engaged to move a flock of sheep between two properties. The deceased's swag revealed that his real name was John Hallahan, from Toowoomba in Queensland. 'Several Queensland Union tickets, voting rights and receipts for money given to recent strikes were also found in the swag. Nothing was known of him locally.'[77] Lawson's sketch intensified the facts in a mix of farce and pathos, focusing his representation on the funeral procession and burial.

The story subverted the rules of reporting into a flat irony: 'We walked in twos. There were three twos. It was very hot and dusty, and the heat rushed in fierce dazzling waves across every iron roof and light-coloured wall that was turned to the sun.'[78] The funeral procession, baked in an unforgiving heat, formed a parade of scant respect. The union-organized observance had started in drunken distraction in a pub, dancing jigs, sky-larking and fighting, a solemn order disturbed, with the wake preceding the formalities. Drunks negligently processing behind the hearse were observed along the route by other drunks, listlessly doffing hats or dozing. Arriving at the cemetery a mourner suddenly announces: 'There's the devil': a Catholic priest, another unsettling reversal of expected roles and forms. Lawson draws the reader's attention to the artifice of his story. 'I looked up and saw a priest standing in the shade of a tree by the cemetery gate. A Church of England parson would have done as well.'[79] Towards the conclusion Lawson again disturbs the account in a laconic description that denied the relief of sentimentality. 'I have left out the wattle because it wasn't there.' There was no 'suspicious moisture' in 'the eyes of a bearded bush-ruffian named Bill. Bill failed to turn up.'[80] The priest is 'callous and business-like' in observing his ritual duties. The unidentified narrator learns that James Tyson was a false name: here Lawson again drew attention to the blurring of reality and fiction; John Hallahan had used that '*sobriquet*', as the *Western Herald* reported. James Tyson was a pastoralist and a 'byword for wealth and a legend in his own lifetime.'[81] By the early 1890s Tyson had amassed a fortune and over two million hectares of property holdings in New South Wales and Queensland. Neither the

Western Herald nor Lawson explained the choice of sobriquet. It was left to the reader to decide if Hallahan and Lawson's 'young union labourer' made an ironic appropriation of a stereotype 'boss' or toyed with a vague hope of emulating Tyson's self-made progress from pastoral labourer to pastoral owner. Although the narrator of 'The Union Buries its Dead' was told the real name, the story tersely ends with a casual negligence that subverts a comforting closure: 'if I do chance to read the real name among the missing friends in some agony column I shall not be aware of it, and therefore not be able to give any information, for I have already forgotten the name.'[82]

'The Union Buries its Dead' describes mateship undermined by the alienated conditions in which men laboured. Published in April 1893, it was one of the first post-Bourke sketches to question – or indeed mock – the ideal of union solidarity and mateship, a theme that persisted until the end of 1894, by which time he had fallen out with the *Worker* and the AWU.[83] In 'The Cant and Dirt of Labor Literature', Lawson issued perhaps his most blunt challenge, lamenting that 'the word "scab" ever dirtied the pages of a workman's newspaper. . . . It should never be used by one man in reference to another, no matter how bad the other may be. . . . It . . . only appeals to ignorance and brutality.' The article appeared in the *Worker* in October 1894, in the midst of a bitterly contested shearer's strike and in which workers and their unions were defeated and forced to concede the rates paid by pastoralists, and the owners prerogative to enforce freedom of contract.[84] Not content with his assault on the language of solidarity, Lawson also took aim at those 'bilious fanatics' who described themselves as 'socialists' and 'comrades'. Most provocatively, Lawson dismissed

> That egotistic word 'mateship' – which was born of New Australian imagination, and gushed about to a sickening extent – implied a state of things which never existed any more than the glorious old unionism which was going to bear us on to freedom on one wave. The one was altogether too glorious, and the other too angelic to exist among mortals. We must look at the nasty side of truth as well as the other, the conceited side.

It was a direct rebuke offered to the sentimental claim by William Lane, who, editorializing in *The Hummer* in January 1892 under the pseudonym 'John Miller', had declared that 'socialism is being mates' and advocated a New Australia, a socialist community to be established beyond the drought and depression wracked colonies (see Chapter 2).[85] In response to Lawson's denunciation of the term 'scab', the labour organizer Arthur Rae admitted that 'the term is nasty, but the thing itself is much nastier', but philosophically added of such 'curses' that 'no one in this age of doubt believes they will have any effect'. Other *Worker* readers scorned Lawson's 'respectable' distaste. 'What name shall we give him then – squatters' saviour, freedom-of-contract martyr, friend in need, champion of the oppressed Capitalist?' Scabs were 'servile and insolent' slaves. 'They crawl and cringe to employers, and fawn to overseers. They travel, eat, drink, sleep, and work under the protection of others like prisoners and not free men.'[86]

Lawson's essay and the reaction to it suggested a clear divide between unionist and scab, policed by an uncompromising repudiation of the servile traitor. Lawson's story 'Stragglers' suggested a more complex relationship. The fictional sketch describes a leftover workforce on New Year's Eve, taking a 'spell' before seeking a 'start' elsewhere, or more likely, delaying the need to face a future wandering the bush tracks without the prospect of work. In an account of a listless day, shearers and shedhands mingled in their accommodation – a 'small, oblong' hut – and described as 'stragglers', almost indistinguishable from the detritus accumulated around them and the sheep they processed in the nearby shearing shed: 'stragglers' was a term that described sheep that had been missed during the main cycle of shearing. Rubbish was heaped by the hut door, 'which opens from the middle of one of the side walls; it might be the front or the back wall – there's nothing to fix it'. Inside the close space, the floor was littered with the straggler's rubbish – 'old wool-bales, newspapers, boots, worn-out shearing pants, rough bedding, &c., raked out of the bunks in impatient search for missing articles, signs of a glad and eager departure, with cheques, when the shed last cut out'.[87]

Even this degraded space reflected how the local was tied to the global economy. The hut formed part of a productive site around the ironically dubbed 'Government House', the home of the station manager, although here, in this otherwise unnamed property, the manager's house was little better than a 'bush hut', 'for this station belongs to a company. And the company belongs to a bank. And the bank belongs to England mostly.' It was a carefully demarcated space: government house stood a mile from the shearing shed and the wool-washing, soap-boiling and wool-pressing sites. The wool shed, opposite the accommodation hut, was built of galvanized iron, 'a blinding object to start out of the scrub on a burning hot day'. The accommodation hut also had a roof of 'the eternal galvanised iron'.[88] By 1892 galvanized iron was a product that sharply signified the ubiquitous European presence in the landscape and one of the cheaply imported iron and steel materials that suppressed local industry, as a deputation of employers and unions complained to the NSW government.[89] Lawson did not share the deputation's desire for encouraging Australian production. 'God forgive the man who invented galvanised-iron, and the greed which introduced it into Australia; for you couldn't get worse roofing material for a hot country.' Drought and the mass processing of hoofed livestock had seared and scored the land. Dead trees stood in 'the broad, shallow sheet of grey water' that constituted the dam; knots of mulga scrub covered the ground 'and, in between, patches of reddish sand where the grass ought to be'.[90]

By New Year's Eve only half a dozen stragglers remained in a hut that accommodated thirty men in two cramped rows of bunks; there was at least a prospect of cadging food from the cook at government house, who was kind to 'travellers'. The men replenished their tuckerbags when the manager 'is likely to be out on the run'. The stragglers were reluctant to submit to the brutal regime of tramping. 'To live you must walk. To stop walking, is to die.' It was 20 miles to nearest government bore and the chance to replenish water supplies. Suspended in an enervating torpor, 'The men lie about in the bunks, or the shade of the hut, and rest, and read all the soiled and mutilated scraps of literature they can rake out of the rubbish, and sleep, and wake up swimming in perspiration, and growl about the heat.'[91] Their search for knowledge was reduced to scrounging in scraps scattered in fragments on the hut floor. Equally, they sought out discarded boots, pants, socks to compare with the worn scraps they wear. Lawson's stragglers are symptomatic of how *fin de siècle* progress seemed to be 'won at the expense of a widespread degeneration'.[92] In 'Stragglers' Lawson presents 'types' symptomatic of this degeneration: the 'Exception', an 'outcast amongst bush outcasts', who 'looked better fitted for Sydney Domain', that is, one of the unemployed 'sundowners' who resorted to dossing down after dark in the Domain; another identity displaced into the bush. Tenuously identified as a 'free labourer', or to use the term Lawson avoids, a 'scab', the 'Exception' is 'a mystery known only to himself', who seems to have a thirst for knowledge: 'He was read every scrap of print within reach.'

The Exception is the most forensically observed of all the identities in the story, although it is the Exception's body, rather than his thoughts or statements, which illuminates character and circumstance.

> He lies on the bottom of a galvanised iron case, with a piece of blue blanket for a pillow. He is dressed in a blue cotton jumper, a pair of very old and ragged tweed trousers, and one boot and one slipper. He found the slipper in the last shed, and the boot in the rubbish-heap here. When his own boots gave out he walked 150 miles with his feet roughly sewn up in pieces of sacking from an old wool-bale. No sign of a patch, or an attempt at mending anywhere about his clothes, and that's a bad sign; for, when swagman leaves off mending or patching his garments, his case is about hopeless . . . [he] now lies on his side, with his face to the wall

and one arm thrown up over his head; the jumper is twisted back, and leaves his skin bare from hip to arm-pit. His lower face is brutal, his eyes small and shifty, and ugly straight lines run across his low forehead. He says very little, but scowls most of the time – poor devil. He might be, or at least *seem*, a totally different man under more favourable conditions. He is probably a – well, a free labourer.[93]

The suffering of the body represented as a patchwork of rubbish, an identity alienated from his peers, barely able to eat – 'his appetite is gone' – and consumed in the refuse of the industrial economy that suspended him in the isolation cell of the hut. The reference to galvanized iron is hardly coincidental nor that the Exception tramped with his feet bound in the scraps of an old wool bale. The scrutiny of the prone body forms the imaginative centre of 'Stragglers'. Lawson bestows the Exception with more humanity than any other character in the story and one who had the possibility of transcending alienation.[94] In observing the isolated Exception, and who might have been 'a totally different man under more favourable conditions', Lawson may have been describing himself. Jim Gordon observed that in the shedhand's hut Lawson was not really a 'mate', lacking common interest with his fellow workers but lay listening to the stories and experiences expressed and enacted around him.[95]

Industrialized process work in the bush reduced men to 'Stragglers'; Lawson's character Mitchell represented a shrewd and resourceful 'type' to which bush workers might aspire. Mitchell's universality is evident in his lack of specific work identity: he is not a shearer, part of the bushwork elite, merely a humble 'Sydney jackeroo who had been around a bit – that's all', part of the mob moving west from the city in search of whatever station work may be on offer.[96] In 'Mitchell: A Character Sketch' and 'Mitchell Doesn't Believe in the Sack', published in the *Bulletin* respectively in April and May 1893, Lawson exercised a terse, concentrated economy (both sketches are barely two pages long in *While the Billy Boils*) to highlight Mitchell's vivid subjectivity, and his cleverness in manipulating station managers and cooks to deliver gratis abundant tucker to his mates and himself, and to defy a degrading redundancy.[97] Mitchell is presented at once self-assertive and cleverly diplomatic, yet 'Mitchell Doesn't Believe in the Sack' outlines Mitchell's spiel to his mate about how he will respond the *next* time he is sacked – refusing to leave the pastoral property, working unpaid (except for rations) until the manager resumes allocating paid work to him. Almost entirely expressed as dialogue, Lawson offers Mitchell's wiliness as model scripts for his readers, although there is also a sense of Lawson drawing attention to the novelty of Mitchell's qualities: not everyone could master these rhetorical skills or project such self-confidence. Mitchell embodied a solitary stoicism, falling back on individual resourcefulness as group mobilization failed.

In Lawson's stories attempts at common bond and purpose often failed in the face of alienating conditions, which confined men together, aggravating their relationships and disrupting a united response to their conditions. Individualized workers might strike back as lone rebels; solidarity threatened to disintegrate into anarchy, and the destruction of prevailing institutions, as many commentators feared in the 1890s. News of anarchist 'outrages' circulated around the globe.[98] In 'The Leader of the Future', an article published in the *Worker* in June 1893, Lawson provided an ironic representation of a dystopian rebel. The leader emerged from within the anonymous ranks of a mob and harnessed their anger into a revolutionary unleashing against established power, although to no identifiable form of liberation. The leader is an expression of body and physical will, rather than mind; not so much a leader but a violent straggler risen out of the mass, a man, not a god, 'gods don't knock round these days', who remains unnamed in the article. Mounted on a barricade, 'He'll most likely come with a blood-stained bandage around his forehead and carry one arm in a sling and a club in the hand of the other.' With 'a brutal cast of countenance' and garbed in the 'uniform of the unemployed', his language will not be 'Christlike, or Gladstone-like' but 'vulgar, and lurid'. He will not stop to reason; 'he'll feel too mad.' Ignorant and narrow-minded, he will stick to a single idea 'as though ideas were scarce in the world and monopolised by companies'. Above all he will seek revenge, to 'comprehensively abolish the society which produces victims like him'. He will depend on no 'league' except 'the union of misery'. The rich, the powerful and the reforming Socialist, 'working against the possibility of his coming', will be consumed in the 'general destruction'. This leader is not the advocate of a coherent movement but an anarchic 'individualist', as are 'the majority of his followers, who will follow him as long as 'the work of destruction goes on and he keeps ahead of it'. Swept along on the tide of chaos, the leader of the future 'won't last long': 'If he drinks, he will celebrate victory with a howling spree, and want to set up as a king on his own account, after the fashion of the Yankee Caesar (he of the "Column"), and then his followers will cut off his head and put it on a pole before he sobers up.'[99]

The *fin de siècle* was characterized by schemes and pleas for 'regeneration'. Many 'proposed solutions contained within itself a quality of desperation and, ultimately, the idea that the only regeneration for a dying culture was through its total destruction'.[100] *Caesar's Column*, which Lawson cited in his article, describes how a working-class 'brotherhood of destruction' overthrows the oppressive power of state and capital. Led by a fanatic who is himself murdered, 'Caesar's column' is a vast tower of corpses heaped in New York's Union Square.[101] Written by the American Ignatius Donnelly and published in 1890, Donnelly's dystopian fantasy was an international bestseller that was widely read in Australia and recommended in the labour press.[102] Under the heading 'Knowledge Is power', *The Hummer* encouraged its readers to obtain a number of works to 'learn more of the world-wide labor movements', including Gronlund's *Co-operative Commonwealth*, Max Nordau's *Conventional Lies of Our Civilisation* and Bellamy's *Looking Backward*.[103] 'Read and reflect upon all the schemes for the regeneration of the world', *The Hummer* enjoined, including 'the horrors and despair of a "Caesar's Column"'. *The Hummer* correspondent wondered if the 'gruesome' terrors described in Donnelly's book would be realized, given the condition of Europe and America and 'the armed millions ready to fly at each other's throats at the word of command', including to 'keep down their own oppressed and rebellious wage slaves – we must ask when, and how, and where will it all end?'[104]

'The Leader of the Future' reflected the disturbing forces generated by *fin de siècle* industrial modernity and which resonated between the international and colonial spheres, and between metropole and periphery. In the aftermath of the 1892 Broken Hill strike, the threat of a violent anarchic reaction loomed over New South Wales. Premier Sir George Dibbs was 'shadowed by armed detectives like a Russian Czar or an Irish Lord-Lieutenant', from fear of reprisal by 'exasperated men'. Non-union labourers had been sent from Sydney to take the jobs of the strikers. 'So long as the land, the mines and all means of producing wealth are in the hands of the capitalist class so long will there be unremitting toil at freedom of contract wage.'[105] As the Broken Hill dispute persisted, the war-like scale of violence that accompanied the great strike of workers employed by the magnate Andrew Carnegie at the Homestead steel mills at Pittsburgh in the United States attracted widespread coverage in the Australian press. In August 1892 *The Hummer* lamented the fate of the Homestead strikers, their struggle against wage cuts and the introduction of non-union labour broken by the massed intervention of the US Army: 'Surely humanity, manhood, and honor are dead, when so-called civilized nations treat the few *men* they have in that way, and permit things like Carnegie to live.'[106] Of the Homestead strike, *The Hummer* declared that 'the first scene of the first act of the drama known as "Caesar's Column," has been played in America'.[107]

The notorious French anarchist Ravachol might have served as a model of Lawson's leader of a blindly furious future. Executed for murder in July 1892, the *Sydney Morning Herald* reported that Ravachol 'met his fate with shocking levity, dancing and singing even upon the scaffold'.[108] Anarchist 'outrages' seemed to be rapidly accumulating. The Australian press reported arrests of anarchists in Spain, Germany and France; anarchists and radicals were also identified and arrested in colonial Sydney, including John Arthur Andrews, whom Lawson knew and who was friendly with another Castlereagh Street radical, John Dwyer.[109] The dynamiting of the Café Terminus in Paris by Emile Henry in February 1894 stirred troubled reflections on the modern world: the Australian press endorsed Max Nordau's verdict that anarchism was a manifestation of a 'hateful moral force' that flowed from the malaise of degeneration.

> Civilised Europe . . . is suffering from nerve exhaustion. A civilised man's environment presses upon him with a force twenty times greater than at any other period in human history, and according to NORDAU, as summarised in the *Quarterly Review*, civilisation is being swept by a tidal wave of hysteria. Nerve degeneracy, trembling on the verge of lunacy, is visible in the art, literature, politics, religion, social habits of the modern world.[110]

The assassination of the French president Sadi Carnot in June 1894 concentrated a fear of anarchist violence. On 14 September 1894 the Sydney *Evening News* published 'Carnot's Death Warrant', an anarchist threat to assassinate the French president that had been distributed months before Carnot's fatal stabbing by the Italian anarchist Sante Caserio. The warrant bluntly promised 'death without ceremony'. In excited, mocking language Carnot was warned: 'Go on! Go on! But not for ever. Justice shall strike you dead, dead. It is now your own debauched carcass, your own hide, that shall be aimed at.'[111] The next day, 15 September, the Sydney *Worker* published 'The Dying Anarchist'. Lawson's sardonic story was modelled on the provocative Sydney anarchist Arthur Desmond, best known for publishing *Hard Cash*, a short-lived periodical that launched scathing and at times libellous diatribes against the colony's banks and capitalists (Desmond also provided inspiration for 'The Leader of the Future').[112] Lawson's anarchist raves from his deathbed over at his fate, the world and his own foolishness, in language that reflected the angry, exclamation-marked diatribes of a desperate manifesto. In broken outbursts the dying anarchist declared,

> I dreamed of revolution with blood and fire . . . wounded and dying – for Freedom – in the arms of a beautiful daughter of the new-born Republic!
>
> I have been through it all, Republican, Conservative, Socialist, Anarchist, Ishmael! Broken idols – or perhaps I broke them myself in my blindness.

A bond of hate – the Anarchists. No, not hating each other: we held each other in contempt – we distrusted one another – but we hated the world!

Losing faith in 'reformation' the anarchist had 'hoped for destruction and revenge', blurting 'Read Caesar's Column. We struck at times, and once we struck a blow that shook the world….' Four dashes that signified distraction, weariness, or idle boast? He regretted his own narrow caste of hate – 'I was blind to all things save injustice!' The bitter confusion of competing causes and ideals collapsed into exhausted enervation. 'I'm tired of it all – I'm tired of ists and isms. Oh, I'm so tired!' At times the disillusioned anarchist sounded remarkably like Henry Lawson. 'Comrade? No! I hate that word now. It has become a word of cant like "Brother," and "Union" – like your "Mateship!" – I am disgusted with it all.' The violence once projected – or imagined – against society and power was now turned on itself, on a subject who 'saw things too plainly' and 'woke up to die!'[113]

Many of Lawson's characters were travelling towards death. The 'Exception' was almost a dead body; 'James Tyson' tracked the bank of the Darling River towards sudden death. A chance encounter with Tyson worked distractedly in the mind of the unnamed narrator of 'The Union Buries Its Dead'. At the beginning of the story Tyson had only fleeting contact with the men, including the narrator, whom Tyson passed while searching for a safe crossing of the river. By the time the narrator was processing behind the hearse, the narrator had forgotten him and Tyson's last words. 'Said it was a fine day', the narrator's friend reminded him. 'You'd have taken more notice had you known that he was doomed to die in the hour, and those were the last words he would say to any man on earth?' The unlucky death, the obligation to respect the stranger and bury him, careless of his name; the unsentimental instability of reality was too much to take in. Of the mourners who set out behind the hearse, and whose numbers soon shrank, 'Perhaps not one of the fourteen possessed a soul any more than the corpse; but that doesn't matter'.[114] According to prevailing conventions, the preservation of the soul mattered above all else.

Preserving the soul was a matter of distracted observance in 'The Bush Undertaker'. The shepherd not only gathered in Brummy but also the remains of another body. After explaining to his sole living companion – his dog, 'Five Bob' – that Christmas dinner will be 'ready dreckly', the old man muses: 'I'll take a pick 'n' shovel with me and dig up that old black fellow.' This startling proposal injects a scrambled confusion of subject and time, as he continues: 'I reckon it'll do now. I'll give it a minet's more bilin' 'n' put in the spuds.' The body of the 'blackfellow' seems to be the meal he has boiling in a pot on the fire, one reality confused with another.[115] After sharing dinner with Five Bob they both set out, the shepherd carrying pick, shovel and an old bag, tramping 3 miles along a ridge to a 'barely defined' mound of earth. After half an hour of digging up the 'supposed blackfellow's grave', the shepherd struck 'payable dirt', a description usually reserved for gold digging: in this case human bones, with which he 'amused himself by putting them together on the grass and speculating as to whether they belonged to black or white or male or female'. Failing to satisfy his curiosity, the shepherd dusted off the bones 'with great care', before putting them into his bag and setting off home.[116] He soon discovers the body of Brummy. The remains of the casually desecrated 'blackfellow' – who is never clearly identified – are promptly forgotten and feature no more in the story.

Lawson described 'The Bush Undertaker' as an account of life in the 'grand Australian bush – the nurse and tutor of eccentric minds'; a remorseless instruction was provided in the punishing and isolated patterns of work that shaped experience. The political economy that governed bush life provided an infiltration so apparently natural that it barely required comment, yet emerged in hints and codes: the old shepherd telling Five Bob to yard the sheep early, 'fetch 'em back', but acknowledging an awareness of transgression: 'The super won't know.'[117] The 'blackfellow's' skeleton assumed the quality of 'payable dirt' and Brummy, the spent shearer who 'cud earn mor'n any man in the colony', but instead succumbed to a premature death.[118] Nothing matters, the old shepherd realizes, haunted by the face of death and a ruthlessly consuming nature, yet he persists in the hope of resurrection, the last and most plangent of the contradictions which Lawson traced through the story: a bleak homily delivered on Christmas Day and characterized as the work of an 'eccentric mind' to ease the message of irreligious despair. The old shepherd was the undertaker of lost hopes and forgotten bodies in the vast domain of the pastoral station.

By March 1893 Henry Lawson had found sufficient inspiration in north-western New South Wales to sustain a steady stream of sketches that would soon appear in the *Worker* and the *Bulletin*. The exhausted novice shedhand 'only thought of escaping the bush', as he observed in his sketch 'In a Wet Season', which described his return journey to Sydney. After shearing 'cut out' at Toorale by the end of 1892, Lawson and Jim Gordon had tramped north to Hungerford, a sparse township on the Queensland border: 'two or three white-washed, galvanized iron roofs start suddenly out of the mulga', surrounded by 'a blasted, barren wilderness that doesn't even howl. If it howled it would be a relief'. Lawson had found another pitiless horizon, which at least provided inspiration for a story but no immediate source of income.[119] On the way to

Bourke in September 1892 Lawson had been dismayed by the arid nature of the bush and the abject towns through which the train had passed. Returning to Sydney, his impression of the country that persistent rain had quickly rendered flood-drenched was 'funereal'. He imagined 'the ghost of a funeral' passing slowly across plains that stretched like 'dead seas'.

Lawson returned to Sydney as a freight object. Stone broke in Bourke after tramping back from Hungerford, he had been forced to fall on the charity of a stock and station agent; he 'haunted' this 'local influence' for a fortnight, enduring 'all the indignities, the humiliation . . . all that poor devils suffer whilst besieging "local influence"' for a pass to ride gratis in a cattle train bound for Sydney – usually these were reserved for drovers required to accompany the cattle.[120] The train took him past accumulating human and industrial detritus. The sodden swagmen's camps that adhered to the towns were scenes of pathetic desolation. From 'a square of calico stretched across a horizontal stick', a 'small, hopeless-looking man' stood with his back to a fire, watching the passing freight waggons. In the trucking yards 'waggons covered with tarpaulins which hung down in the mud . . . suggested death'. He observed a swagman 'struggling away from the town, through mud and water', accompanied by a 'low-spirited dingo'.

> The 'traveller's' body was bent well forward, from the hips up; his long arms – about six inches through his coat sleeves – hung by his sides, like the arms of a dummy, with a billy at the end of one and a bag at the end of the other; but his head was thrown back against the top end of the swag, his hat-brim rolled up in front, and we saw a ghastly, bearded face which turned neither to the right nor the left as the train passed him.[121]

Lawson described a body barely capable of forward motion; it might have been on its way to the fate that greeted the old shepherd in 'The Bush Undertaker', except this desperate swaggie would not be felled by thirst as he struggled through the fringe of the 'ghastly ocean' that constituted 'the "dominant note of the Australian scenery"', accentuated 'by naked, white, ring-barked trees standing in the water and haunting the ghostly surroundings'.[122]

The 1896 publication *While the Billy Boils*, the major compendium of Lawson's fiction that would be regularly reprinted and expanded across the remainder of his life, provided a powerful source of his personal legend as a 'voice of the bush'. While much of the colonial press exulted how economic value could be extracted from the fragile environment of the far west, the bush that Lawson described in his sketches seemed barely fit for human habitation. Humans were also permanently altering the landscape with their impact, decimating forest and ringing the plains with fencing and filled with alien livestock. Lawson was accused of obsessing over the 'ugliness' of bush life.[123] As he wrote from Hungerford to his Aunt Emma in January 1893: 'You have no idea of the horrors of the country out here. Men tramp and beg and live like dogs.'[124] Yet in his sketches Lawson was also capable of capturing the humour and stoic endurance of bush life. Out of these adversities Lawson fashioned a kind of resurrection, although his audience may have chosen to overlook the horror that he found in the bush and in the unforgiving accelerations that humans had imposed upon themselves. Lawson's work did not reflect a morbid obsession with death. Lawson was fixated on the struggle to live, to survive, and how death snapped that struggle.

The *fin de siècle* and the second industrial revolution closed in on Henry Lawson, shaping his experience and perceptions of identity, place and work. Lawson was not a political activist, although he hoped that exposure of the conditions that he described would lead to a transformation of social conditions, fostering empathy between bushman and city worker, unionist and non-unionist. The resurrection, or regeneration, he offered men and women was a focus on their sufferings and an affirmation of their emerging identities and mobilization – tempered by his warnings that these mobilizations and forms of identity might lead to new oppressions. By drawing attention to problems that appeared to be at the periphery, Lawson wanted to show that these problems were central to the culture and economy inhabited by Australians. When Henry Lawson travelled to Bourke he travelled to the heart of *fin de siècle* modernity.

Lawson revealed an industrial zone of turbulent energy, generating product and refuse. Perhaps all modern systems are ultimately self-destructive, inflicting violence on the humans who find themselves processed by production to the point of redundancy and reaction; blindly destructive leaders of the future, spent stragglers discarded, shifted to the margins or ruthlessly relocated – to the next shed, the next start, from exhausted selection and back to town, in order to renew the cycle. Henry Lawson's immersion in *fin de siècle* acceleration exposed the blunt impact of making a modern world and which, in its relentless processing, was torn between the potential for transformation and a troubled suspicion that nothing matters, nothing ever does.

2

Rose Summerfield imagines a New Woman

Agitate! Agitate! I hope I'll die with that word on my lips.[1]

'I defend the new woman,' Rose Summerfield declared in an address before a Sydney audience in February 1895. The political and radical feminist embraced an identity that had only recently emerged in the public sphere. Passionate and intensely determined, Summerfield stood before a crowd receptive to the challenge that she championed, although scornful voices shot through the cheers. In Leigh House, the headquarters of the Australian Socialist League – of which she was a leading light – Summerfield provoked her audience's preconceptions about gender discriminations and roles, and 'derided the contention that man was a superior being either mentally or physically. "It is only in the minds of the ignorant, the vicious, the prejudiced, that woman ranks as an inferior mentally, morally, or physically."' At which declaration a *Daily Telegraph* reporter noted: '"Hear, hear", ejaculated a muffled male bass voice. Its owner evidently knew,' reflecting the tone of sardonic derision that characterized the *Telegraph* report and the resistance that Rose Summerfield's agitation would face as she defended the ideal of the New Woman.[2]

By 1895 Rose Summerfield had developed a theatrical and prophetic discourse of labour radicalism. Her embrace of the New Woman was consistent with the roles and identities that she took up: autodidactic acts of self-invention, accruing influence from peers and her own readings of books, pamphlets and journals which were themselves being invented in the period – the secularist, temperance and suffrage publications, the labour press, *Dawn*, *The Hummer*, the *Worker*. Her reading reflected the self-fashioning available at the *fin de siècle* and how the individual could challenge class and gender discriminations. 'Woman's role variously as a wife, a mother and a sexual object were all under scrutiny in the debates on the New Woman at the *fin de siècle*.'[3] In many of her own speeches and articles, Rose Summerfield often focused on the subjective nature of class and gender, although conscious of the broader contexts which shaped experience and identity.

Rose Summerfield hoped to overturn discrimination and injustice by force of her agitation; the technological, industrial and discursive conditions of the *fin de siècle* provided her opportunity – although she was also forced to campaign on terms she could not control. Rose Summerfield agitated in colonial New South Wales at a time when a global crisis of capital had collapsed prices for commodities, such as wheat and wool, and closed banks and building societies, throwing unprecedented numbers of workers into unemployment – perhaps 25 per cent of the workforce – and triggering street protests by the unemployed and industrial unrest, including bitterly contested strikes on Sydney's wharves and in the bush pastoral industry.[4] Like Henry Lawson, Summerfield found herself compelled to the colonial periphery, where work and the second industrial revolution had directed labour. Unable to control the space in which she and other workers functioned, Summerfield imagined another sphere that promised the transformation she desired: the dream of a New Australia.

Rose Summerfield was an embodiment of late nineteenth-century radicalism triggered by a youthful religious dissent. Summerfield joined the Australasian Secular Association in her native Ballarat at age twenty-one in 1886. In that year, Rose Stone married the freethinker and clothing manufacturer Henry Summerfield in Melbourne and settled soon after in the Sydney suburb of Waverley, and she apparently enjoyed a life of relative affluence in 'Ivanhoe', one of the 'Summerfield Terraces' in Porter Street. A son, Henry, was born in 1888; Henry senior died in 1890.[5] It is unclear whether Rose needed to work after that time; she soon went in search of networks and colleagues with whom she could develop her social and political activism. Within a few years she turned from freethought to womanhood suffrage and temperance and socialism. Katie Spearritt observed that feminism became an integral element of heightened political and cultural debate in the 1890s, manifesting in women's participation in 'women's clubs, literary associations, temperance societies, suffrage leagues and workers' unions'.[6] Rose Summerfield displayed an ability to articulate the language of provocative political engagement. In May 1892 she delivered a fiery address, 'Master and Man', in Leigh House, in which she declared that workers must no longer acquiesce as 'social slaves' but accept the responsibility of transcending their circumstances. Your 'masters' are 'your self-constituted owners', who have reaped the rewards of your harvest, she told her audience.[7] Rose Summerfield was a messenger of the emerging mobilization and restless political ferment issuing from the radical labour domain of lower Castlereagh Street in southern Sydney, which generated the proselytizing and lectures in Leigh House and the Protestant Hall by the Australian Socialist League, the radical reading culture nurtured in MacNamara's bookshop, and in the awakening of feminist activism reflected in the 1888 launch of Louisa Lawson's periodical, *Dawn*.[8]

Delivering her address in Leigh House in February 1895, Summerfield railed at this 'bureaucratic-governed demagogue-ridden country. . . . The new woman's field of work was humanity. The new woman led her assaults on cant, humbug, and commercialism.' The *Telegraph* reporter was troubled that this 'dangerous language' was met with 'widespread applause'. Summerfield knew that she could expect a relatively sympathetic hearing, particularly, the reporter claimed, as 'there were several young ladies in the audience'. 'Either they were curious spectators or they hadn't found sweethearts yet. It is only when a woman gets near the other side of 30 that she begins to have "views" on the marriage question.' It was on 'the marriage question' that Summerfield made some of her most provocative observations. 'Every day brings forth fresh evidence of the enormities of the wrong-doing caused by conventional marriage. . . . The god which joins most people together . . . is the god of Mammon, the spirit of selfishness, and the dominion of lust. That is the rule upon which marriage is contracted nowadays.' Summerfield hoped for the 'good days of socialism' when 'the cant of religious ceremonies should be cast out, and the miserable strife of a sordid commercialism should be banished, then marriage would be placed on a "rational" footing'.[9] For the first-wave feminists of the 1890s, rejecting conventional marriage and maternity constituted a necessary step, Susan Margarey argues, in fulfilling 'the logic of women's emancipation'.[10]

The *Telegraph* reporter observed that in her address Summerfield quoted 'the authors whose feminine creations excited her admiration. Ibsen was among them.' In Australia, Henrik Ibsen's play *A Doll's House* (1879) had perhaps the most penetrating impact in the period. *A Doll's House* 'marked an early intervention in the portrayal of the relation between the sexes as Nora [Helmer] dramatically slams the door of the family home in an unprecedented bid for freedom at the play's close'.[11] By the mid-1880s *A Doll's House* was embraced by London radicals including Eleanor Marx and George Bernard Shaw, and its influence soon found its way into the colonies; the first Australian production of Ibsen's play was staged in Melbourne in 1889.[12] This identification was concentrated in 1894, when the idea of the New Woman first found expression in the public sphere of the British world. The publication in London of Katherine Mannington Caffyn's novel *The Yellow Aster* in 1894 dramatically focused attention on this new conception of women's identity. Written in Australia, where Mannington Caffyn

Figure 6 A New Woman: Katherine Mannington Caffyn, the author of *The Yellow Aster*, may have served as the model of the sorceress in Charles Conder's *Hot Wind* (1889), adorned in the props that she had lent him. National Gallery of Australia.

lived until the early 1890s, and published under the pen name 'Iota', *The Yellow Aster* was written 'as a protest against a loveless marriage' and attracted sharply polarized responses in Britain and Australia, being both 'savagely condemned' and 'extravagantly praised', for its depiction of the Nora-like awakening of its heroine, Gwen Waring, 'from the "torpor" of a dull life'.[13] In Melbourne in the 1880s Katherine Mannington Caffyn and her husband Stephen, a medical practitioner who also published fiction, were said to enjoy anything but a dull marriage, living in a bohemian, 'Oscar Wilde' atmosphere.[14] In 1889 the young artist Charles Conder was drawn to their home; Katherine lent Conder a number of decorative items, muslin draperies and Liberty silks for his Melbourne studio. Conder painted a portrait of Katherine, in a colouring 'beautifully soft and clear' but now lost.[15] Katherine portrayed Conder as the character Charles Byrdon in *The Yellow Aster*, an artist of 'soft voice' and 'passionate' nature who dressed his studio 'in dolls house style'; 'Conder's bent towards Symbolism seems to have been strengthened by the theatrical and literary personalities with whom he came into contact.'[16] Ibsen's play, the cultivation of the New Woman and the artistic subjectivity of Symbolism forged new connections between individuals and stimulated activism and inspiration, reflecting the innovative and diverse ideas at work at the *fin de siècle* (Figure 6). Katherine Mannington Caffyn may have served as the model of Conder's *Hot Wind*, adorned in the props that she had lent him.[17]

Summerfield's 1895 address demonstrated how quickly a new identification of gendered self-expression and awareness was taken up and contested. The New Woman became a key battlefield of *fin de siècle* gender conflict in Australia and 'provided a vital testing ground for the radical ideas of the *fin de siècle*'.[18] In the mid-1890s the terms *fin de siècle* and 'New Woman' provided codes for signalling the inappropriate behaviour of women. In 1895, the Sydney *Evening News* published an attack on the New Woman by the British anti-feminist campaigner Eliza Lynn Linton. In rejecting 'the shaping force of motherhood', Linton argued that this new form of identity, 'under the names of *fin de siècle* and new woman, she is all wrong from start to finish, and a national disaster rather than a domestic blessing and a social ornament'. Foreign literary works identified as promoting the idea of the *fin de siècle* New Woman such as Ibsen's *Ghosts* and *Hedda Gabler* and Leo Tolstoy's *The Kreutzer Sonata* were also decried in the Australian press as 'impure', a threat to mothers and the healthy 'regeneration of the race'.[19]

In 1895 the *Australian Star* disputed the reality of this disruptive conception.

> Does the New Woman exist? ... For nebulous she certainly is, melting away into thin vapour when one demands of her who and what she is. ... She is supposed to look with a certain disfavor on domesticity, to go about with a chip on her shoulder among old-fashioned people who fancy that a woman's natural sphere is in the narrow world of home.... Whatever a man may do this product of a *fin de siècle* fancy is said to insist upon doing.[20]

In her Leigh House address Rose Summerfield faced a similar scorn from 'A hard-headed Scotchman named Sinclair', who confronted her from the floor. 'If woman was the equal of man, why didn't she, in this age of competition, enter the open field with him and show it? asked the Scotchman.'[21]

The idea of the New Woman that Summerfield stirred into life was confronted by the reality of working-class women compelled to hard labour in the family home and in an often ad hoc, improvised range of casual and permanent paid roles. In the Australian colonies in the 1890s women were denied property rights, rights within marriage – including equal rights in relation to income, divorce or the guardianship of children, access to contraception – and, with the exception of South Australia, the right to vote. Women were discouraged from full-time employment, although women laboured in factories, bootmaking, the clothing trades, laundries and the retail sector, and almost always for wages lower than those earned by men.[22] In an appeal published in the *Sydney Morning Herald* in 1893, Summerfield asked, 'How many hundreds of married women, mothers of families, have to enter any avenue of employment open to them, in order to maintain, not only themselves, but their children and husbands, plainly indicating the possession of great strength of body as well as brave determination?' The women's movement for equal political, economic and social rights gathered strength in the late nineteenth century, represented by the Womanhood Suffrage League (WSL). Women's participation in political life would 'assist poorer women and children to a fairer and happier life'.[23]

Summerfield was active in the NSW WSL following its formation in 1891. A political voice for women was crucial. 'If we had a voice in electing representatives to Parliament, I venture to maintain there would be no starving poor in our congested cities; there would be fewer divorces, and our children would be physically and mentally superior to the present generation', as a consequence of the suppression of child labour. Summerfield believed that if women were released from 'economic thraldom', then

> the biggest part of the woman question will soon be solved. . . . Those amongst us who are mothers would be very loth to allow girls of tender years to enter the factories and workrooms of the city. We know it is through rank injustice that any child under 17 years of age should be forced into the labour market.[24]

In asserting a right to organize and agitate, Summerfield observed that the WSL was 'not a body of women meeting together for amusement, but banded together to add our voice and work to that of the foremost guard of politicians who are prepared to treat females as rational human beings'.[25] It was difficult to find such politicians. In 1894 Summerfield joined a WSL deputation, including leaders Maybanke Wolstenholme and Rose Scott, that urged NSW premier George Reid to introduce legislation to extend the voting franchise to women. Reid 'expressed his sympathy with the object of the League' but dismissively added that 'the pressure of more important legislation' prevented anything be done at present. 'If the agitation were renewed in about twelve months' time they might be successful in securing some advance.'[26]

Like Summerfield, Rose Scott suffered the consequences of a prominent public profile, as the *Worker* noted in a front-page 'portrait', in text and illustration, of the 'untiring' WSL secretary in 1894. 'Those who entertain the vulgar prejudices against woman's rights advocates are fond of representing them as masculine-minded women who are anxious to usurp the proud position now occupied by the Lords of Creation.' Scott came from a family well connected with public life and Sydney society, and with whom she networked in prosecuting the WSL campaign, including attracting the support of the labour movement and a wider realm of political and social allies in the struggle for women's rights.[27] Scott corresponded with 'advocates of the enfranchisement of women in all parts of the civilized world, and is possessed of a fund of information and argument which never fails to convince all those who converse with her'. Rose Scott, the *Worker* declared, was 'one of those earnest patriots who wish for a vote . . . that she may use it in advancing the prosperity, the happiness, and the morality of her fellow women, and through them of all future generations of the Australian Nation.'[28] Both 'vulgar prejudice' and apathy proved stubborn obstacles. Maybanke Wolstenholme later described the 'ordeal' of campaigning for women's suffrage in the 1890s and which would not be achieved in New South Wales and across the Commonwealth until after the turn of the century. 'Indifference was a much more difficult enemy than open opposition.'[29]

Rose Summerfield believed that women's rights, and greater rights for the working class, could only be won through persistent 'agitation'. The labour press celebrated Summerfield's agitation.

> Say, *Hummer*, you ought to have heard Mrs Summerfield lecture at Leigh House the other night on Socialism. She made a really good speech, and to tell the square-toed truth my . . . adoring heart tickled the apple in my throat during the whole of her address. When the women folk make common cause with man the Revolution will heave ahead. A feminine boycott of scabs and sweaters would be more powerful than dynamite.[30]

Although the unions often discouraged women in the workforce, the labour press regularly represented their views, and women's place in the workforce was keenly observed and debated. In November 1892 the *Worker* criticized the 'conservative folly' of the typographical unions in the various colonies attempting to exclude women compositors. These women were part of an emerging network of 'brain workers' on whom the labour movement itself was relying to expand its mobilization. 'Nothing that the compositors have done will . . . prevent women setting type for non-union offices. Thus the associations have gone the right way to make blacklegs of the smartest of our women workers – and that is not Unionism.'[31]

Summerfield's proselytizing had turned to action in 1892 as an organizer of the Women's Division of the Australian Workers' Union, and she travelled to Bourke to mobilize women workers.[32] On 21 September, the day that a young Henry Lawson arrived by train in Bourke, *The Western Herald* advertised the addresses, including 'the Gospel of Discontent', that Summerfield would deliver in Drew's Hall in the first week of October.[33] Summerfield was intimidated by her first experience of the outback; she lamented that people did not 'revolt' against being compelled to work in the 'dry and dusty west'. 'Travelling across these great weary plains in the train I found myself thinking of man's consummate stupidity in allowing his desire for change, or his reverence for existing institutions, which? – to lead him out into a wilderness.' Summerfield wanted to stir her fellow workers out of a dejected resignation with being pulled into the gravitational orbit of capital that turned even a remote and arid space into production, whatever the consequences for those labouring in 'an atmosphere bordering on the mythical heat of Hades'.[34] In Bourke she set about her task with in a flurry of activism and incitement. Summerfield helped to establish a co-operative laundry staffed by women working under union pay rates and conditions. She established a branch of the AWU Women's Division and announced an intention of forming a branch of the Australian Socialist League. Most notably, she made a powerful impression as 'a rattling lecturer . . . full of fire and energy', as she returned to the theme that she had previously addressed in Sydney.[35]

On 3 October 1892 Rose Summerfield stood on the stage at Drew's Hall, and before an audience of 300 people delivered an address chaired by Hugh Langwell, elected as the first Labor Member of the NSW Parliament for Bourke in 1891. Summerfield urged her audience to a discontent with their circumstances.

> Are not the majority landless? Are not the majority just one step above being homeless? . . . Are you workers not wholly and solely under the thumb of the capitalists and monopolists? Are they not wrenching the screw a little tighter, trying desperately to force you into the acceptance of lower wages? . . . Can you not see it?

Although in order to understand their own condition, 'we do not need to read the cablegrams about the unfortunate ironworkers who earn the riches for inhuman wretches like Carnegie'. Summerfield stressed the global nature of the discontent that must be mobilized into action.

> I see in America, in England, all over the continents of Europe and Australia thousands and thousands of workmen becoming more and more dissatisfied with their surrounding conditions. I see millions of toilers, of every nation looking toward the future with a sickening dread. Some of them weary and distressed, plod on and vainly endeavour to cast all thinking aside, obeying their masters' mandates like poor caged animals in want of food, their keeper, standing over them with a stout whip.

Summerfield appealed to her audience to organize in their own interests and imagine a better world. 'If your bodies were free from the heavy manacles of endless toil your minds would have leisure to enjoy intellectual freedom. Discontent is freely spreading itself over the whole of the civilized globe, may it spread and flourish, may its seeds take deep root in healthy soil, it will lighten the almost superhuman tasks the social reforms have begun.' In her Leigh House address, 'Master and Man', in May 1892, Summerfield had worked herself into a passionate reverie, as if she could animate the superhuman energy required for a breakthrough transformation: 'Agitate! Agitate! I hope I'll die with that word on my lips,' she had declared. In Bourke this energy was unleashed in a prophetic plea.

> I wish I was possessed of the fire and eloquence and reason of a God so as I could force the knowledge of your wrongs upon you; so as I could make you feel as I feel the indignity, the injustice and shame that is forced upon you by a barbarous tyrannical society. We can go back to the dark ages and surely then no greater wrongs were done than now.[36]

At the conclusion Summerfield was 'heartily applauded'. Langwell thanked the audience 'for allowing me to preside at the first lecture ever given by a woman in Bourke'. Over 100 of the audience were women.[37] A fortnight later, 'a woman who heard the two lectures' delivered by Summerfield composed an equally forceful response to the scornful dismissal of 'anarchical and socialistic old women's meetings' that had been published in the local press, which she described as 'an insult to the great number of intelligent men and young women who attended these lectures'. Summerfield was not a 'he-female screeching in favour of anarchy'; Summerfield had urged discontent with parliamentary representatives who pretended 'to work in the interests of the toilers'. Neither was Summerfield's second lecture on 4 October 'anarchical' but

> was delivered with the intention of inducing the working girls to break from existing conditions, which crush and oppress them, and form a union for their benefit and protection. The laundry workers, for instance, who are sweated and badly paid, have turned 'anarchists' so far that they are about to start a co-operative laundry, where Chinese labour, sweating and long hours will be unknown.

The outraged correspondent hoped that 'the females will grow and flourish and spread the gospel of discontent in every town and city of Australia'.[38]

Summerfield's gospel was enflamed with racism. In 'Master and Man' she dramatized her visceral fear in Sydney's Belmore markets, amid Chinese 'almond eyed slaves', Syrian and Indian hawkers, Italian beggars in the lane ways. 'Ugh! The smell, the dirt, the unwholesomeness! If you are a woman you hear loud laughter, expressions of "welly nice", "welly good", from the lips of Chinese gamblers, and lewd eyes are fastened upon you by these creatures who are allowed to live huddled together like beasts instead of human beings.'[39] Lecturing across New South Wales in 1892, Summerfield laced her accounts of economic and political oppression with lurid images of 'the alien Mongol, the Chinese with their leprosy-breeding vegetables ... their vile opium dens, where so many of our sisters go to destruction'. This racial threat formed part of 'the reign of monopoly and tyranny' to which the white working class were compelled to submit.[40] Summerfield made no comment on the punitive discriminations experienced by the Indigenous, and neither acknowledged their existence in Sydney or the 'wilderness' of far western New South Wales. Her conception of a utopian arcadia or 'New Australia' was idealized as the inheritance of a white working class in which no other race had a legitimate place.

The report on Summerfield's 'Gospel of Discontent' address and her own account of arriving in Bourke were published in the pages of a significant labour movement innovation. The first edition of the *Worker* appeared on 24 September 1892. Incorporating *The Hummer*, and published by the Amalgamated Shearers' Union (ASU), the *Worker* was a more ambitious projection of a labour voice that would within a few months be published from the colonial capital. The emergence of the labour press was a product of technological innovation and a relative efficiency of industrial process that brought the possibility of regular weekly publication within reach of the new mass membership unions. The *Worker* also reflected 'the second industrial revolution of the mind', the product of 'brain workers' and 'nervous energy' mobilized in pursuit of social justice and hovering in the distant promise of transformation.[41] Both Rose Summerfield and Henry Lawson would feature as important contributors to the *Worker*, Summerfield from late 1892 and Lawson a year later; and both absorbed the tensions at work in the *fin de siècle* and projected them into their narratives. In the fledgling *Worker* Summerfield contributed her 'sister's column' under the pen name of 'Rose Hummer': 'One would prefer to be a HUMMER rather than a WORKER.' Summerfield identified with the thrum of agitation rather than the 'distasteful' drudge of work, of which 'we have all too much of it to do'.[42]

After helping to unionize the laundresses in Bourke, Rose Summerfield left to continue her agitation in other country centres before returning to Sydney. In Gundagai, a centre of the pastoral industry in southern New South Wales, Summerfield reminded her audience of their connection to the global system of capital and the struggles of workers against its oppressions, whose intensity she had never previously witnessed.

> The terrible conflict raging between capital and labour not only in Broken Hill at the present time but at the iron works in America, among the workers in France where the municipal council nobly stepped in and assisted the men on strike, the state of the starving poor in London, the general and very great distress existing

in all the colonies from Melbourne northwards to Brisbane, suburbs looking miserable through the poverty of the people ... all point out that something is radically wrong, that change is needed.

On the banks of the Murrumbidgee River which ran through the town, 'where miles and miles of the beautiful stream is enclosed, practically owned, by the tyrant squatters. . . . Who owns the beautiful hills around you, the beautiful green health giving country for miles distant? Who owns it all? Is it you, the people, the workers, the wealth-producers, or is it your masters, the tyrants, the monopolists?'[43] With 'fiery eloquence so characteristic of her sex', a reporter observed how in her Gundagai address Summerfield

> fiercely attacked the wrongs, the injustices, and the corruption of the age. 'Monopoly', warmly exclaimed this lady, with reasonable anger, with its attendant curse, competition, written in letters of blood on the gown of 'Liberty', is the flag that flies from every portal of state nowadays; it is flying from Parliament House, where Dibbs, McMillan, Burdekin, and Co. kneel down and worship it, and from the palaces where mock justice is dispensed it catches the breeze and rouses dismay in the minds of the toilers.

Although capital and its agents in Parliament were primarily responsible for the sufferings inflicted on the working class, in her addresses Summerfield provocatively drew the attention of her audience to their tolerance of this misrule. 'Are not you the people – the busy bees – to blame for a lot or the miseries you endure?' Working men and women had to take responsibility for changing the face of the world.

> Until you learn the lesson I have tried to explain to you to-night, you will have worse ills to undergo, more hardships will be forced upon the toilers throughout Australia. Take heed of the example set you by the barbarous treatment of your Broken Hill brothers, of your unionist leaders. Organise, agitate, federate, and use your best endeavours to destroy the reign of monopoly and tyranny. (Cheers.)[44]

Organizing and agitating were demanding tasks for working men and women, and all too often generated a punishing reaction. In late October 1892 a *Western Herald* correspondent complained that employees of the largest private laundry in the town had been discharged for 'the terrible crime' of attending a lecture on the economy and joining a union – almost certainly references to Summerfield's activism.[45] The Bourke Branch of the General Labourers' Union (GLU) hastily established a co-operative laundry to provide work for the discharged women. By mid-1893 the GLU reported that the co-op had not been as successful as anticipated, 'owing to the cut in prices by the privately-owned firm'. Paying union rates, the co-op struggled to compete with private laundries.[46] Nonetheless, the co-op was still functioning in October 1893, with the staff joining the annual eight-hour parade. 'The appearance of women workers in the line of procession for the first time was greeted with some wild cheering by the other participants and their sympathisers on the side walks.'[47]

The first woman to deliver a public address in Bourke had helped mobilize the first women to join a union and march in an eight-hour parade. Yet maintaining industrial and political activism required a commitment that Rose Summerfield found difficult to sustain in the 1890s. While participating in various bursts of activism in the labour movement, the Women's Suffrage League and the temperance movement, her disillusionment also grew, particularly with Australian workers and Labor politics. In the mid to late 1890s Summerfield's activism seemed subject to abrupt shifts, evident in short bursts of involvement in a number of groups; her participation in the WSL seemed to lapse in 1896, just as she became active in the Independent Order of Good Templars (IOGT) 'Heart of Oak' Lodge in Waverley. The IOGT campaigned in working-class communities, and temperance appealed to her ideal of fashioning a self-disciplined working class capable of its own transformation: 'the desire for strong drink' reflected 'the present deplorable condition of our working people'. However, her active participation in the IOGT seems soon to have lapsed.[48] Summerfield also resigned from the Australian Socialist League in 1897, bitterly lamenting workmen 'gulled' by the 'farce' of manhood suffrage.[49] Sheila Rowbotham observes 'the new spaces for heterodoxy' that enabled women in the period to embrace reform aspirations, ranging from 'extreme forms of individualism' to collectivism, as anarchists or socialists, bohemians or 'eugenic enthusiasts'.[50] This novel and experimental heterodoxy could also make it difficult to identify the most effective or desirable course of action or sustain what could seem a lonely and unrewarding activism.

Perhaps workers could not live up to the intensity of her vision and which contested with other analyses and prejudices churning in the *fin de siècle* public sphere. In 1894 the press observed the conflicted interpretations of the New Woman, at a time when this barely established identity seemed already to be shattering into a myriad of conflicting elements.[51] This scrutiny was spurred by the visit to Australia by Annie Besant, who had first won fame and notoriety in England as a champion of contraception and secularism, then turning to socialism, and agitation to redress the cruel working lives of London's match girls. In these vibrant challenges Besant had also influenced a number of

Australian feminists and radicals. In a profile that announced her forthcoming Australian tour, the Sydney *Daily Telegraph* observed that Besant's life story reflected four distinct phases: Christianity, atheism, socialism and Theosophy. 'One uses the word distinct phases deliberatively; for the first three, in their turn, were as paramount and absorbing as Theosophy is now to this deeply emotional and ardent woman.'[52]

The first three phases were already behind Annie Besant. By 1894 Besant toured Australia as the 'high priestess' of Theosophy, the vague alternative religion that promiscuously borrowed from Eastern mysticism. Besant had assumed leadership of this spiritual movement in Britain and had abandoned her leading position in the Social Democratic Federation, which she had helped to form. Like a number of her *fin de siècle* contemporaries, Besant was on a restless search for liberation and self-expression that could trigger abrupt shifts in identity and faith or produce a curious hybrid of loyalties and activism, as Rose Summerfield had embraced a range of campaigns and causes since the mid-1880s. Summerfield had followed a similar transition from freethought and women's rights to temperance and socialism, although she did not embrace alternative religious faith, even as Theosophy began to attract followers among working-class radicals in Sydney such as John Dwyer.[53] Evidently Besant 'has parted from the sect of the New Woman', although she would yet be remembered 'as one who led the revolt' against 'female bondage'. Besant seemed to represent a disruptive if creative element of woman 'genius' that was the subject of the dubious yet influential psychological assessment provided by the famed Italian criminologist Cesare Lombroso, as an editorial published in Broken Hill's *Barrier Miner* described. Women geniuses were 'organic anomalies' who can 'hardly be said to be females', lacking the physiological capacity for true male genius:

> The New Woman . . . has been in a most degrading bondage . . . the outcome of the absence of master minds among womankind, and the presence of a multitude of mere copyists lacking originality . . . it is because of this aptness at copying that the New Woman – 'the shrieking sisterhood' in all grades – is become so numerous in so short a time.[54]

The New Woman was subject to a harsh gaze, an identity drafted into a gender battle intensified by undisciplined pseudo-scientific assertions that often characterized the flux of new ideas at work at the *fin de siècle*. The New Woman Rose Summerfield looked into her own society with an agitated scrutiny. It was not an abstract assessment of class and capital but was steeped in subjective perspective, interpreted through the immediacy of her experience. Summerfield's racialized radicalism was most vividly expressed as her own instinctive responses, as she passed through the Belmore market or the streets of Sydney, a daily experience that also stirred other tough judgements. In September 1895 Summerfield described spending 'a few hours in Sydney streets'. 'There is always something to pain one in a busy city', and often it seemed to Summerfield to be the sight of women struggling to maintain their roles and appearances. Her observations were torn between scorn and sympathy, of women 'with hair like tangled hemp that showed of dyer's aid, with cheeks that aped the lily or the rose, tawdry imitations that scarcely could deceive'; or the well-dressed who 'give orders in the smartest shops' to shop girls with listless gaits from 'long hours of standing'; 'the sickly gas has given them unhealthy hue' as they 'parrot utterances': 'A beautiful glove, indeed.' Summerfield felt oppressed by a merging human type 'understood as "Civilisation"'.

> On my way home the faces ran into each other: The match vendor, the old wrinkled-orange seller, the blind singer, the paper runner, the fashionably dressed lady, the shop girls, the bread-and-butter misses, the carriage dames, the skinny bundle woman, the money-lender's greasy partner, the liquor-vendor's spouse, they all ran into one composite portrait. Upon analysis I found 'twas a sickly face, the outcome of false delicacy, greed, gluttony, unchasteness, avariciousness, canting hypocrisy, and unnatural surroundings.[55]

This composite face was not unlike the alienating racial types that confronted her in the Belmore markets. Yet these women were struggling individuals whom Summerfield believed needed to be moulded to the common purpose of political mobilization and rebirth as new women. 'A few hours in Sydney streets' reflected Summerfield's disillusionment not only with capitalism but modern urban industrial life and the potential of workers to transform their circumstances.

In the *Worker* in February 1899 Summerfield derided parliamentary politics and expressed doubts that the movement towards the federation of the colonies as an Australian nation would benefit workers and their families. It was not the 'commercial men who advance their country's good . . . it is not the men in State offices but the dreamers and thinkers' who could realize 'the vast possibilities that a well-ordered community would yield to every man, woman and child that formed it. Educate and agitate till the dreams become realities.'[56] Yet as Summerfield expressed these views the editions of the *Worker* were filled with reports of the labour movement's active participation in colonial democracy and which urged workers to obtain elector's rights.[57]

From early in the decade, a divide had opened within the labour movement over whether to continue to pursue reform within the colonies or seek a 'New Australia' beyond its shores. Rose Summerfield had long been interested in William Lane's New Australia socialist co-operative settlement in Paraguay, established in 1893. In May 1892 Summerfield imagined 'an industrial hive', created by 'our great socialist reformers'. In 'Master and Man' she had envisioned a community in which 'freedom, social equality, individual independence for man and woman is willingly acknowledged the law of the land'.[58] Summerfield returned to this theme in an October 1895 address to a meeting of the Social Democratic Federation. Summerfield argued that 'the basis of injustice was land monopoly . . . any attempt that might be made by organised labour to better their condition would be futile while land was privately owned and worked for the benefit of a few'.[59] The fledgling Social Democratic Federation had only formed a few months earlier and struggled to make an impact on the fractious politics of the labour movement. With her address meeting a 'somewhat critical' reception, it seemed that she would have to look elsewhere to realize her dream of an industrial hive.[60]

While Summerfield was in Bourke in October 1892, the *Worker* had published a 'friendly criticism' of Lane's scheme. The *Worker* felt that Lane, the fiery and persuasive editor of leading labour movement journals, and author of the popular and provocative fictional account of labour's struggles *The Workingman's Paradise*, was offering a vague dream.

> The disappointing feature in the New Australia Movement is, at first sight, the conviction on the part of its founders that Communism will have a better show on the soil of a South American republic than on our own soil. The majority of us fancy that Communism has just now as little chance of striking root in one part of the world as another.

It was doubtful that the settlers would be able to overcome entrenched acquisitive instincts. 'The majority of us are not materially interested in watching a handful of settlers trying to look good tempered over an equal division of profits . . . a piece of self-effacement that may be all very well for the few but which is all together beyond the morality of the many.' The *Worker* also wondered why the New Australians deemed 'it better to establish themselves amongst a Latin people where the distinctions of race will emphasise their identity'.[61]

New Australia, as it had been conceived by Lane, promised socialism, equal rights for women, temperance and racial exclusion. Yet by mid-1894 the community that Lane and his fellow pioneers established in rural Paraguay had already acrimoniously splintered. Lane was autocratic and intolerant of dissent, and many colonists struggled to adapt to the isolated rigours of a settlement in the humid Paraguayan hinterland. As one disillusioned pioneer wrote: 'Paraguay is no place for a white man to work in, as under the most favourable conditions he will not obtain sufficient to provide him with the necessaries, not to speak of comforts, of life.'[62] The *Worker* published an idiosyncratic self-justification penned by Lane, couched in religious language and explaining nothing of the cause of the split. 'I am sinful, as we all are.' The *Worker* reported that Lane had led his loyal followers away from the New Australia colony to establish a new settlement, Cosme. 'Possibly the division of the settlers into two camps may not be a permanent disadvantage, but it is easy to see that in the present and for some time to come it will greatly complicate operations.' With evident satisfaction the conservative *Sydney Morning Herald* reported the disintegration of the New Australia colony. A vision of happy brotherhood had vanished 'like a mist on the mountains'. 'Government', the *Herald* concluded, 'of some kind on the old-fashioned pattern seems to be a necessary evil, even to the most freedom-loving people.'[63] *Worker* editor James Medway Day could not contain his frustration with a project that had distracted the movement from the need to reform 'Old Australia'. 'Neither the individual nor the State is to be lectured out of vice or scolded into virtue. And neither the individual nor the State can jump into a better state of things in one act, nor will they do so by simply changing their location.'[64]

Lane's dream did not entirely vanish. In November 1897 he claimed that Cosme represented 'a workingman's paradise'. It was a colony of teetotallers (Summerfield would have been pleased to hear) working for 'the common weal': 'Only think: for thirty-six hours of work per week the happy communist is supplied with all the necessaries and perhaps with some of the luxuries of life. During two and a half days each week he dances, sings, and plays cricket!'[65] In January 1898 an anonymous 'New Australian pioneer' claimed that the 'Paraguayan colonies' were doing well and were fulfilling the ideal of co-operation. 'Workers should realize that union for protection against capitalistic combination is not sufficient. Union for production is the real solution.'[66]

Summerfield clung to Lane's vision throughout the 1890s. In February 1899, doubts of parliamentary reform contrasted with a lyrical reflection on flowers that summoned a vision of communal arcadia. 'Thoreau, Emerson, and others revelled in a life among flowers and trees in the open,' she told a lecture audience. 'A paddock of wild flowers – of course, it was paddock, as nearly all the beauty spots were fenced in – was a real object-lesson. There without costly governments, taxes, rulers, or policemen, they lived amicably together, giving of their perfume and beauty in return for sustenance and room to live.' Humans were like flowers and 'required land to live on, and with free land and the money, or exchange system – at present a great power for evil – taken out of private hands we should be well on the road to the millennium – that to which Socialists aspire'.[67] A month later she lamented the frustrating contrast provided by the reality of Australian colonial life. 'What a pity the masses are so slow in grasping the idea of the benefits that would accrue from Unionism and co-operation'.[68] By then, frustration with Australia had already resolved in a decision to engage with a great experiment. In April 1899 Rose Summerfield and Jack Cadogan set out together for New Australia. She had married the former shearers' cook and mine manager in September 1897. Labor MP George Black presided at their send-off, which included AWU president William Guthrie Spence and the socialist and feminist May Hickman. 'The company present included representatives of every section of the reform movement, united in the common desire to do honor to Mrs. Cadogan, whose earnestness arid singleness of purpose manifested during more than thirteen years of service in the reform movement in Sydney has won the respect of all.'[69]

New Australia was a product of powerful forces at work at the *fin de siècle*: utopianism and globalization both spread as cultural and political influence via the new communication technologies of telegraph and undersea cable, which facilitated the rapid transmission of news and new ideas.[70] The arcadian socialist fantasizes of writers and artists like William Morris helped to nurture longings for an 'earthly paradise', as Morris styled the ideal rural commune, free of the industrial grime of city life that he popularized in *News from Nowhere* (1890). 'In Morris's visionary Nowhere, England became a physically beautiful place, full of attractive people who enjoyed their work.'[71] Even as division and sheer exhausting labour were undermining the New Australia settlements in the late 1890s, in the pages of the *Worker* its evangelists persisted in claiming that in these colonies Morris's utopia had been made real. Throughout the late 1890s Morris's work appeared in the Australian labour press. His poem 'The Voice of Toil' was regularly reprinted in the *Worker* in 1898–9, an emblematic talisman of the struggle for justice.[72] Rose Cadogan's Morris-style motivational verse was also published in the *Worker*. 'Here and Now' bore more than a little similarity to Morris exhortation to maintain the struggle. 'This is our moment – there's none other,' she reminded readers in January 1898.[73] The will to seize her moment had led to New Australia (Figure 7).

Paraguay intensified Rose Cadogan's alienation. Lane's experiment had foundered in permanent division. As the Cadogans arrived in Paraguay in

Figure 7 'This is our moment – there's none other.' The will to seize her moment led to William Lane's New Australia settlement in Paraguay in 1899. Rose Summerfield, portrait photo. Undated. State Library of New South Wales.

1899, Lane departed, never to return. In November 1901 Rose wrote to the *Worker*, from a small hinterland town, Los Ovegas, 'where her husband keeps a store', which was worked by his wife, as she raised their children. Rose Cadogan warned readers not to believe all they heard about Paraguay. 'It is a fine country, but, owing to the ignorance, indolence, and superstition of the natives, it is a poor place to live in, and anyone may do better in any part of Australia. One regrets that such good workers in the reform cause should be buried among strangers and retrogrades.'[74] New Australia proved an illusion; as much as it represented aspiration and hope, her image of it was also formed in her reaction against Sydney, a port city exposed to the infiltration of foreignness, an insidious alienation that through New Australia she had expected to escape. The forces at work at the *fin de siècle* were unruly and heterogeneous, reflecting the acceleration into a modern world in which technology and capital, new ideas and people themselves spilled the boundaries of nations and communities. Rose Cadogan's escape from strangers might have been realized within the closed borders of a White Australia, enacted as a consequence of the creation of the Australian nation in 1901 and the passage of the Immigration Restriction Act.

In the 1890s Rose Summerfield had embraced the *fin de siècle* promises of innovation and self-invention offered by the New Woman and New Australia, bursting the bounds of restraint that oppressed women and the working class. Yet she embodied the tension between tradition and innovation, reflecting and internalizing conflicts that seemed within reach of resolution – and almost impossible to resolve. The *fin de siècle* often held out elusive promises of transformation. Her vision of the contented future of the 'civilization' of a fulfilled woman was essentially traditional. In contrast to the sickly composite face of women she encountered in Sydney's streets, she also imagined that

> Sometimes when gazing on them the eyes of the women seem to soften and glow, and the mouth quivers as with a pure desire, the shapely bosom lifts and falls, and it may be but fancy – a melodious voice whispers, 'We mothers, wives, sisters, daughters, look back on the past with sorrow that we endured so long; farther back we glide and from every era take a pattern. We look into the eyes of harlots whom men worshipped – into the hearts of the women who bore their children. We learn a mighty lesson. We go into the fields and see fine limbed women reaping at their husband's side, women full of health and beauty suckling shapely infants, holding husband's hearts – and back again to the present we come, the patterns in our hands; and soon we women will choose and mould – and soon the world will be clothed in womanly beauty.' And methinks I see an answering look of welcome in the eyes of men.[75]

She had high expectations of women to embrace self-improvement, a standard hard-pressed working women might have struggled to live by.

> It is fully time that women began to learn their economic ABC. It thus behoves intelligent women to study the economic question. The matter of rent, interest, and wages is a vital one affecting them all to more or less extent, and the charm of a form of society where labor was freed from economic slavery, where the vileness of competition was eliminated through industrial unity and co-operation, should commend itself largely to their sympathy and attention. It is high time women made a powerful effort on behalf of suffering humanity.[76]

In 1896 Summerfield described a Morris-like contrast between a rural arcadia, 'A miniature world with seas and lakes, long stretches of beautiful country, fields of waving corn; the harvest fields were golden, the orchard lands were full of beautiful trees laden with fruit, and surely that glittering, moving show was a crowd of well-apparelled people!' By contrast the city was represented as 'this inferno . . . sucking in new victims', an inferno that drew together all the evils that animated her activism and her imagination. 'The refuse boxes stood at the front doors poverty in all its unloveliness stalked around. Stuffy drink shops added their unsavory smells – the very dregs of human society here debauched and orgied. White and black and yellow scum huddled and banded together, steeped themselves in opium and poison drink, that for a while blunted their misery.'[77]

Angelique Richardson has argued that the 'New Woman' was 'a contentious term, seeking to bring together, and limit within a single definition, a number of social and political positions, as the voices of women themselves, or those sympathetic to the women's cause, vied with their opponents'.[78] In *fin de siècle* Sydney women reflected a heterogeneous welter of experience and response, new attitudes and beliefs vying with tradition and familiar practice, negotiating the grind of toil. Rose Summerfield transferred agitation into her perception of those around her, the racially vilified, the social slaves mired in misery and not least the women of whom she expected so much; her observations of men were often less harsh, although it was men in whose interest the social and economic system functioned. 'Educate and agitate till the dreams become realities,' Summerfield urged in 1899.[79] Agitation reflected an anxious pressure to transform imagination and circumstance, a hard burden to shoulder as the accelerating energies of capital and radicalism collided in the last decade of the nineteenth century, driving one new woman from Australia in pursuit of an elusive dream.

3

The wanderer

Christopher Brennan's two lives in *fin de siècle* Sydney

> Harsh mother, thou hast drunk our soul unborn;
> take now this outworn flesh and our despair:
> within thy lap at least we shall not care
> if here no grove of pillar'd arches warn
> some wanderer above our moulder'd bones
> how once we dream'd beside these uncouth stones.
> *Christopher Brennan, Twilights of the Gods and the Folk.*[1]

In July 1902 a visitor from Melbourne recorded his impressions of Sydney: a busier metropolis than its southern cousin, confined by its hilly and irregular terrain. A population as large as Melbourne packed into half the space of the 'great plain' of the Victorian capital. Hurrying throngs funnelled down narrow city streets and swarmed into electric trams, so that 'one longs to get far from the madding crowd, and for a time listen to . . . the gentle lullaby of the waves as they ripple along the shore' of Sydney Harbour. The 'watery indentations penetrate the city in a puzzling fashion to strangers', opening space for trade and shipping, the drunken cavorting of sailors – 'Jack ashore is not a teetotaller', and 'the unchecked solicitation of women on the streets', seeking the company of carousing Jack. The unnamed Melburnian was also confronted by the rowdy Sunday afternoon ritual in the broad open space of the public Domain, 'thronged with thousands of people, who are addressed by stump orators on all kinds of conceivable and unconceivable subjects', demanding 'the nationalisation of wealth' or extolling the virtues of 'The New Thought' or the 'Gospel of Love'; a 'snarling philosopher in the shape of an illiterate German', 'scoffed at everything, except his own words'; a young man with 'shrill voice' and 'staring eyes, was speaking on – one scarce knew what. He had been in gaol, etc., etc., but from what we gathered, he was not like Japhet in search of a father, but was looking for the bones of his mother, she died at Elmore, etc.' The visitor found himself immersed in 'a strange Babel.... These babblers were all intensely in earnest. Freedom of speech seemed to have run mad.' Once more it was a relief 'to walk along the sea, and being on the placid waters of the harbour', to hear sailors gathered on the stern of a man-of-war, singing 'the sweet words' of 'Abide with Me, Help of the Helpless, Oh, Abide with Me'.[2]

Sydney was a city of its harbour, a basin of beauty into which poured dreams and raw sewage. In the winter of 1902 plague rats were still found among the ramshackle stores and industrial wharves of Darling Harbour, although another outbreak like 1900 was thought unlikely.[3] The 'pressing evil' of the pollution of the harbour was a menace to the 'thousands' who passed over it, not least by crossing the new steel swing span bridge opened at the beginning of the month and which linked Pyrmont Point with the city at Market Street. Thousands converged to celebrate the opening of the bridge, squabbling and snatching for patches of the ribbon cut by the Lady Mayoress.[4] Later that month crowds milled for the nightly illuminations strung along the facades of public and private buildings to celebrate the coronation of Edward VII. Above the ferry wharves at Circular Quay, the inscription 'Australia Greets the King' beamed from the Customs House, 'a beautiful sight' viewed from the harbour. The Town Hall and the General Post Office were 'brilliantly illuminated', although misty rain and a cold wind blowing up from the water could extinguish the gas jets, the traditional source of light; the streets were 'sloppy and muddy'. From some facades, new electric globes blinked 'defiance to the elements'.[5] The elements could implacably impose; winter fogs enveloped Port Jackson 'in a thick heavy haze', obscuring the view eastward until mid-morning.[6]

The divide between nature and human activity was part of the display and experience of Sydney Harbour. Anyone crossing the harbour by ferry or walking its overlooking rises could absorb it into the memory of being, as a wanderer drew his solitary evening steps beside 'this wayside harbour'; so the poet Christopher Brennan described the site of his lonely vigil in his 'Wanderer' series of poems.[7] The wandering in Brennan's poems was defined by the topography of its own traces, 'following the ridge ... alone with night', a dark space in which the self dissolved in its steps, as he described in the first of this series, published in the jubilee edition of *Hermes*, the University of Sydney's magazine, in July 1902.[8] In the early 1890s the university graduate and poet seemed poised on the cusp of a brilliant career, a talented language scholar travelling to study in Berlin. By the turn of the century Brennan's 'Wanderer' poems reflected the search of a wanderer 'on the way to himself', although trapped in frustration, unable to secure a teaching post at the University of Sydney, as controversies over his personality and his poetry blocked his path. Brennan felt suspended in a colonial by-water of the intellectual ferment sweeping the globe, a culture preoccupied with the narrow insularity of nation building following the federation of the colonies in 1901 as the Commonwealth of Australia.

The imagined identity of the wanderer was much on Brennan's mind in the early years of the new century. In 1903 Brennan told the University of Sydney's Philosophical Society 'that man is a wanderer by nature', that is, 'in process of becoming self-conscious'. Brennan seemed to embrace a radical relativism of identity: 'man is no fixed type, but a transitory product of the continual flux and transformation of species.'[9] The continual flux of shaping identity had proved dispiriting. By 1902 the 'Wanderer' poems expressed an ambitious quest already exhausted, caught, in Brennan's own poetic style, between the appeal of new Symbolist ideas and the pull of Victorian tradition. A decade of pursuit had found, according to the last of the sequence of poems published in *Hermes*, 'no ending of the way, no home, no goal', left divided between two lives, as he later ruefully acknowledged, of the dreaming realm of the mind and a tawdry reality.[10]

Christopher Brennan was born into a working class, Irish Catholic family in the Haymarket district of Sydney in 1870; his father was a brewer by trade. Brennan was educated by the Jesuits at St Aloysius' College from the age of eleven. He won a scholarship to attend Riverview College from 1885 and again under the tutelage of the Jesuit order: 'I had no hope of getting to Riverview without assistance.'[11] Often disregarding the set curriculum, Brennan immersed in classical Greek and Latin literature.[12] By 1888 he was student at the University of Sydney and was soon editing the literary journal *Hermes*. His reading remained 'wide . . . I roamed around the old library where you could pick the books off the shelves'. He read Tennyson, Swinburne, Hugo, Balzac and Gautier. Brennan made a vivid impression on teachers and friends alike, physically tall with a shock of dark hair swept back from an imposing brow and intense blue eyes, declaiming verse and opinion in a resonant voice as he embarked on his bold and iconoclastic course.[13] At the university he abandoned his vocation for the priesthood; in his nineteenth year he seemed to be searching for a 'religious experience – which wouldn't come'.[14] Lapsing from Catholicism, Brennan then 'spent the rest of his life trying in philosophy, love and poetry to establish a new kind of absolute', which Brennan rendered with a capital A, to symbolize his efforts, as a twenty-year-old philosophy student in 1890, 'to elaborate a special epistemology of the Unknowable, which was the Absolute'.[15] Brennan's quest for the Absolute was stimulated by the award of a travelling scholarship to study at the University of Berlin in 1892–4, after graduating from the University of

Figure 8 A wanderer 'on the way to himself'. Christopher Brennan, c. 1898. A portrait gift to his friend John Le Gay Brereton, with whom Brennan collaborated on the short-lived *Australian Magazine* in 1899. State Library of New South Wales.

Sydney with honours in Philosophy and Classics. For Brennan, the quest for the Absolute involved a search for an Eden on earth; from the mid-1890s, he explored under eclectic influences the *fin de siècle* literary and artistic code of Symbolism and which found a belated assertion in his self-styled *livre composé*, *Poems*, the collection of his work published in 1914.[16] Brennan never precisely defined the terms of the quest or what its final goal might look like (Figure 8).

The Melbourne visitor of July 1902 had delighted in the 'small fleet of swift ferry boats' that 'ply to and from scores of bays' and which had helped facilitate the growth of new suburbs, including Mosman on Sydney's north shore, and 'much cheaper than in Melbourne'. Splendid freestone homes were 'being erected in all directions' at Mosman and connected with the city by ferry and electric tram.[17] By mid-1902, Brennan was regularly crossing the harbour from his home at Mosman to his employment as a librarian in the Public Library of New South Wales. Returning from Berlin in 1895, Brennan remained with the Public Library for fourteen years. By 1902 his material circumstances had recently been secured in promotion to the position of cataloguer and from the arrival from Berlin of his mother-in-law, who had purchased a property and built a new family home.[18]

A measure of recognition as a serious poet was also provided by the substantial space allocated to Brennan's work in *Hermes*. It was a gesture that stood in contrast to the repeated denial of an academic post at the University of Sydney, a rejection largely due to his Bohemian reputation since the late 1890s; it was not until 1909 that he was finally appointed Assistant Lecturer in Modern Literature. Both Brennan's creativity and his marginalization were sourced in his quest for a breakthrough in literary success drawn from a transformed consciousness. Brennan explored this search in the poems written between the mid-1890s and the early twentieth century and was further outlined an important statement of his ideals and literary influences in a series of lectures, 'Symbolism in Nineteenth Century Literature', delivered in 1904. It is these texts that illuminate Brennan's immersion in the *fin de siècle* imagination. Scholars have richly explored the symbolic terrain of Brennan's poetry and the identity that he had hoped to locate in the Absolute.[19] There has also been debate about identifying Brennan as an incipient modernist – that is, projecting Brennan beyond his time, as a harbinger of the future.[20] There has been less focus on the 1904 lectures and in approaching the development of Brennan's ideas and work in the context of the intellectual and material ferment of his own time.

The selection of poems published in *Hermes* in 1902 and the Symbolism lectures delivered two years later reflect the 'double consciousness' of the *fin de siècle*: an 'emphasis on the pluralistic nature of human consciousness, in contrast to the penchant of many Victorian thinkers to represent the self as rational, unified, and stable'. A perception borrowed from the Romantics, and not least the poet William Blake, had a significant influence on Brennan. Under the influence of the French poets Charles Baudelaire and Stéphane Mallarmé, Brennan turned to the *fin de siècle* perception 'in which traditional, hierarchical oppositions – rational and irrational, masculine and feminine . . . disenchantment and enchantment' were found to be 'co-terminous, existing in tense equilibrium'.[21] A tension evident in the unresolved conflict in Brennan's poetry, which turned between the dual influences and inflections of nineteenth-century Victorian poetry and the arch elisions of the Symbolist movement flourishing from the late nineteenth century. Greg Melleuish has observed Brennan's contemporaries contesting the meaning of the poet's legacy, 'what the Master embodied', as either 'a bearer of an aesthetic religion that derived from the European pagan tradition', the 'Catholic Latin tradition' or 'the moody Celt who had lost his faith'.[22] Perhaps all these elements contested in Brennan's imagination. Brennan struggled with the *fin de siècle* divide between the clamour of new ideas and the relief of tradition, as he sought a new path: towards the Absolute, then in accepting that he must turn from it – a duality evident in his self-conscious sense of difference as an isolated intellectual and poet, apparently disinterested in Australian nationalism and its culture.

Yet Brennan was part of the strange Babel of *fin de siècle* Sydney, the metropolis hovering in the flicker of gas jets and the flare of electric light. In July 1902, the newspapers and periodicals that reported the publication of *Hermes* also noted the monthly meeting of the Universal Brotherhood and Theosophical Society, during which addresses 'from the Theosophical standpoint' were given on 'The Meaning and Purpose of Life', 'Harmony', 'Life, and Not Death' and 'Capital Punishment'. 'Musical selections were rendered at intervals.'[23] There was excitement over the commencement of the Australian tour of 'the modern Hercules', Eugen Sandow, whose feats of weightlifting and lion wrestling excited audiences around the world.[24] The famed German-born strongman's books on physical culture and bodybuilding were international bestsellers and addressed an anxiety over degeneration and the decay of male vitality; exciting the interest of a portly George Reid, the former NSW premier and federal political leader was much mocked in the press for his embrace of Sandow's physical exercise regime.[25] Embracing eugenics, Sandow was the bearer of a virile modernity: 'his system offered a rational, scientific program for reform, a way for everybody to cope with the stresses of modern society.'[26] Some imagined an even more impressive figure to represent Australian modernity. In early July it was reported that the New South Wales Minister for Works, E. W. O'Sullivan, had suggested to the trustees of the will of the late Cecil Rhodes that the sum of £100,000 should be gifted as a donation to erect a 'colossal' statue of 'Australia Facing the Dawn' in Sydney Harbour.[27] Fantasies of the past fed fantasies of the future. Considered in isolation, Brennan's work may seem aberrant in the culture of *fin de siècle* Sydney; it is better understood as an intense expression of it.

It was in Berlin that Brennan discovered the works of the Symbolists, particularly Mallarmé, and a wide range of contemporary French Symbolist writers, including Joris-Karl Huysmans and Villiers de L'Isle-Adam. He also read the romantic poet Novalis; he had found his way to Baudelaire prior to leaving Sydney.[28] Symbolists believed that absolute truths could only be accessed by indirect literary or artistic methods. They wrote in a highly metaphorical and suggestive manner, endowing particular images or objects with symbolic meaning and aiming 'to free themselves from the perceived drudgery of normative existence'.[29] The Symbolist manifesto published in France in 1886 by Jean Moréas announced that Symbolism's goal was to 'clothe the Ideal in a perceptible form' – what constituted this ideal was not clearly defined, although what was important was not so much the goal as the process of transcendence itself.[30]

Gabriele Fahr-Becker observes that 'The Greek word *symbolon* describes the secret signs by which those sworn to mystic cults recognised one another. Thus the symbol as a bearer of coded messages to a chosen few has the power of revelation.'[31] The Symbolists 'attracted Brennan because they were something of a private discovery. Mallarmé especially was almost unknown in Australia, and even in France, where he was better known, he was as a rule hardly understood.'[32] The impulse of shared secrets and private discovery points to a contradiction in Brennan's work: between communicating with a wider audience while expressing his message in a symbolic language that only a few – perhaps only himself – could really understand.

Brennan's interest in Symbolism did not entirely evolve in isolation. The work of several of Brennan's contemporary Australian poets reflected Symbolist influence that seemed to flourish as Brennan's quest flagged. Hugh McCrae's poetry drew on Greek myths and the medieval past and was 'full of satyrs, centaurs, unicorns, fauns and nymphs', including 'Courage to Conquer', published in *Lone Hand* in December 1907 and which described an apparently ancient, legendary tale of the narrator summoning the resolve to overcome a threatening archer, the courage to conquer evidently a lesson necessary to impart to his fellow Australians.[33] Victor Daley's dream of a feminine 'Muse' who 'weaves a wild, sweet magic rune' was published in *Lone Hand* in August 1907, as was Bernard O'Dowd's 'Fate', illustrated with a young maiden contentedly coiled in the Art Nouveau curve of a pair of snakes; in Symbolist works, women ambiguously represented innocence and temptation. The 'many incarnations' of fate lure 'the voyaging soul' and whose 'avatars' included 'Augustine, Calvin, and Mahound'.[34]

Symbolism was one of the European ideas and artistic styles that influenced the Australian sculptor Bertram Mackennal, whose *Circe* (1892–3), the beguiling bronze of the woman as sorceress, was internationally recognized. The artist Rupert Bunny's embrace of Symbolism provided him with access to the Paris salon, integration denied Brennan.[35] The work of the artist Sydney Long and the illustrator David Henry Souter reflected Symbolist and Art Nouveau influences; both Long and Souter collaborated with Brennan in 1899 on *The Australian Magazine*, discussed later, and illustrated Brennan's verse. Brennan's work influenced the imaginative stylizations of Long's major work, *Spirit of the Plains* (1897), immediately associated with an incipient nationalism, described as 'essentially Australia, beautifully decorative, and full of feeling'.[36] A naked maiden piper leads an elegant arch of dancing Brolgas (Australian cranes), within spare towers of ghost gums: a moment of transcendent magic fixed beneath a brilliantly lit sky. The delicately coloured poetic representation of *Spirit of the Plains* is considered a 'masterpiece' of Australian Art Nouveau, populating 'the prosaic Australian bush with nymphs and fauns', an adaptation of sinuous dream-infused lines. 'Art Nouveau emphasised the verticals and the rhythms of our ti-tree, spindly eucalyptus, long grasses and reeds.'[37] The work of the artists Tom Roberts and Arthur Streeton impressed Brennan. Streeton adopted Symbolist ideas and Art Nouveau motifs in *The Spirit of the Drought* (1896), as did his fellow Heidelberg artist Charles Conder's *Mirage* (1889). Conder functioned as a 'conduit' for Symbolist influences on Streeton; in both these works the mythic maiden conjured not dance but the bleached-bone death of drought.[38] Symbolism also incited scorn and bafflement. 'It is very nice to be a Symbolist', *Truth*, Sydney's caustically deflating satirical periodical, declared. 'You have only to say something, and the readers or hearers of your work supply as many meanings as the heart of man could desire . . . beautiful interpretations [may be] drawn by some critical conjurer out of the apparently empty hat.'[39] To supply as many meanings as the heart may desire aptly describes Brennan's quest.

Symbolism represented Brennan's narrative construction of his aim to live beyond good and evil, and the mean dualities of existence. Reflecting that life consisted not only of 'high movements' like poetry but also of weeks and months of dullness and mediocrity, Brennan observed in his 1904 Symbolism lectures:

> There are, as most of us keenly feel, two lives: that lies in the brightness of truth, this stumbles in error; that is radiant with love and beauty, this is vexed with its own littleness and meanness; that is unfettered, lying beyond good and evil, this is caught in the quagmire.[40]

Brennan seemed to attract 'meanness', denied a university post although he 'was at that time better read in, and a more original critic of, European literature than anyone else in Australia'.[41] Counting against Brennan was the reputation that followed the publication of *Towards the Source: XXI Poems* in 1897. His first published collection of poems was a slim volume of work composed since 1894, in a small print run of 200 copies. *XXI Poems* proved a commercial failure, receiving a hostile reception in the press and even among some of Brennan's circle. *XXI Poems* apparently scandalized respectable opinion, not least the University of Sydney's professors and senators, with innocuous lines like 'We sat entwined an hour or two together (how long I know not) underneath pine-trees'.[42]

Since his undergraduate days Brennan had a difficult relationship with conservative university officialdom. In September 1899 senior members of the University of Sydney Senate declared Brennan's verse 'immoral' and reflecting a 'gross mind' when they decided to pass over Brennan for a lecturer's position.[43] In 1897, Brennan responded to the scorn heaped on *XXI Poems* by composing the playful 'Prose-verse-poster-algebraic-symbolico-riddle musicopoematographoscope', a large format, hand-written composition across several pages which mocked his critics, set out in the style of the French Symbolist poet Stéphane Mallarmé: words sparsely scattered across the white space of the page, tumbling down and across in short smatterings and erratically varied in size and style, and through which were shot single large capitalized words that spelt out, across the pages of the work, 'I don't give a tinker's damn for the public and they return the compliment.'[44] Yet 'hidden behind the bravado of the disparaged Australian poet are some of his deeply-held poetic aspirations'.[45]

The reaction to Brennan's mild verse reflects the resistance waiting to be directed against challenges to prevailing norms. Brennan's verse oscillated between tradition and innovation, at once pulling in the new direction of ideas and language developed by the French Symbolists, but also highly attached to the older forms of nineteenth-century Victorian poetry to which Brennan remained loyal – Swinburne, Keats and Coventry Patmore. Brennan's poetry was 'enmeshed in the stylistic mannerisms of the late nineteenth century'.[46] In 'Epilogues', written in 1897, Brennan outlined, in symbolic and metaphorical terms, his quest for the Absolute and the 'Source' for which he was seeking, 'Deep in my hidden country', that only Brennan had 'the skill to seek'. Only from intense solitude could the poet summon 'the fire from heaven' and achieve transcendence.[47] The exterior world was in contrast represented as a decayed environment, 'rows of heartless homes and hearths unlit', and 'dead churches', the pavements filled with 'the haggard shades' of the crowd.[48] Brennan was aware that his project did not harmonize with the self-consciously nationalist culture developing in Australia. In a poem he composed at the time he apparently addressed Australian society when he declared, 'Count me not of yours.'[49] Brennan could not see transformation in nationalist or political terms; it had to be expressed within the self, and the influences he drew upon came from a rarefied and metaphorical discourse sourced from Europe.

Brennan enjoyed a significant, if fleeting, moment of connection with this transnational discourse. In August 1897 Brennan had forwarded a copy of *XXI Poems* to Stéphane Mallarmé, the 'central figure' in French Symbolism, who drew a range of artists and writers under his influence, from Édouard Manet and James McNeill Whistler to Paul Gauguin, Edvard Munch, Huysmans and Paul Verlaine.[50] Brennan saw in Mallarmé's 'heroic devotion' to poetry a model for his quest, which Brennan eulogized in an essay following Mallarmé's death in 1898: 'To his lot fell the heavy duty of thinking out afresh the whole poetic problem, of envisaging the poet's task in its rarest form.'[51] Brennan received a warm and generous response from Mallarmé in September, which Brennan took as a polite but perhaps standard correspondence with a fellow poet. In fact, Mallarmé rarely responded so fulsomely to the work of others, particularly those previously unknown to him. Mallarmé greeted Brennan as 'a wonderful poet'. *Towards the Source*, Mallarmé declared, was no empty title; Brennan moved through 'the every day current of poetry towards its rarest source. Words, choice words, you use just insomuch as they are needed'. 'I can truly sense that your song has passed through our own', and as a result 'there is between you and me some dreamworld affinity'.[52] The gift of affinity was not lightly bestowed. Mallarmé's own emphasis on 'words, choice words', and his insistence on their precise allocation in the 'carefully engineered discontinuities' of his verse (most radically represented in 'A Dice Throw at Any Time Never Will Abolish Chance', published in the same year as his correspondence with Brennan and the poem which inspired the confronting Symbolist style of Brennan's *Musicopoematographoscope*), provided an extraordinary appreciation of Brennan's work.[53] The fact that Brennan could not grasp the deep sincerity with which Mallarmé responded to *XXI Poems* reflects Brennan's distance from the European literary scene. Australia's literary and intellectual circles offered little encouragement. Reviews of *XXI Poems* in the daily press reflected a mystified hostility, although *Freeman's Journal* looked favourably on Brennan's 'thin sheaf of poems' and the poet's 'deep spiritual, original genius', even if his verse suffered from 'occasional obscurities'.[54]

Brennan's work provoked derision from even those apparently sympathetic to it. In 1899 Brennan helped to found and edit *The Australian Magazine*, a journal intended to highlight the work of a new generation of Australian artists and poets including Brennan's close friend John Le Gay Brereton, Sydney Long and D. H. Souter. Brennan's poem 'Secreta Silvarum' was published in the April edition and was illustrated by Sydney Long. Although Long's painting such as *The Spirit of the Plains* and *Pan* (1898) provided emblematic expressions of Symbolism in Australian art in the period, Long confessed his bewilderment at the Brennan verse he illustrated.[55] In June 1900 a friend of Brennan's, Dowell O'Reilly, published a satire of Brennan's poetry in the *Bulletin*'s Red Page, ostensibly devoted to promoting Australian literature:

> Come! Let us rail at Cyrus Brown,
> The poet pale of Sydney Town;
> His form is frail, his eyes hang down,
> His hat suggests a martyr's crown,

He must not fail to win renown –
As a Symbolist!⁵⁶

The Red Page was edited by A. G. Stephens, another friend of Brennan's who published and promoted his work, and who seemed to take some pleasure in mockery of Brennan's style and literary ambitions. In 1899 Brennan took Stephen's published scorn of Mallarmé personally: defending 'his favourite author's work', Brennan challenged Stephens: 'Isn't the difference from Prose to Poetry principally one of the greater concentration of mental energy? Things seem more in shorthand, analysis suppressed, ellipsis everywhere? And isn't that exactly Mallarmé?'⁵⁷

The Australian Magazine flirted with the spirit of the transformative quest of Symbolism, most evidently in the illustrations provided by Souter, who employed the varied stylizations of Art Nouveau to represent an imagined 'land of fair promise' – which Souter also described in prose, of pilgrims seeking a 'Fair Country' but finding only 'the darkness of eternal night' and 'the hill of delusion'. Deploying the emphatic graphic line and heroically Nietzschean themes of German *Jugendstil*, Souter illustrated the shadow of death hanging over the dream of transformation: of men, 'naked, aboriginal, exultant, scorning the earth which had exhaled them' and joining in a 'universal shout': 'Behold! We – we create a New Heaven and a New Earth!' In the accompanying text Death plucked the narrator by the sleeve. 'They are but children at play.'⁵⁸ Brennan's poem 'Secreta Silvarum', the secret woods, was published in the same edition and evoked a medieval dream world; within its web of self-conscious obscurities was nonetheless evident the journey from hopeful quest to disillusionment. 'No silver bells about the bridle-head ripple of any quest . . . the knights are dead' (Figure 9).⁵⁹

The Australian Magazine lasted only a few months and a handful of editions in 1899. It captured a moment of creativity whose promise was difficult to sustain, as either collective enterprise or individual development. The press response was both warm and wary; the *Illawarra Mercury* hoped its first edition might help nurture a 'national literature', although '[t]he characteristic black-and-white drawings of D. H. Souter are still too Beardsleyish to be really artistic'. In August the *Daily Telegraph* thought the magazine had improved over time, yet 'strives to cover rather too much ground'.⁶⁰ The September edition proved to be the last. Australian artists like Sydney Long continued to travel to Europe in search of markets and inspiration; Souter carved out a living as illustrator of the *Bulletin* and *Lone Hand*, and for a time edited *Art and Architecture*, a more successful publishing

Figure 9 *The Australian Magazine* flirted with the spirit of the transformative quest of Symbolism. D. H. Souter, 'a new heaven and a new earth', *Australian Magazine* illustration, April 1899. State Library of New South Wales.

venture.[61] Brennan's participation reflected a willingness to help develop a local literary community and culture while also standing apart from it. Brennan was conscious that 'for all purposes of art and culture Australia was suburb of that provincial town, London', as he wrote in an essay published in the jubilee *Hermes* in 1902. 'Nature', Brennan observed, 'had not been good enough to hurry up and fashion a race pervaded with the spirit of the soil.' Hence the 'Australianity' of its literature 'was mainly addressed to mythical individuals called Bill and Jim'. The *Bulletin*, the principal journal of local literature since the 1880s, had 'grown old and hide-bound in its convention of aggressive irreverence'. These remarks were presumably directed at the *Bulletin*'s cultivation of writers like Henry Lawson, whose work was assimilated with an emerging bush nationalism cultivated in its pages. Yet Brennan was not entirely jaded in his assessment of Federation Australia. He seemed hopeful in 1902 of the transformative energy of 'the people', breathing spirit 'into the dry bones of politician-made Constitutions' and with a 'real democratic instinct' restoring art to 'her proper place in the national life'.[62]

Brennan struggled to find a place for his identity within the nation. Personal circumstance may have intensified alienation: from the turn of the century

Brennan became increasingly isolated and unhappy in family life. His 1897 marriage to a young woman he had met in Berlin, Elisabeth Werth, soon deteriorated.[63] This rift, and the difficulties associated with trying to achieve self-transformation, in poetry and professional career, resulted in Brennan seemingly abandoning his quest for the Absolute by 1902. Yet the poetry he composed at the turn of the century under the titles 'The Labour of the Night', the 'Lilith' poems and 'The Wanderer' constituted some of his finest work and included 'Twilights of the Gods and the Folk', which described an exhausted wanderer, whose dreams will be forgotten among the 'uncouth stones' of a cemetery.[64]

Brennan dwelt on this fate in the 'Wanderer' poems. An initial 'horror' at being cast adrift to face a 'horrible dawn' is resolved in accepting the disillusioned reality of a 'clear grey day', a 'transformation of consciousness', as Terry Sturm argued, as 'the wanderer of many years' who, in the final of the eight poems published in *Hermes*, 'cannot tell if ever he was king or if ever kingdoms were', and cast adrift beside a wayside harbour and the realization that life lacks a goal: there is no arrival at the Absolute. The 'Wanderer' poems also capture the dynamic tension of the *fin de siècle*: new knowledge and experience eroding a capacity to cling to 'sentimental feelings and beliefs'.[65] The 'Wanderer' poems reflected Edward Said's conception of late style: lateness as a form of exile – 'late style is *in*, but oddly *apart* from, the present'.[66] Brennan's poetry seems to stand apart from an identifiable context of society, suspended in the space of his imagination, unresolved and unquiet. The 'Wanderer' was represented in 'a limbo of defeated glory', yet in this state 'I feel a peace fall in the heart of the winds/and a clear dusk settle, somewhere, far in me'. Said argued that 'late works quarrel with time'. In the 'Wanderer' a consciousness of lateness generated a creative response, as Brennan seemed to resolve his quarrel.[67]

In 1898 Brennan defensively refuted that he was a Symbolist. In correspondence with A. G. Stephens, Brennan had conceded '*some* tendencies that way . . . one must live in one's age'.[68] Despite disillusionment Brennan did not entirely abandon the Symbolist cause or an impulse to engage with the intellectual currents of the age. In June–July 1904 he delivered the 'Symbolism in Nineteenth Century Literature' lectures, organized, as his biographer suggests, to advance his scholarly cause and future prospects for employment at the University of Sydney; they were presented as university extension lectures, chaired by Mungo MacCallum, the professor of Modern Literature who had, along with the university Senate, once again denied Brennan's appointment as lecturer only a year earlier.[69]

In the first of the lectures, delivered in the Royal Society's rooms in Elizabeth Street on 15 June, Brennan acknowledged the confusing heterogeneity of his subject and a long history of literary symbolism that ranged from antiquity to the intensity of the movement emerging from the mid-nineteenth century under the influence of the Romantics and Charles Baudelaire's *Les Fleur du Mal* (1861). 'In the majority of minds', the word 'symbolism' did not correspond 'to any definite, consistent, identifiable conception'. Yet the Symbolist saw his doctrine as 'one and definite . . . every artist who follows the law of his imagination is bound to create symbols'. In modern times this esoteric doctrine had become explicit; 'if it is dangerous, then so is all art.'[70]

Brennan defined Symbolism as a form of correspondence between the natural and spiritual worlds. Brennan surveyed the historical development of Symbolism and the idea of correspondence from Ecclesiasticus, 'all things go by opposed couples' and the Gnostics, a progress 'choked' by the Renaissance and the Reformation. Symbolism as 'a determining aesthetic theory and principle belongs to the last days of the eighteenth century, when the French Revolution stirred up the poets'. Brennan invoked the Romantics, John Keats, William Blake and particularly the German poet Novalis and his aphorisms: 'Man is a source of analogies for the universe.' Symbolism came to maturity in France through Baudelaire, 'the most profoundly original poet . . . and one of the acutest thinkers on art that his century has produced' and directly influenced by the philosopher Swedenborg's *Heaven and Hell*: 'the whole natural world corresponds to the spiritual world' – a theme taken up Baudelaire's sonnet '*Correspondences*' and cited by Brennan: 'man walks amid wild-woods of symbols which look upon [him] with looks that he recognises as kin.'[71]

It was in Mallarmé that Brennan identified the most intense maturity of late nineteenth-century Symbolist vision and style, invoking Mallarmé's 'statement', which acknowledged that nature's sufficiency and man's merely material additions – 'cities, railways and certain other inventions which constitute our stock in trade' – leave only a line of action 'to simplify the world in accordance with some inner mood, which we are driven to extend beyond ourselves. This is the equivalent of creation: we grasp at the notion of some new object, which escapes us, and whose lack we deplore.' The symbol provides the method towards this end: 'The symbol is simply that image which, for the special purpose in hand, condenses in itself the greatest number of correspondences', although the symbol is more than 'a mere metaphor': 'A real symbol directs and governs its poem: it is at once starting-point and goal, starting-point as plain image, goal as symbol: the poem rises out of it, develops within its limits, and builds it up by successive correspondences.' Brennan described this process as a form of Art Nouveau dance, 'a kind of Loïe Fuller tissue of alliances and deductions': 'Aesthetically, we must view the world in a somewhat Pythagorean way, as a system of answering rhythms, rhythms differentiated into melodies, as a counterpoint, a repeating arabesque.'[72] The Parisian dancer Loïe Fuller's swirling, evocatively illuminated 'serpentine' performances were the subject of awed tributes from Mallarmé and Yeats.[73]

Brennan described his first lecture as a dry exposition of the 'grammar of Symbolism'.[74] Delivered in the 'merely material' domain of the city on 15 June 1904, it shared cultural space with a 'public entertainment' conducted by the Theosophical Society and the YMCA's annual tea and concert at the Scot's Church; the 'Darling of the Gods' at Her Majesty's Theatre, 'The Rose of the Riviers' at the Lyceum; and a 'Gas Cooking Demonstration' at the School of Arts.[75] The following day, a terse acknowledgement was buried in news summaries on the *Sydney Morning Herald*'s editorial page: 'It was claimed for Symbolism that it was a theory latent in the poetry and art of all ages, and was alone capable of explaining the facts of artistic experience.'[76] In the *Australian Star* a rather bewildered summary shared space with reports on 'the Turf', cycling and rugby. 'The subject was somewhat mystical and abstruse, but it was evidently dealt with by a master of art and literature, and a profound student.' A 'fairly numerous' audience listened intently.[77] Introducing Brennan, Professor MacCallum offered a somewhat backhanded appreciation. 'Whatever might be thought of it, all now agreed that Symbolism at any rate offered one striking apercu of the truth of God.'[78]

Brennan's lectures drew on a range of *fin de siècle* thinkers, artists and ideas, as he attempted to reconcile the traditions of Western culture with the new forces at work in his own age. Of Max Nordau's repudiation of Symbolism – in *Degeneration* (1892), Nordau argued that 'the *fin de siècle* disposition' reflected in works of Symbolists were producing neurasthenia and hysteria, and devoted a chapter to condemning this 'remarkable class' of 'degenerates' – Brennan listed the targets of Nordau's diatribe to expose its reductive monomania:

> Pre-Raphaelism, Nietzsche, Wagner, and Tolstoi, by saying degeneration, degeneration, and again degeneration; showing, to his own satisfaction at least, that Rosetti's use of the refrain is just a phase of echolalia; that the elaborateness of Mallarmé and the simplicity of Verlaine, the altruism of Tolstoi and the ego-worship of Nietzsche are all indifferently variations of a single modern disease; we begin to find the explanation rather stretched and thin.[79]

Brennan's lectures reflected an ambiguity towards Nietzsche; Brennan 'prized this thinker and poet for his extraordinary honesty' and equally noted the 'fallacious' nature of his 'historical method' in relation to the history of philosophy; yet Brennan clearly admired, and perhaps recognized, how Nietzsche

> made his mind a battlefield for all the conflicting tendencies of his time and allowed it to fight the battle with a ruthless logic. He began as an idealist, of a kind: and after his system had been wrecked, owing to extra-philosophic, artistic reasons, he became the sworn enemy of all idealism.

Brennan's attempts to construct an integrated, historically framed analysis of Symbolism was sensitive to 'the wreck of systems', and divided consciousness, alluding to Nietzsche's epigrammatic repudiation of modern rational systems in *Twilight of the Idols*: 'The will to system is a lack of integrity.' One of the wrecked systems Brennan identified, and 'scattered over the earth', was the quest for the 'Absolute'. 'Man is not meant to be build lasting structures in this world.' Even 'systems of symbolism' are 'never more than an experiment, an attempt to see in how far the results we have reached agree with one another'.[80]

Dualism, division, provided the metaphors of Brennan's experimental system. To achieve some sense of transcendence, and authenticity of experience, Brennan argued that it was necessary to follow the idea expressed in William James's *Varieties of Religious Experience* (1902), 'which I heartily recommend to everyone here', and 'plunge into an altogether other dimension of existence', as Brennan cited James: 'the mystical and supernatural region'. 'The sea of subconscious' could bridge the gulf between 'our discursive mind and our true self'.

> The transcendental self in us is not something abstract but a concrete reality: only, its full potency is not manifested, it is yet in process of development. The mind, like the material world, is going through an evolution. It is by coming to know the world that we come to know ourselves: the double process is still going on, each aspect of it acting on and helping forward the other.[81]

Symbolism and poetry provided a path to the transcendent self. The influence of Nietzsche and James reflected the infiltration of vitalist thought in Brennan's search for new sources of creative energy and 'which might enrich every part of man's being and life'.[82] Yet Brennan was too aware of human fallibility to entirely embrace vitalist optimism. 'For every presentation of that which transcends our broken, imperfect life, our divided, discursive consciousness, is a symbol: it cannot be anything else.' Brennan added: 'For since poetry passes beyond the divided, analytic, everyday life and symbolizes the complete, perfect, eternal self, it must follow that it presents what cannot be presented in any other way.' Poetry provided a mode of being independent of 'the world in the dust of whose things we are frittered away'; poetry is 'the birth of new worlds'. In working his way to this idealistic assertion, Brennan could not suspend an awareness that 'our life consists not merely of high movements and hours in insight, such as give birth to poetry, it consists also of days, weeks and calendar months of dullness and mediocrity, that outer weariness which made Baudelaire a maniac'. And it was here that Brennan confessed the feeling of living two lives, between truth and error, love and meanness. These two 'facts of poetry' could be simply rendered as happiness and unhappiness: 'but these simple names involve universes.'[83]

Brennan's lectures reflected the importance of romanticism to the *fin de siècle* imagination, which renewed 'the Romantics valorization of the Imagination as a faculty that was equal, rather than subordinate, to reason'.[84] In two successive lectures Brennan focused respectively on the poet and artist William Blake and 'Novalis', the German aristocrat Friedrich von Hardenberg, the author of classic romantic poetry and essays, including 'Hymns of the Night' (1799–1800); both poets functioned as creative influences on the international Symbolist movement at the *fin de siècle*.[85] Brennan's lectures explored the linkage between Novalis and Mallarmé in pursuit of a 'higher power' transcendent of symbolic representation.[86] Brennan endorsed the Romantics mystic Symbolism against rationalism and reason: 'Blake revolts against the rationalism of his day. Reason cannot create'; it is 'a cruel tyrant', severed from life by abstraction; 'life can only exist in minute particulars' that could be reached through poetry. Novalis, 'the one man of genius whom the romantic school produced', believed that through a mystic poetry, man could realize his true nature.[87] In support of his claims, Brennan offered his audience his own translation of extracts of Novalis's *Ofterdingen*, 'one of those absolute masterpieces which comes perhaps but once in the lifetime even of a great poet', which captured both the intention and language of Brennan's own quest: the search for 'the innermost soul of all life' by 'splendid wanderers with eyes of meaning'.[88]

Drawing together his thoughts on Novalis and Blake, Brennan observed: 'we are divided. We are under the dominion of science, which is the result of our needy condition.' This divided condition was 'the seed of Urizen'. Urizen was a central figure in Blake's complex cosmology, the symbolic system that structured his poetry and his prodigious output of striking and allusive engravings and watercolours. One of Blake's four Zoas, 'a cast of characters' that dramatized 'the dynamics of psychic experience', Urizen was 'beared and patriarchal', God-like, the symbol of authoritarian reason, a 'judgemental father figure'. In Brennan's lecture on Blake, Urizen functions as a symbol of division, 'dividing the nations, family by family'.[89]

Brennan's Blake lecture of 29 June 1904 has survived in partial transcript, terse fragments and notes, into which substantial extracts of Blake's texts were inserted, all to guide the audience into the vast and intricate domain of Blake's imaginative system:

> And the fault Blake lays at the door of reason:
> *Europe*, 8, 16-23
> This leads us directly to Blake's myth and his system of symbols.
> Man a harmony of four great moods or states.[90]

Which led to a detailed summary of the Zoas and their characteristics, forming only a part of the exhaustive survey of a poet who rivalled Mallarmé as a significant influence on Brennan.[91] The correspondent of the *Australian Star*, and who provided the only contemporaneous account of the lecture, reduced Brennan's survey to a perhaps stunned paragraph: 'The main lines of Blake's symbolic system were sketched out and illustrated by numerous quotations from his works; longer passages were also read to support the claim that Blake's Symbolism, for all its complexity, did not lead to obscurity, and that his poetry was eminently characterised by epic breadth and grandeur.'[92] Brennan's imaginative quest had to contend with the difficulty of translating symbolic metaphors into plain language and into the system of press accounts circumscribed by the prosaic grids of the public school football competition, and a calendar of June days memorable for Australians: the discovery of the Hawkesbury River, the riots at Lambing Flat and the capture of the Kelly Gang.

Of all the Symbolism lectures, the reflections on Blake provided a window into Brennan's elaborate imaginative archive, which remained otherwise hidden, except as it found expression in his poetry. Brennan's archive consisted of a compendium that has survived from the period in which the lectures were composed: a discarded volume that the librarian had repurposed, turning the reverse, blank pages of the Sydney Free Public Library's Catalogue of Books 1869–87 ('Part II, with index') to the compilation of his varied inspirations.[93] For reference purposes, Brennan may have hauled the large and heavy volume to his lectures: hand inscribed by the official title page was the request, 'please return to Chris: Brennan Public Library BENT Street.'

Over page after page, in his tidy and tiny, spidery hand, Brennan provided a summary of the biographies and major works of his influences. Brennan began with Blake.

> To hear a man talking or to watch his gestures, is to study Symbolism, and when we restore our impressions in what are thought to be straightforward and scientific sentences, we are in reality giving <u>a more limited, and therefore more graspable</u>, <u>symbolic</u> [underlined twice] statement of this impalpable <u>reality</u> [underlined thrice].

This paragraph was a quotation from *Works of William Blake* by Edwin Ellis and W. B. Yeats. Brennan was drawn to the *fin de siècle* revival of interest in Blake represented by its 1893 publication. Yeats was powerfully influenced by Blake.[94] Brennan likened the Irish poet to Blake and perhaps Brennan also had himself in mind, as 'a symbolist grown up on his own soil without foreign influences'. Brennan referred his audience to Yeats's *The Wind among the Reeds* (1899), which featured some of Yeats's most characteristic works in the late nineteenth-century Symbolist style, including 'The Song of Wandering Aengus', 'The Valley of the Black Pig' and 'The Secret Rose', the latter reflecting Brennan's symbolic language in describing 'the proud dreaming king who flung the crown/And sorrow away, and calling bard and clown/Dwelt among wine-stained wanderers in deep woods'.[95]

In the volume of his notes Brennan set out Blake's system in a grid of Zoas. A rudimentary hand-rendered table represented Blake's elaborate schema. The section on Blake was followed by a detailed publication history of Yeats's poetry and essays.[96] This was followed by a single-page bibliography for the works of 'WILDE, OSCAR FINGALL O'FLAHERTIE WILLS, Born'.[97] Brennan's calligraphy was precise enough to register subtle distinctions in font size. Another two pages carefully categorized the publishing history of the works of the French Symbolist writer Villiers De L'Isle-Adam: 'published in periodicals', 'not reprinted', 'published in volumes edited by others'.[98] Some inscribed names signalled entries that were never completed: 'WELLS, HERBERT GEORGE' and 'WHISTLER, JAMES ABBOTT MACNEILL'.[99] Other categories were only fragmentarily noted, particularly of classical literature and mythology: entries for Dionysus and Virgil tersely listed locations from the ancient world associated with them – 'Thrace: Delos: Crete: Astium' – there was no indication of how this was to be developed.[100] There was a fragment of verse[101]; there was a long draft of a talk, in which Brennan ruefully reflected on the disappointments of modern urban life and the divide between imagination and experience. 'Dreary suburbs prolonged by monotonous ways to the central absence of anything extraordinary, of anything divine or sprung up from this artificial soil to compensate us for the leagues of asphalt, which we must trudge once more to escape.'[102] Brennan attempted to escape into knowledge. Across the final, long section were pages of dense notes largely devoted to German literature, philosophy and spirituality, focusing on Klopstock, Wieland, Winckelmann, Lessing and Herder, the eighteenth-century founders of the 'Greek revival' in German intellectual life.[103]

An exhaustive survey of Mallarmé's life and works spanned ten pages of Brennan's notes, and a passionate defence of the 'difficult' French poet provided the subject of the penultimate lecture of Monday 18 July 1904.[104] Brennan's lecture sketched Mallarmé's biography and focused on a dedication that some of Brennan's friends might have recognized: Mallarmé 'worked quietly at his self-imposed task in poetry, in his scanty leisure: never caring much to publish, waiting to complete and perfect his intentions'. Mallarmé died in 1898, not long after retiring from the 'drudgery' of teaching, and was unable to complete his *oeuvre*; 'his work consequently remains a fragment'. While influenced by Baudelaire, Mallarmé avoided the former's 'perversity'. 'Mallarmé is characterised from the start by an abstract purity of thought: more than the trouble of the world the eternal splendour of the ideal possesses him.' A quest that found a critical point of development in *L'après-midi d'un faune* (1876) and which spurred Mallarmé's identification of the 'law of correspondences' as 'the unique spiritual activity of man'.[105] Mallarmé's work attracted charges of 'obscurity' and 'sterility', even 'enmity to life'. Brennan retorted to these critics: 'And life – what do they mean by it? Most of them commit the modern error of confounding it with rush and turmoil – ideal, the motor-car. . . . Flowers don't grow by making a noise in the world.'[106] Soothing the modern world of division and turmoil was a theme Brennan returned to in his final lecture. The abstractions of the law of correspondences that he had described as governing literary symbolism were 'in fact a spiritual reading of the world', of the relationship 'between our imperfect self and our perfect or transcendental self . . . to introduce more harmony into the world and into our consciousness: to heal the sundering of Urizen, to heal the division and substitute peace for the war in ourselves, to bring life into the body of death'.[107] A *fin de siècle* quest that sought not an end but renewal in a new beginning.

Dorothy Green objected to Axel Clark's characterization of Brennan as a 'deeply divided man'; Green wearied of both the phrase and the commonplace claim that man is a divided creature.[108] In poetry and prose Brennan emphasized the dilemma of the divided self:

> The 'first and most patent' of 'the living facts of poetry . . . has to do is the imperfection of our life: and this involves the contrary fact of its possible perfection. Out of the conflict of these two facts poetry is born: and its office is to exasperate or reconcile that conflict, indeed both to exasperate and reconcile it. The imperfection is in ourselves; the imperfection of a divided consciousness, a divided life; war within us and war upon the earth.'[109]

From the early 1900s, Brennan attempted to keep some element of the transformational quest alive in his life, recreating the world of the Parisian café scholar-bohemian in Sydney, despite the derision that he would sometimes attract. Brennan was active in the Casuals Club in the years prior to the First World War. 'A remarkable conversationalist', Brennan attracted a number of people who expressly attended to hear him and his prodigious learning; he could also lapse into the role of the inebriated and opinionated bore, rousing the ire of his fellow members. One of these objectors at the Casuals Club in 1908 was the journalist and literary critic Bertram Stevens, who argued with Brennan about the significance of the work of Charles Baudelaire. Stevens 'objected to any member monopolizing the talk, and using the club for discussion of esoteric literary subjects in which some members had no interest'.[110]

Brennan was influenced by Baudelaire as a poet and as life model of the café bohemian, holding court and exciting controversy with unconventional opinions. Brennan observed that Baudelaire was 'the great type of his generation', the most profoundly original and influential, powerful French poet of the nineteenth century; and Brennan's identification with Baudelaire is suggested in Brennan's observations that 'It was evidently difficult for [Baudelaire] to write verse' and persist with composing the works brought together in *Les Fleurs du Mal*.[111]

In December 1914 Brennan was finally able to realize the dream of publishing his poetry in a form that reflected his ambitions. *Poems* fulfilled the Symbolist ideal of a 'single concerted poem', a *livre composé*, as advocated by Mallarmé: an integrated body of poetry that followed a series of related themes, rather than a disparate collection of individual poems. The poems were usually untitled within each series and were dramatically interposed or linked with brief, italicized verses and strategically deployed subheadings, so that the graphic design, the presentation of the stanzas on the page and the typefaces selected became part of the integrated and flowing composition. In an explanatory note Brennan observed that of the 105 pieces in the volume, fewer than a dozen dated from after 1902, although most were previously unpublished. 'That publication had been so long delayed was due to what humanity is vaguely accustomed to call "'Life", or the "circumstances", which it likes to imagine beyond its control . . . the fault was the authors.'[112]

Life and circumstances conspired to overwhelm *Poems*. It was a limited edition, funded by subscription; a review by Bertram Stevens in the *Lone Hand* captured the cool tone of grudging and bemused respect which characterized contemporary response, in a nation preoccupied by the outbreak of the First World War in August 1914: the book 'makes no claim whatever on Australian interest, and depends solely on the intrinsic poetry of its contents', contents which were at times 'difficult to understand' and all of which had 'evidently been written to please the author himself, without even half an eye to an audience'. Stevens noted that Brennan also 'pleased himself to use capitals only as in prose, and to omit pagination and titles'. The poems, however, were often 'musical' and reflected 'an intensity of passion', and Stevens favourably compared Brennan's work with Yeats. 'He has produced some things of beauty for which we are all thankful, and for which Australia will some day call him blessed.' The review was accompanied by a caricature by the cartoonist David Low of Brennan's busy if ageing bulk, clutching his broad-brimmed hat, scurrying with papers and bag.[113] *Poems* represented a delayed conclusion of Brennan's pursuit of the Absolute, somewhat cruelly but appropriately appearing at a time when the world was being driven along a new and calamitous course, which would leave behind the dreamworld quests of the *fin de siècle*. *Poems* made no impact on the public or the popular imagination and received virtually no attention beyond Australia. Katherine Barnes has observed that it is easy to overlook Brennan's remarkable achievement: '*Poems* grapples with some of the most profound thinking of the Romantic and Symbolist movements, exploring the notion of a higher or transcendent self-constituted by the union of the human mind and Nature.'[114]

By 1914 Brennan may have reconciled with the failure to fulfil his vision of the Absolute. Veronica Brady has argued that the 'Wanderer' poems reflected Brennan's reconciliation with an inability to identify 'the Absolute'. There was an acceptance by Brennan of 'incompleteness', and that identity is not to be found 'as something for or within itself but by being open and vulnerable to others'.[115] Brennan's poetry, and the ideas that he outlined in his 1904 lectures, certainly exposed his vulnerability to others and contributed to his rueful reflection on living two lives; the reconciliation expressed in the 'Wanderer' poems was hard to live by. Brennan's marginalization may have been sourced in his own personal dilemmas and idiosyncratic ideals, which struggled to find a place in Federation Australia. Yet Brennan's acknowledgement of Australian provincialism was also accompanied by awareness that this fate was part of a wider and global degeneracy. 'The nineteenth century ... threw art out of life altogether and left it merely as a luxury to be enjoyed by the Pierpont Morgan's in the pauses of their real strenuous living. The artist was informed that he might exist, but that he was not of those who lived.'[116]

The extraordinary dynamism of *fin de siècle* capitalism, represented by the global reach and repute of the New York banker John Pierpont Morgan's role in creating the richest and largest transnational corporations ever constructed, while lavishly accruing art and culture as luxury commodity, seemed beyond Brennan's context; yet he was evidently aware of its oppressive impact.[117] It was also evident in the division that Brennan regretted in 1904 and which contextualized the reporting of his lectures: 'war upon the earth' was not merely an abstraction that Brennan observed of humanity's divided nature but a blunt reality, 'THE WAR', daily headlined in the press. The public mind was gripped as the extraordinary conflict between Russia and Japan played out in the siege of Port Arthur and reported across the period of Brennan's lectures.[118] 'The war without is a correspondence of the war within', he observed in his second lecture while anticipating that 'we are working our way through error'.[119] Brennan hoped, in his reflections on the role of the university in 1902, that at the advent of a new century, it had helped to restore the place of literature in national life. Brennan struggled to find a place either in the university, national life, or in the transnational literary discourse of which he was perhaps the most eloquent of the creative agents of the Australian *fin de siècle*.

4

'A modern Eve'

Vida Goldstein stands for Parliament

I am a modern Eve. (Loud laughter.) I offer you an apple – (laughter) – but an apple of a different kind – the apple of harmony – the idea of a woman going into Parliament. Take and eat of it, and you will find you will develop a relish for more apples of the same kind. (Renewed laughter)[1]

On Tuesday, 22 September 1903, a reporter from the *Advertiser* stood on the platform of Adelaide railway station as the Melbourne express pulled in. The reporter believed that a 'prominent member of the National Council of Women' might be aboard the train. 'When the cars pulled up, Miss Vida Goldstein, of Victoria, was received with womanly warmth' by a trio of ladies from the council. '"Is that Miss Goldstein?" observed a bystander. "Well, well, I had formed the impression that she was a crabby-looking old maid. Why she's quite young and pretty."' Shaken from his reflexive condescension, the reporter noted that Goldstein was 'clever, and has a magnetic personality, and these attributes should be of material assistance to her in her coming political campaign as a Senatorial candidate'. Requesting an interview, the reporter asked Goldstein how her 'Christian name' was pronounced. '"Most people address me as Veda", she answered, "but it is Vida, with an accent on the I".'[2]

Goldstein arrived in Adelaide on the same day that the press speculated on the date to be chosen for the federal election, soon settled as 16 December.[3] Having decided to contest the elections as a Senate candidate in Victoria, Vida Goldstein was compelled to define herself in the public sphere. Given her unusual status as the only woman in Victoria to stand for the elections, Goldstein had also to clarify the space of the woman's sphere of politics following Federation. As a consequence of the passage of the Commonwealth Franchise Act in June 1902, the elections were the first in which women could vote and stand for office, a reform that helped to establish Australia as 'laboratory' of social policy – of the world's nations, only Australia and New Zealand had granted women the right to vote.[4] The *Advertiser* did not underestimate the fact that 'the coming federal elections will be absolutely unique in the history of constitutional government and the annals of civilisation'. Even though South Australia had extended the franchise to women in 1894, 'taking the Commonwealth as a whole a reform has been brought about that is equal in its possibilities to a revolution'. The *Advertiser* felt sure that 'Miss Goldstein's presence in Adelaide will no doubt develop interest among women in the political questions of the day'.[5] Yet only four Australian women felt sufficiently supported as potential candidates to offer themselves for public office, even as the innovation of women's right to vote made its impact on national life.

Responding to her *Advertiser* interviewer's 'delicate question' – 'people are enquiring how old you are?' – Goldstein acknowledged that 'people are very anxious to know my age – I am 32'. Goldstein told the reporter that she had been interested in 'the woman's movement' since she left school. 'My active association with it commenced in 1899, when I first spoke in public. I have been hard at it since then.' Born in the 'sleepy, unprogressive town' of Portland' on Victoria's south coast in 1869, Vida Goldstein was the daughter of middle-class, reform-minded parents who engaged in public activism and charity work, sometimes in collaboration with the iconoclastic social and religious reformer Charles Strong, the founder of the Australian Church, a 'free religious fellowship' that broke away from the Presbyterian Church.[6] It was Strong who, according to *Table Talk*, shaped Goldstein into 'a battler for social order . . . Strong interested her in land reform, penal reform, social reform of all kinds'. Goldstein's search for reconciliation between religious faith and a progressive, rational politics led her in 1902 to a lifelong embrace of Christian Science, which taught that 'to be spiritually minded is . . . to be scientifically minded'. It was also a sect which equally recognized women in its structures.[7]

Goldstein's father Jacob operated a store in Warranambool, also on Victoria's south coast; he encouraged her education at Melbourne's Presbyterian Ladies College. Goldstein claimed that she was born a suffragist. 'I believe that the State is only an extension of the family . . . everything that makes for the good government of the home makes also for the good government of the State, and the State cannot afford to do without the direct influence of women any more than the home can.' Vida's mother Isabella was a supporter of women's suffrage. Vida's first political activism involved collecting signatures for a Woman Suffrage petition in 1890.[8] Goldstein also embraced the causes of penal and social welfare reform, and equal pay for women. Her politics gravitated towards the socialist spectrum, although she steadfastly maintained her independence from party politics and the labour movement. In February 1902 Goldstein attended the annual convention of the National Woman Suffrage Associations of America, immediately followed by the inaugural International Woman Suffrage Conference conducted in Washington; she then toured the United States until August. In the American capital Goldstein addressed a congressional committee on women's suffrage and was part of a delegation that interviewed US president Theodore Roosevelt, who questioned Goldstein about Australia and New Zealand.[9] By 1903 Goldstein had developed into an experienced and impressive public advocate of women's rights and social reform.

In order to appreciate the skills Goldstein brought to her Senate candidature, it is necessary to first explore the development of her activism and the causes she embraced. The heterogeneity of the causes in which Goldstein immersed was a reflection of an explosion of new ideas, faiths and social movements. The 'New Woman' was among the most provocative of the identities to emerge at the *fin de siècle* and in Australia became a target of hostility and derision.[10] 'Christened in 1894', the New Woman was 'a journalistic phenomenon', identified as over-educated, emancipated and a threat to the institution of marriage.[11] Spreading rapidly in Western societies as a narrative identity in books, pamphlets and the press, the New Woman 'was an anarchic figure who threatened to turn the world upside down and to be on top in a wild carnival of social and sexual misrule'.[12] Embodying the idea of the New Woman, Goldstein's self-creation in the public sphere coincided with a moment when the possibilities of a new identity were unprecedentedly open for first-wave feminists and hence sharply contested.

Goldstein's activism was part of a wider mobilization that included women's rights campaigners like Maybanke Anderson (née Wolstenholme) and Rose Scott, who formed the Women's Political and Educational League in New South Wales in 1902. Mobilizing a woman's right to a political voice increasingly assumed the established forms of class politics. Annie and Belle Golding, together with Kate Dwyer, formed the left-leaning NSW Women's Progressive Association, in part a reaction against a perception of Rose Scott's support for non-Labor election candidates. Liberal women's political organizations also emerged, such as the NSW Women's Liberal League. In Victoria, the staunchly conservative Australian Women's National League would later prove to be a fierce opponent of Vida Goldstein's politics and candidature.[13] Goldstein's political activism proved a difficult path to follow; as Janette Bomford observes, Goldstein's 'challenge' as she emerged as a public figure from the late 1890s was 'to find new ways of achieving social, political and economic equity, while preserving the strengths of womanhood'.[14]

Goldstein dramatized her activism with the launch in September 1900 of her own monthly journal, the *Australian Woman's Sphere*. The *Woman's Sphere* argued that the extension of the federal franchise required women to acquaint themselves 'with the principles of right government'. 'When women come to be fully alive to the fact that on them, as well as on the men, rests the responsibility for the affairs of the Commonwealth ... [t]hey will begin to take broader views, to advocate wiser methods of action, and to formulate a higher patriotism.'[15] There was no shortage of demanding issues to address. A commitment to penal reform responded to the unjust treatment by the courts of mothers and children. In September 1900 Goldstein appealed to the Victorian government to separate young girls, first offenders, from 'hardened criminals' and appoint matrons to city lock-ups, 'so that she and not the constables should attend to the women who were locked up at all hours of the night'.[16] Goldstein served on the committee of the Criminological Society of Victoria. Having visited a number of US penitentiaries in 1902, Goldstein sought the introduction of New York's Elmira system. 'There indeterminate sentences are given and the prisoner is liberated when cured. Crime is treated like the liquor habit as a disease.'[17]

At the National Council meeting in Adelaide in September 1903, Goldstein urged the adoption of a 'bond of union' which she said had been agreed 'by the members all the world over':

> We, women of all nations, sincerely believing that the best good of society will be advanced by strong unity of thought, sympathy, and purpose, and that an organised movement of women will best conserve the highest good of the family and of the State, do hereby band ourselves together into a confederation of workers to further the application of the Golden Rule for society, custom, and law.[18]

Attracted to idealized abstractions, Goldstein claimed the National Council of Women was strictly non-political, although she also acknowledged that it 'takes up matters of social and industrial reform'. 'All women were warmly welcomed in the fold of the National Council, irrespective of creed or nationality': she assured the council's inaugural annual meeting that it was this non-political openness that had built a movement of over seven million women worldwide.[19] Yet Goldstein also highlighted injustices that would require direct political interventions to redress.

Goldstein was a tireless advocate of equal pay for women, at a time when the emerging Commonwealth industrial arbitration system 'reinforced existing market inequalities' against women, who were in weaker sectors of employment and were under-represented in union hierarchies and bargaining strategies, which favoured men.[20] Even where men and women worked side by side, gender bias undermined equality. Goldstein decried the fact that women teachers in Victoria were 'shamefully sweated', paid only half the rate of their male counterparts. 'While the men teachers were liberated from duty at 4 p.m., the women were expected to remain behind till as late as 7 p.m., getting the sewing lessons ready for the next day. For all they did the women workers received a "miserable pittance".'[21] The lower wages paid to women undermined both sexes; women denied a living wage, while 'the employment of women in industrial pursuits was a growing and serious menace to organised labor and the rate of wages' paid to men. Equal pay could only be realized by the mobilization of women into trade unions. 'Some women thought it would lower their status to belong to a union, but that was not so.' Parliamentary action was also required to compel employers to accept equal pay for women, a political intervention that required women to embrace the right to vote extended to them by the passage of the Franchise Act. 'One woman making shirts worked 18 hours a day for about 5/ a week, and if that sort of thing existed, could anybody say that women did not want the vote?'[22]

The growth of the international women's movement and its ambitious reform agenda represented key *fin de siècle* developments that Goldstein urged Australian feminists to emulate. The *Australian Woman's Sphere* provided its readers with a regular stream of intelligence about international developments and the opportunities opening up for women. In 'The World Moves' column, published in each edition, the *Woman's Sphere* reported in December 1900 on the Congress of Electricity held in conjunction with the Paris exposition: 'the paper which attracted most attention at the congress was one read by an English woman electrician.'[23] In February 1901 it was reported that 'the women of Budapest have won the right to enter the University', although they had to endure 'the coarsest jeers and insults' of professors and students alike as they took their places in lecture theatres.[24] In America, women's clubs were taking up the study of social and political economy. The Women's Club of Denver, Colorado, had organized a study programme, 'The New Industrial World', followed by a focus on John Stuart Mill, 'On Liberty' and 'On Women'; trade union history and present development; and John Ruskin's economics and its relation to art theories. 'We commend this program to our Progressive Leagues,' the *Woman's Sphere* commented.[25]

At Goldstein's instigation the National Council of Women adopted the position of its American counterpart in its commitment to international arbitration to peacefully resolve disputes between nations.[26] Goldstein hoped that a system of arbitration would result in 'abolishing war', supporting the international campaign that led to the hopeful Hague peace conferences of 1899 and 1907, which ultimately shipwrecked 'on the rocks of government intransigence', the refusal of rival states to have resort to military might be restrained.[27] Goldstein returned from the United States awestruck by the dynamism and organizational strength of the American feminists, as she told her *Advertiser* interviewer.

> It seemed to me that they are head and shoulders above the women I have met in Australia. . . . Now, the American women might be specialists at the University, and yet take up the work of social reform, and be thoroughly democratic. The American women are wonderful conversationalists, and no matter what the subject is they are able to take an interest in it, and in a dozen sentences they can express as many original views.

By contrast

> Australian women seem more inclined to get into grooves . . . in Victoria our University women are exceedingly narrow-minded. There is too much 'cram' about the system, and the women have to give up all their time and thoughts to University work. Now, American women, having won high distinction in universities, afterwards take a leading position in the social reform movement.[28]

These 'narrow-minded' Australian women were among those whom Goldstein would appeal to for support in the forthcoming election campaign.

Goldstein found herself at the centre of international women's activism in Washington. She was elected secretary of the International Woman Suffrage Conference, serving alongside conference president Susan B. Anthony, the famed American feminist. Anthony provided a model of courageous activism: for the cause of women's rights, the *Australian Woman's Sphere* observed, Anthony had endured 'abuse, ridicule, persecution and even violence' over the course of fifty years of agitation. American women who enjoyed college education, the right to property and custody of children, and 'the chance of earning an honest living' owed 'these sacred privileges to Susan B. Anthony beyond all others'.[29] Goldstein was also a member of a sub-committee tasked with drawing up a declaration and constitution for the new International Council of Women. In outlining plans to further the cause of women's suffrage, the conference was declared a great success; conducted over six days, with over 200 delegates attending, 'the public meetings were packed to the door'. The account of the conference published in the *Woman's Sphere* observed that 'Miss Vida Goldstein seems to have quite captured the hearts of the other delegates', an enthusiasm reflected in the song composed for the 'youthful delegate' by Alice S. Blackwell, the editor of the Boston *Woman's Journal*, who represented 'Australia's infant Commonwealth':

> We see her slender, girlish grace,
> Her vivid, keen, and sparkling face;
> From her clear eyes, intelligence,
> Looks forth, with wit and common-sense;
> No manly air can we perceive,
> She looks as womanly as Eve;
> We think the 'Antis' must be doting,
> For girls are *not* unsexed by voting.

The 'dark, alert, slender girl from Australia' was also the focus of a number of American press reports. The *Salt Lake City Tribune* enquired what Miss Goldstein thought the women's sphere should be. 'Anything that a woman feels she is fitted to do, and her sex should not debar her from pursuing any profession she desires.' The *New York Herald* published an interview with Goldstein, which also featured her portrait.[30]

Goldstein's visit to America and participation in the Washington conferences reflected a shared spirit of progressive era reform that was exchanged between the two white settler societies in the period.[31] Goldstein's attitude to American women revealed an enthusiastic embrace of modernity, drawn into her self-invention, a process in which her trip to the United States played a stimulating role: using innovative technology – photography and slide projections – in the creation of her narrative of herself and her responses to her experiences. By September 1903 her self-styled 'lecture entertainments' on her US trip had been periodically conducted for almost a year and were 'illustrated by a number of stereopticon slides, which Miss Goldstein brought from America for the purpose'.[32] In a lecture delivered in October 1902 'Miss Goldstein suggested that when (with a big emphasis) the site of the Federal Capital was decided on, Washington might well be taken as a model. America is the land of superlatives. There are no half measures about the American.' Goldstein fell in love with the 'wonders' of New York. She recounted how 'going into an office, she stood by accident on the top of hot air register, by which means the rooms are heated. Miss Goldstein thinks she might be excused for expressing her astonishment in an acrobatic manner.'[33]

Goldstein's American visit provided an engagement with an unprecedented transformation, a 'heightened awareness of firstness' evident in an era of 'gas, railways, steamships, telegraphs, evolution, the spectroscope, bacteriology', as a commentator noted at the end of the century, on the 'intrusion of the new'. Peter Fritzsche observed that extraordinary industrial and technological changes were not only large movements or abstract constructs but impacted on the individual.[34] This subjectivity intensified at the *fin de siècle*, together with technological and communication innovation, helped to shape a space for women in the public sphere and created more capacity for self-fashioning, providing Goldstein with her moment.

Goldstein was selected as the Senate candidate of the Victorian-based Women's Federal Political Association at a meeting on 14 August 1903, by a vote of 29-8. Although overwhelmingly endorsed – and no other candidate contested the selection – some resistance was based on a view that the association should not support candidates standing for election; while Goldstein served as the association's president, it did not financially assist her candidature.[35] Nor did the influential Women's Christian Temperance Union (WCTU) in Victoria support her candidature, declaring that women should not stand for Parliament: 'such action would prejudice the interest of the women's cause at the present juncture.'[36] There was also a concern that her candidature would 'prejudice the granting of the State franchise to women', as Mrs Trundle, the 'superintendent of the franchise' for the WCTU in Queensland, acknowledged in a letter supporting Goldstein's candidature. Trundle dismissed fears of prejudicing voting reform in the state of Victoria as 'groundless'. 'Do we get any sooner what is justice for us to have by waiting, and striving to conciliate the feelings of those who bitterly oppose us? I think not.'[37] The deeply conservative Victorian Legislative Council (its members were appointed, not elected) stymied the extension of the franchise to women voters in state elections until October 1908. Women could not stand for election for the Victorian Legislative Assembly until 1923.

Goldstein's decision to formally open her Senate campaign in her family hometown of Portland on 13 October 1903 – over 350 kilometres from Melbourne – was made practical by rail and communications technologies. Newspapers and cable news reported her election launch in the next morning editions; beginning in an unorthodox setting attracted attention.[38] Her persona and the groundbreaking nature of her candidature also drew press attention as she campaigned across regional Victoria. 'A lady politician is a very different person. Here then is Miss Goldstein: Dark hair, dressed low upon her forehead, but not absurdly low, merely becoming; sparkling dark eyes, which are very much on the alert, especially when an elector ventures upon a question; prettily flushed face, nicely featured, and a very attractive smile.' After several years of reform activism Goldstein had developed a lively and confident style as a public speaker, able to deftly field audience questions and deflect interjections.

> Her composure when signs of disturbance appear and the way she has of getting off a slap at the other side without in the least descending from the pedestal she as a lady stands on are worth seeing and hearing . . . her delivery could hardly be better; her magnetism – well, those who go to scoff at future meetings will remain to admire.[39]

Shearer West argued that 'one of the strongest focal points of early feminism was the idea that women should be in control of their own bodies.'[40] Goldstein took control of the presentation of herself in the public sphere: in the discursive intervention represented by the publication of the *Australian Woman's Sphere* from 1900, in her skilful performances as a public speaker and in the presentation of her body and dress. In person, image or print, Goldstein's dress and physicality drew attention. Goldstein exploited gendered judgements about women's appearance to her advantage. In Adelaide her platform interrogator immediately registered the signal sent by her dress.

> Miss Goldstein is a dress reformer, and on her arrival it was noticed that she did not wear a long skirt, but one which just tipped her ankles. She said, 'I think of the practice of women wearing the drawing-room train in the streets is simply disgusting. It is the worst possible taste to wear in the streets a long dress which is suitable only to the drawing-room.'

Goldstein's self-representation made for arresting photo portraits and illustrations that were reproduced in newspapers and periodicals, and not least in portrait photographs published in the *Woman's Sphere*, as in the image that dominated the cover of the November 1903 edition. The 'first woman candidate for the Senate' stood in a long white drawing-room dress that emphasized height and poise. Her gaze was confident and calm, one hand assertively on her hip, the other holding a copy of her own journal. The *Woman's Sphere* apologized to readers for the 'unavoidable' reprinting of 'another portrait of Miss Goldstein'. 'We were inundated last month with orders for the copy of the *Woman's Sphere* containing the portrait and manifesto from towns where she had recently spoken, and from towns where she was going to speak.'[41]

In April 1903 the *Woman's Sphere* published a large cover page illustration that dramatized the forces that Goldstein's election campaign confronted, and the gendered and racial tensions concentrated at the *fin de siècle*. The cartoon presented a multitude of men of all types in a massed parade of rich and poor, decrepit and callow, rough pugilist and effeminate snob, the drunkard, the businessman and racial stereotypes arrayed under the banner adorned with the blunt assertion 'MANHOOD SUFFRAGE', framing a device of a brimming beer tankard and crossed smoking pipes. Above the mocking male crowd was isolated womanhood standing on a podium, chained to a wild haired 'mad woman' and a coarse male convict who both knelt in distracted subjugation (Figure 10). 'THOU SHALT NOT VOTE WOMENHOOD MADNESS CRIMINALITY' read the sign that loomed over the degraded types, and the erect figure of woman, her defiant gaze and clenched fist signal a determination to assert a right of self-expression. In the distance shone the sun of 'women's suffrage', breaking through the clouds over a silhouetted city.[42] The figure of the elegantly attired and dark-haired young woman was clearly modelled on Goldstein.

Some forms of resistance could prove more intractable than outright hostility. At her Portland campaign launch on 13 October, 'Miss Goldstein had a good reception, and several of her points aroused genuine appreciation, but the audience showed a disposition to evince a lack of seriousness.'[43] A month earlier,

Figure 10 Goldstein's 1903 election campaign reflected the gender and racial tensions concentrated at the *fin de siècle*. Cartoon, *Australian Woman's Sphere*, April 1903. State Library of Victoria.

news of Goldstein's intending candidature inspired the mocking rhyme, 'Veni! Vida! Vici!':

> When it comes to the ken
> Of a Senator's wife, could he chide her
> If she kicked up a row with her tongue
> and her pen
> On the boldness of brainy Miss Vida?
> For a lass
> Is a lass
> But, alas! should it pass
> There are ladies who'd call her a spider!
> And although we may cheer
> Still I fear
> It is clear
> We must bid you 'Good morning,'
> Miss Vida![44]

Derision could prove a powerful tool for belittling women's participation in the public sphere and was often enlisted to scorn the ambitions of the New Woman. A mocking rhyme appeared in several regional Victorian newspapers in the period before the 1903 election, of a New Woman 'who lived under pressure that rendered her dizzy', exhausting herself in a flurry of causes and interests:

> She served on a School Board with courage and zeal;
> She golfed and she kodaked and rode on a wheel;
> She read Tolstoi and Ibsen, knew microbes by name;
> She approved of the franchise, thought sewing was tame
> And died of shock at finding herself with an hour free.[45]

The New Woman was described in a hostile Australian newspaper report as a 'composite creature'.[46] Sheila Rowbotham observed that by the end of the turn of the century, 'growing numbers of middle-class women found themselves with one foot in the conventional world and another in the unexplored territory of "new womanhood". The arrival of these "odd women", hovering between the established parameters of class and gender, unsettled the status quo: they did not fit within the established structures of society, and their singularity inclined them to dissent.' Yet 'unconventional behaviour put women in a precarious position'; activists like the British feminist and labour reformer Beatrice Webb wanted to avoid the 'damaging stamp' of 'eccentricity'.[47] Goldstein was a self-consciously composite modern creation: 'Vida not Veda' had to define herself, and she had ample talents and financial resources to realize her ambitions, although she necessarily had to struggle against the gender and structural obstacles cast before her.

In the election campaign Goldstein confronted 'the prevailing prejudice amongst many of the electors to a woman taking part in affairs of State'. Her manifesto declared that 'I believe that women should enter Parliament as representatives of the home, and to voice the opinions of women on important domestic and social affairs, which the increasing specialising of labour, educational, industrial, and social, is bringing more and more into the political arena'. It was perhaps that intimidating sense of an encroaching specialization, and an intervention in the traditionally male sphere of politics, that compelled Goldstein to frame a manifesto that reflected relatively conventional priorities, despite the novelty of her candidature, and the wide range of issues she embraced as an activist. Goldstein felt constrained to focus upon her positions on immigration restriction, industrial arbitration, protection versus free trade, her views on the naval agreement with Britain.[48] The policy programme that Goldstein outlined was primarily that of radical protectionists such as Henry Bournes Higgins, who stood for the House of Representatives North Melbourne seat in the 1903 elections.[49]

On 'the fiscal question' Goldstein stated, 'I am a protectionist. I believe in freetrade absolutely – as a theory.' Yet the latter was 'impracticable in a young country', as 'the world's workshops' were 'forging ahead with high protectionist tariffs'. Compulsory conciliation and arbitration were 'preferable to the barbarous methods of lockouts and strikes'. Australia should be protected against the cheap labour of other countries, although adopting the principle of equal pay would be preferable to 'drastic and restrictive legislation'. Goldstein seemed to be advocating a universal application of equal pay, regardless of race or gender, although she qualified her stance by adding that equal pay would reduce the 'keen desire for unrestricted immigration, with all its dangers to health and morality'.[50] In these measures Goldstein embraced a defensive spirit of contraction before the threats posed by the world, while exhorting electors to risk a new openness by endorsing her candidacy.

Goldstein sometimes struggled to clarify the nuance of her policy positions, particularly as she continued to hesitate over fulsomely supporting the racial imperative of a White Australia, so fundamental to Australian national identity at Federation.[51] Campaigning in the Gippsland region in November, Goldstein was accused of contradicting her White Australia stance by endorsing the intermarriage of whites and non-whites. 'If a white woman takes a fancy to a black man let her have him! . . . It was in vain that electors called out, "What about a White Australia?". . . . As a woman legislator we may take it for granted that Miss Goldstein would not oppose the replenishment of the husband market from alien sources.' Goldstein also struggled over the question of the annexation of New Guinea, under either Australian or British control.

> She replied to the query that she was not in favor of taking the Blacks land away from them and that she was 'altogether opposed to the grab-all policy of Britain.' The fact that but for the empire's expansion which she called the 'grab-all' policy there would be no Canada, or New Zealand, or Australia today, did not appear to occur to her.

Perhaps it did, but Goldstein at times gave an impression of naivete. Her derision of women wearing expensive dresses did not always meet with a sympathetic hearing. 'Miss Goldstein's vehement assurance that if she ever saw a woman wearing such a skirt she would go up and tell her what the first-class dressmaker got for making it' was 'received in silence'.[52]

Goldstein expressed a strong disapproval of party politics. 'Party government was government by machine, and party government meant the creation of unthinking voters and the dictation of party organisations, which was the most serious menace this young democracy had to face.'[53] Reaction against mass, working-class democracy and the rise of working-class party 'machines' that displaced an elite liberalism was one of the anxieties of *fin de siècle* politics.[54] The Australian Labor Party (ALP) returned the rhetorical fire. Labor steadily built its electoral success in the post-Federation decade by developing a nationwide political machine that was the envy of its non-Labor rivals. Stephen Barker, a Labor Senate candidate for Victoria, asked a public meeting in October

> to consider the candidates from the standpoint of reformers; but they were not to be confounded with those spurious reformers who were endeavoring to throw dust in the eyes of the people. . . . The Labor party had battled for the women's vote when those who were now giving political drawing room parties – (laughter) – were fighting against it. There was only one love that the women politically should have, and that was the Labor party. The party's interests were the women's interests.[55]

Goldstein's election campaign attracted wide press interest across Victoria and the nation. It was Goldstein's intelligence that both confronted and impressed her audience at the hectic schedule of election meetings that she maintained from mid-September until 16 December. 'Miss Goldstein is rather too practical, downright, matter-of-fact and brainy to be spoken of in a light way. She is nice to look at, and absolutely delightful to listen to. The quick, eager way she has of rising to answer questions has its charms, for you see there the enthusiast; her smartness at repartee is a rare gift.'[56] Stressing her charm could serve as a device for dismissing Goldstein, if it were not for her skill in turning audiences and awkward questions to her advantage. Asked at Portland of her objection to maintaining the agreement whereby Australia paid a £200,000 subsidy for British naval protection, Goldstein crisply replied that 'the Commonwealth should endeavor to establish a navy of our own. (Applause.)' Goldstein explained that she favoured preferential trade with Britain 'in the broad sense, but it seems that Britain standing alone against the world was magnificent but not common sense'. Of deporting Pacific Islanders who had been brought in to work in the Queensland sugar industry, 'these people have been civilised, christianised, educated, and there is no reason to force them out. She was decidedly opposed to colored people coming in. Those who were going for a White Australia were going bald-headed for it (Laughter.).'[57]

It was unfortunate that Goldstein did not forge strong links with the labour movement as part of her electoral strategy, as her agenda reflected such common cause with it. On the basis of shared outlook, Labor declined to nominate a candidate to oppose Higgins in North Melbourne at the 1903 election.[58] In the cultural politics of the *fin de siècle*, Sally Ledger observed a complex dynamic between feminists and socialist parties in Britain: on the one hand, 'a lack of common ground' on key issues such as equal pay for women, while a number of women were actively involved in the labour movement, including active feminists.[59] A similar, contradictory dynamic was at work in Australia. As an agent of the future, Goldstein was attracted to the labour movement as an innovative force of reform. Despite her hostility to machine politics, Goldstein could serve as a conduit for transmitting intelligence between the feminist and labour movements. In September 1902 Goldstein gave an address in the Melbourne Trades Hall on American industrial conditions, outlining the 'stiff battle the trades unionist has to fight in America'. In a hall 'packed to the doors' Goldstein

> was able to give details of several important events in the commercial and industrial world, which are referred to only in the briefest words by the daily papers. The methods of American labour organization, immigration, the operations of the iniquitous Beef Trust, the ins and outs of the recent coal strike in the hard-coal region of Pennsylvania, and the tramways strike in San Francisco, factories legislation, arbitration and child labour were reviewed.

At the conclusion of her address 'three cheers were given for Miss Goldstein'.[60]

The blur of issues and events reflected the turmoil and opportunities churning as a consequence of global '*fin de siècle* industrial transformation'. The second industrial revolution of the late nineteenth and early twentieth centuries had seen production and the reach of unprecedentedly vast corporations and trusts expand around the world, generating spectacular wealth and ruthless exploitation, and the reactions in Australia that produced tariff barriers and immigration restriction.[61] Goldstein was a code sharer of this transformation, both enthusiastic of the potential for change and troubled by the scale of the reform task. In surmounting these difficulties Goldstein understood that the labour movement provided a crucial organizational tool. In December 1902 a *Woman's Sphere* editorial expressed frustration with the decision of the recently formed Victorian Women's Federation to deny membership to the Trades Hall Council. Excluding an organization that had done so much to support the struggle for women's suffrage was a 'blunder'. The establishment of a coalition of organizations reflected the web of connections in the issues that faced them, even if these connections were not always immediately obvious. 'The platform of the Trades Hall does very materially concern itself with the interests of women and children; their advocacy of equal suffrage, of factory legislation, of old age pensions – yes, and of an unimproved land values tax – can anyone be found bold enough to say that the interests of women and children are not touched by these?'[62]

The most dynamic of Goldstein's self-representations in the 1903 campaign was the presentation of herself as a 'modern Eve' at an election meeting held in the Melbourne suburb of Prahran on 13 November. With another month of demanding campaigning still before her, Goldstein began her appeal to the 'crowded' hall of electors defensively, compelled to offer what the *Argus* described as 'a personal explanation', in 'true parliamentary style' – as if Goldstein had already been reduced to the familiar status of just another politician. Goldstein defended her decision to charge admission to her election meetings by the payment of a silver coin – a more expensive contribution than copper pennies. 'It was all very well, she said, for a great luminary like [Free Trade party leader] Mr. G. H. Reid to charge for admission. Nothing was said about that,' while she faced 'severe comment'. Goldstein said that she was not 'a moneyed woman' and was determined to avoid going into debt, given the lack of financial support from the Women's Political Association. Goldstein was 'rope-able' at the charge that her candidature 'would imperil the chances' of women's suffrage for the Victorian state legislature, and that women standing for Parliament was described as 'a horrible revolutionary idea which would upset creation'.

Goldstein also responded to the warning made by 'a federal Labor member' that 'the ladies not be led away by "high sounding claptrap and humbug"' about casting a 'thinking vote' – an appeal that Goldstein often made to women voters during the campaign. 'What on earth did he mean?' Goldstein retorted. 'Did he want the women to cast an unthinking vote?' Despite Labor hostility, Goldstein appealed to the women in the audience 'to arouse enthusiasm for social and industrial reform'. While the home was 'the woman's sphere', women should also work outside it, dealing with issues that impacted upon the home. The home was also the man's sphere, Goldstein added, which 'he often neglected'. Provocatively, Goldstein asserted that 'the men of the country were what the women made them', which seemed to blame the victim for male behaviour, as one 'voice' in the crowd readily concurred: 'That's very true (laughter).' Although Goldstein promptly added, 'yet how was it possible for women to make men good citizens unless they were good citizens themselves? No doubt woman's sphere was the home. But so was man's (Cheers and laughter).' Goldstein led her audience to their own instinctive prejudices and then subverted them, often to the sound of laughter. Addressing the men in the audience, Goldstein urged them to cast their minds back thousands of years, to the Garden of Eden, 'where peace and love and happiness reigned until woman tempted man, and he did eat the apple of discord (A Voice. – "So he did.")'. Then she asked them

> to bring their minds back to the present. I am a modern Eve. (Loud laughter.) I offer you an apple – (laughter) – but an apple of a different kind – the apple of harmony – the idea of a woman going into Parliament. Take and eat of it, and you will find you will develop a relish for more apples of the same kind. (Renewed laughter.) I may not be all that a member ought to be, and I have not exalted my own capacity, but I am perfectly certain that I could not do worse than some of the men you have sitting in Parliament (Loud cheers).

In this startling and unexpected peroration Goldstein recast frustration and hostility as an opportunity for breaking with outmoded prejudice – even as she invoked the oldest parable of the 'discord' between men and women.[63]

Aleida Assmann has described advocates of modernity creating 'the fiction of a new beginning' by inventing narratives that ordained a decisive break with the past.[64] From the claims of her unprecedented candidature to the range of reforms Goldstein advocated – including a fundamental rethinking of the relationships between men and women – the place of women in the public sphere, and a host of social and economic reforms, Goldstein cast a modern Eve as a breakthrough voice of the future. Gail Marshall argued that 'there is some debate as to the extent to which the New Woman existed beyond the pages of the novels, short stories and newspapers of which she was an integral part'.[65] Vida Goldstein embodied the challenging spirit of the New Woman, a narrative expression of the *fin de siècle* invented to break with the past.

It was little surprise that following the election on 16 December, the *Woman's Sphere* reported that Goldstein 'polled highest wherever she had spoken'. Attracting 51,497 votes in a potential statewide electorate of 600,000 eligible voters, Goldstein was ranked fifteenth of the eighteen Senate candidates, with four elected. Without the benefit of the financial and organizational support available to the Protectionist, Free Trade or Labor parties – and lacking the support potentially provided by the WCTU – Goldstein nonetheless made a significant impact that was only partly captured in polling figures. The leading Melbourne newspapers, the *Age* and the *Argus*, also imposed what the *Woman's Sphere* described as the 'tyranny of the ticket', prominently endorsing, respectively, their own preferred Protectionist and Free Trade candidates, lists from which Goldstein was excluded. There was press praise for her campaign, her eloquence and grasp of the policies she advocated. The Bendigo *Evening Mail* observed that 'Miss Goldstein handled the topics of the day with the skill of an old campaigner'. Goldstein seems to have appreciated the views expressed by a Miss Amy Tomkinson, who wrote to the *Woman's Sphere* praising Goldstein's 'splendid polling', significant of the progress of

> a departure so new in political history. It speaks so much for the educative effect of your arduous campaign, and surely must be accounted a virtual victory for you. The thanks of the women of the Commonwealth, first and foremost, are due to you for so valiantly pioneering the way, encouraging them to think for themselves on matters of vital concern to humanity at large, and, in fact, to realize the responsibilities of enfranchisement.[66]

As the Senate vote was counted, the *Age* observed that 'Miss Goldstein's vote must have appeared an astonishingly large one even to her most insistent supporters', polling better in regional centres than in Melbourne and possibly as her personal appearances made a greater impact.[67] The *Age* also reported that 'women polled in great numbers' while lavishing condescension on anecdotes of their unfamiliarity with political affiliations and voting procedure. Goldstein entered her local polling station promptly at 8.00 am and 'probably holds the distinction of being the first woman to exercise her franchise in an Australian election – unless other enthusiasts were quicker with the blue pencil than she was'. The returning officer 'was so impressed with the incident that he intends to preserve the ballot-box . . . this plain white pine-box is to be handed down to posterity and perhaps will be an object of curiosity in the Smithsonian Institute of Australia, 1,000 years hence'.[68]

Reflecting on 'the humour and pathos' of her campaign experiences, Goldstein regarded her 51,000 votes 'as a tribute to the cause she advocated', the pursuit of 'educational propaganda among the men and women of Victoria'. Goldstein lamented that 'the apathy shown by Victorian people, particularly professional men . . . many prominent citizens, doctors, barristers, and others had declared that they would not go across the road to record their votes'.[69] Voting in Australian elections was voluntary in 1903 and conducted on an ordinary day of the working week; federal officials struggled with the task of compiling voting rolls for each electorate to include the hundreds of thousands of women voters in each state, and to generally prepare for the still novel and enormous task of an Australia-wide election. Perhaps these factors helped to account for little more than half the potential votes polled in the House of Representative seats, as the *Age* noted, and that the people did not take an eager part in the contest, presenting further obstacles for Goldstein to overcome with her pioneering candidature.[70]

In the period between 1903 and 1914, Vida Goldstein again ran for the Senate, at the 1910 elections, and twice ran for the House of Representatives seat of Kooyong, a middle class and politically conservative constituency in Melbourne, in 1913 and 1914. Goldstein contested these elections as an independent candidate with the backing of the Woman's Political Association, of which she remained as president. All these campaigns were unsuccessful. Her 1910 Senate campaign attracted only slightly more voters than her 1903 candidature. She might have allied with 'one of the great parties' but she stood for principle rather than personal ambition: 'she despised party government'.[71] As the candidate for Kooyong, she attracted over 10,000 votes in 1913 and repeated a similar result in 1914.[72] Firmly established as a champion of women's rights, her politics also fixed more sharply as an advocate of socialism, although one who formally stood apart from the machine politics of the Labor Party, an outlook projected from 1909 in a new periodical, *The Woman Voter*, of which she was editor and proprietor. The WPA's idealistic manifesto included a commitment to 'equal rights in the disposition of property'.[73] A harder edged ideology, lacking a strong base in a larger political organization, may account for the plateau that she seemed to reach in electoral support in her various campaigns. Goldstein also laboured against stubborn male prejudice and was unable to accept that the Victorian people 'are not yet anxious for that equality of the sexes which Miss Vida Goldstein made part of her programme', as Melbourne's *Punch* explained

'A Modern Eve' 105

Figure 11 Goldstein defied the claim that the Victorian people 'are not yet anxious for . . . equality of the sexes'. Postcard produced for Goldstein's 1910 election campaign. Museum Victoria.

following the 1910 election (Figure 11). 'In truth, Nature long ago decided against the idea of equality, when she gave woman a smaller brain-pan, and smaller and weaker limbs than man.'[74]

Goldstein also faced the growth of modern forms of government and political mobilization that constrained her appeal. In 1904, the Australian Women's National League (AWNL) emerged in Victoria. Supported by the Victorian Employers Federation – itself the product of a reorganization in 1901 to more effectively resist trade union mobilization – the AWNL was staunchly conservative, establishing an effective branch network across Victoria and a membership of over 50,000, far rivaling the fringe WPA, which struggled to resource Goldstein's campaigns. In the weeks prior to the 1913 election the *Woman Voter* appealed for 'speakers, organisers, canvassers, paper sellers, assistants in the office'.[75] As the election loomed, the AWNL's council passed a resolution 'repudiating Miss Goldstein's claim that she speaks for the women of Australia'.[76] During the 1913 campaign the AWNL supported Goldstein's Liberal Party opponent, Sir Robert Best, in Kooyong. The AWNL stood 'to protect the best interests of the home' and opposed the election of women in Parliament, supporting 'men of high principle and ability'. Goldstein was denounced as a 'militant suffragette' who was 'in accord with the principles of Labor's socialism'. The AWNL 'deplored' the methods adopted by 'our misguided sisters in England', the suffragettes who had resorted to violent demonstrations in support of their campaign for the vote.[77] The freedoms offered by the model of the New Woman had generated a powerful reaction.

Across the post-Federation period the women's vote increasingly divided along class lines. The fusion of the Protectionist and Free Trade parties in 1909 to form a more cohesive non-Labor organization was prompted by the increasing political success of the ALP, which won control of both Houses of the Commonwealth Parliament in 1910; machine politics was evolving into more disciplined and effective forms. Goldstein's agenda of creating an Australia of independent women able to exercise personal and political freedom, with opportunities created by access to full-time work and equal pay, was also inhibited by the privilege accorded by the institutions of the new federal state to the male family breadwinner. Between 1907 and 1914, a series of industrial arbitration decisions, beginning with the Harvester judgement of 1907, paid a family wage to the male breadwinner while assuming that women would remain at home, serving the nation as mothers. Goldstein had hoped that the creation of a compulsory industrial arbitration system by the Commonwealth Government would lead to the expansion of a workplace regime based around a principle of equal pay for equal work by men and women. In July 1912 Goldstein applauded a Commonwealth Arbitration Court judgement that seemed to promote equal pay for women, although the *Woman Voter* noted the ambiguities of a 'most signal victory'. 'The Judge saw clearly that, where a man and a woman did exactly the same work, the pay should be equal.' The Fruitpickers judgement, as it was called, entrenched wage discrimination against women – as the court's president Justice Henry Bournes Higgins intended. Higgins only awarded equal pay to women fruitpickers as he could not avoid doing otherwise. The court preserved a discrimination against accepting women as breadwinners on behalf of the family. 'It is a grave error to suppose that women wage-earners are not responsible for the support of home and dependents,' the *Woman Voter* warned.[78] State and federal industrial jurisdictions adopted Higgins's gender discriminations as precedent.[79]

The modernity that emerged from the *fin de siècle*, and which Goldstein hoped to creatively harness to establish a new domain of freedom, had reassembled established practices and prejudices into more efficient forms. The New Woman was itself a discursive formation of the second industrial revolution; Goldstein's

1903 campaign was a projection of that modern discourse. *Fin de siècle* culture evolved from the new communications technologies that democratized knowledge production and dissemination – the cable news system, the cheaper production and distribution of news and ideas in books, pamphlets and journals, which trade unions, radicals and feminists were able to produce. To publish your own newspaper is to produce your own instrument of self-creation. Vida Goldstein succeeded in projecting herself in the public sphere as the author of her own life and narrative: a transmission that was also projected back at her, in praise and vilification. The subjectivities of surveillance and the demands of political activism often proved too much for many advocates of change. Vida Goldstein maintained an iconoclastic activism that ran into the post-First World War period, even as the accelerations of modernity, in industrialization, militarism and gender discrimination, threatened to overwhelm the spirit of self-expression and idealism unleashed at the *fin de siècle*.

5

'Some disquieting symptoms'

Alfred Deakin's nervous breakdown

On Monday, 8 July 1907, newspapers in Melbourne and around Australia reported on 'some disquieting symptoms' experienced for several days by the prime minister, Alfred Deakin.[1] Feeling 'slightly indisposed' on the previous Thursday, Deakin had left early a sitting of the House of Representatives, in the Parliament building on Spring Street, and returned to his home, 'Llanarth', in South Yarra.[2] On Friday, his 'indisposition' seemed 'somewhat more serious': 'seized with dizziness' at an Executive Council meeting and exciting anxiety among his colleagues. Deakin was persuaded to forego the Lieutenant-Governor's official dinner that evening, to mark the resumption of Parliament on 3 July.[3] On Saturday, Deakin was unable to attend his office. Called to Llanarth, Deakin's physician Dr Marcel Crivelli detected symptoms of 'serious physical and brain fag' and ordered complete rest.[4] The press reported Deakin's 'partial nervous break-down' and 'nervous exhaustion' as a consequence of 'the strenuous life' and overwork during his recent extended trip to England. In April and May, Deakin had represented Australia at the Imperial Conference, the gathering of the white Dominion leaders of the empire in consultation with the ministers of the British government. On 10 July Deakin left Melbourne, travelling by train around the wide arc of Port Phillip Bay to 'Ballara', the family retreat he had built at Point Lonsdale, where he would remain for at least a week. 'He has virtually worked himself to a standstill.'[5] It would be nearly four months before Alfred Deakin fully resumed his duties as prime minister. During which time Deakin felt compelled to immerse in an intensive scrutiny of his relationship with 'the way of action' in the world, conducted in prayer, reading and reflection, including the ethically charged and testing Hindu text the *Bhagavad Gita*, while struggling as the subject of a relentless public exposure.[6]

Press accounts of Deakin's disquieting symptoms were matched by the dogged persistence of his own surveillance, tersely recorded in his private diary.

Deakin had noted a 'first skip' – heart palpitations – as early as 9 March, just after the steamer *Marmara* bearing him and his wife Pattie to Europe had left Port Adelaide. At a reception on his return to Australia on 26 June, Deakin appreciated, 'with much feeling ... the "grand help" which Mrs. Deakin had given him' during the trip, although given a demanding schedule, he had to acknowledge 'the little that he had seen of his wife during their stay in London'.[7] On 29 June he noted in his diary another 'skip': 'Fagged', 'Unwell office' were noted on 3 and 4 July, then on the 5th, he scrawled, 'Early office – giddy Forrest and Navy Lunch Fox Office Giddy Crivelli found heart and eyes affected injection.' On the 10th he inscribed the refuge reached: 'Ballara', on the Bellarine peninsula, 103 kilometres (64 miles) from Melbourne, which could be reached by either train or ferry within a few hours. The bay held the dimly glittering night-lit city at a distance. Entries for the remainder of July tracked persistent suffering. 'Rather depressed', 'giddy injection', 'poor night', 'attack of dizziness', 'palpitations'.[8]

Steeped in illness, the private Deakin seemed to merge with the public persona. '[G]iddy Forrest and Navy Lunch Fox Office Giddy' registered a blurred code of distress and duty: presumably, Deakin joined the Lt.-Governor at the luncheon on board HMS *Powerful*, the flagship of the Royal Navy's Australian station squadron, berthed in Melbourne as part of its visits to the state capitals in July.[9] Either side of that commitment Deakin met with his Treasurer, Sir John Forrest, and the journalist and political confidante Frank Fox, who in 1907 became editor of the recently established periodical, *Lone Hand*, the voice of a new cultural nationalism.[10] With Forrest and Fox, Deakin processed the ceaseless demands and manoeuvres of keeping his minority Liberal Protectionist ministry in office; Deakin's party had lost five seats at the December 1906 elections and was even more dependent on the Australian Labor Party's support in the parliamentary session that was about to commence. Labor preferred – or at least tolerated – Deakin's reform agenda to the stridently anti-labour stance of George Reid's Free Trade Party.[11] Only three days earlier, the federal Labor caucus had met and, crucially for Deakin, decided to renew the 'general support' it had extended to the government in Parliament since July 1905, when Deakin had become prime minister for the second time. 'Things will go on as before,' Labor's leader, John Christian Watson, reassured an *Age* reporter.[12]

That things were going on as before was the dilemma that immediately confronted Deakin on his return to Melbourne from the Imperial Conference on 25 June. In both London and Melbourne Deakin was overwhelmed by an 'avalanche' of commitments which chimed in his diary: in London he recorded 'the avalanche descends' of callers and letters on 9 April; 'nervy' and 'hard pressed' signalled the internalized impact a week later.[13] The punishing demands of work generated a private crisis that in the months between July and October at times stood exposed in the public sphere. That his symptoms and the progress of his convalescence were intensively tracked in the press and private diary reflected the demands of public life and liberal modernity's requirement of scrutiny, assessment and control.

The liberal 'rule of freedom' cultivates subjects who are 'reflexive and self-watching', finely balancing responsibility and rights.[14] As prime minister, Alfred Deakin was a skilled manager of this balance, sourced in the management of himself: projecting a coherent, rational identity capable of governing – a performance which by mid-1907 Deakin was unable to maintain. The Australian press scrutinized Deakin's illness and absence from public life, and diagnosed 'neurasthenia . . . another modern addition to the list of humanity's troubles'.[15] Neurasthenia, or weak nervous system, was conceived as an 'imprecise' definition of an elusive malady in 1881.[16] New York doctor Margaret Cleaves published *Autobiography of a Neurasthene* (1910), in which she identified 'a peculiar condition of nervous exhaustion' that afflicted the modern subject. Cleaves identified 'periodic electrical storms' in the nervous system and which presented sufferers with a dilemma: 'the conservation of energy'. Neurasthenia was a symptom of a defining characteristic of the *fin de siècle*: 'the experience and consciousness of accelerated change'. A second wave of global industrialization saw 'the emergence of a new constellation of energy sources as well as systems of production, transportation, consumption, and communication'. As Andreas Killen observes, 'It was also not lost on observers that similar transformations were occurring at the level of the body', which could generate 'heightened output' or 'pathological exhaustion'.[17] Deakin's private archive plunges us into a mind struggling with the stresses threatening to unravel the physical self that had to keep moving forward in time, possessed of the energy and will to act, as Deakin crossed another personal threshold in 1907: the onset of the physical and mental decline that increasingly shadowed his last years of public life.

In 1907 Deakin was exercised by the complexities of implementing a contentious legislative programme while leading a minority government and managing Australia's place in the British Empire and the wider world. His participation at the Imperial Conference in London showcased his leadership and oratorical skills. On his return the *Age* declared that Deakin had overcome an English 'cold shoulder' for colonials 'as the Australian orator gained their ears and then their hearts'. That Deakin had impressed was also a testament to hard work. 'Through long series of early morning interviews, through long Conference sittings, through brilliant midday luncheon speeches, through banquets at night – every one with its separate demand for a speech – the days went by. Nor did this comprise all; for far into the hours of the night the work went on, studying documents, answering questions and giving or promising audiences.' Unaware of the collapse to come, the *Age* added that 'it meant a demand for work that might have broken down a man who had not Mr. Deakin's great capacity for sustained labor'.[18] In London Deakin faced resistance from Campbell Bannerman's Liberal government over his ambitions for an Imperial Secretariat to represent the Dominions in London and over his support for preferential empire trade.[19] In Australia, Deakin faced vigorous opposition from the Free Traders over his interventionist programme of tariff protection and compulsory industrial arbitration.[20] Yet whether or not agreeing with his policies, Deakin's oratory 'carries an audience away, because his hearers feel sure that the man so eloquently addressing them thoroughly believes that his proposals are necessary for his country's salvation'.[21] Deakin drew upon these skills to manage Australia's response to an accelerating globalization of trade and intensifying international rivalries between empires and nations; the racial anxieties of a white nation in the Asia Pacific region were heightened by the rise

Figure 12 Alfred Deakin in London, 1907. His participation at the Imperial Conference 'might have broken down a man who had not Mr. Deakin's great capacity for sustained labor'. The breakdown came on his return to Australia. National Library of Australia.

of Japan, particularly in the wake of its humiliating defeat of Russia, a European imperial power, in the 1904–5 war. By 1907 Deakin had cast off a liberal's disquiet to embrace a programme of compulsory military training for men and male youths, and the creation of an Australian Naval Squadron, compelled, as he said, by the circumstances of time and situation, and which he announced in a major Defence Statement in December.[22] But first Deakin had to reconstruct himself (Figure 12).

John Jervis described how 'a culture becomes "modern" when it manifests a degree of understanding of how its own processes intervene in the world, exhibiting the cultural power of the means of classification and control'. By the *fin de siècle* 'this reflexive awareness is increasingly turned inward as well, on to the self, producing an increasing sense of crisis'.[23] For Deakin, managing the public self required the steady construction of an archive of memory and reflection. Born in Melbourne in 1856, Deakin had from his early years began to record and gather the details of his thoughts, life and ambitions, as he made his way from university to a career in the law, in journalism with David Syme's *Age*, one of Melbourne's major daily newspapers, and then to politics, serving from 1879 in both the Victorian and Commonwealth Parliaments. Deakin was a key architect of the Federation of the Australian colonies in 1901, assuming the position of Attorney General, and serving as prime minister, for the first time, for several months from September 1903: 'Deakin believed that it was the duty of those who had argued for federation to make it work.'[24] His collected papers in the National Library of Australia constitute an extraordinary archive of self-surveillance.[25] Deakin maintained a daily diary between 1884 and 1916: 11,680 days lived over 32 years. Each individual page of the *Rough Diaries* published by Sands and McDougall that Deakin preferred provided space to record three days of his life. Each day was encrypted by Deakin in a staccato knot of references, tentatively chained together with hyphen strokes as they dashed forward in his scrawled hand. Another dense constellation of scrutiny was contained within each diary between 1906 and 1914: in the blank note pages at both the beginning and end of each volume, Deakin had the habit of recording each book he read during that year. In 1907 Deakin recorded the titles and author's names for 100 books, almost his exact annual average.[26] Deakin also maintained a series of notebooks on which he brooded over spiritual and philosophical questions, animated by concern for the soul and the ethical dilemmas of engaging in the world.[27] The tendency to surveillance discreetly infiltrated the public sphere: Alfred Deakin was also the anonymous 'Australian Correspondent' of the London *Morning Post* for over a decade from 1900, providing more than a million words of commentary on Australian politics – and the progress and struggles of 'Mr. Deakin'.[28]

Yet the man 'who rules a continent, and has arrested the attention of an Empire', was most content in South Yarra, 'that little suburb enclosed in its ring of parks' – where he had grown 'as youth and man; married there a graceful woman, who is in all things a fit mate for him; dwells there now in a simple villa, close by his aged mother, next door a married daughter, whose infant son is his playmate'. This 1907 profile published in *Lone Hand* described Deakin's 'whole happiness': 'his family, his books, the occasional visit of an intimate, the fine Fitzroy Park or Botanic Gardens for an eager, striding walk'.[29] The world colonized Deakin's domain in the books lining room after room of Llanarth – 'political', 'history', 'biography', 'essays', 'religious', 'travel and exploration' – in the study; 'educational' in the breakfast room; a concentration of 'French books' in the study, spilling out into the breakfast room and the landing; novels and 'agricultural' on the landing, 'poetry and drama' and 'religious' in the drawing-room bookcase – a list of 1,500 titles that does not exhaust the content or household distribution of Deakin's library.[30]

Deakin's reading provides an astonishing survey of the *fin de siècle* imagination and an immersion in 'a heightened awareness of the constructed nature of self and world'. Deakin's reading reflects how 'apparently oppositional ideas . . . operate in creative tension with each other', in shaping an emerging modern consciousness.[31] Illness hardly flagged his dedication to his annual reading tally and presumably provided respite and the basis of maintaining some continuity of interests and identity. Deakin unfailingly listed his reading in sequence from the beginning of the year, so it is possible to estimate what he read as the months unfolded.[32] In 1907 he caught up with books published in previous years, some stretching back to the late nineteenth century; he also seized on new works and in some cases literally as they were available. As his notebooks attest, Deakin's reading was drawn to spiritual mediations, including Eastern mysticism. He was also drawn to philosophy, particularly the current vogue for idealism; Deakin was sensitive to the relativities of experience and perception. In 1907 Deakin read the American philosopher and pioneer of psychology William James's *Human Immortality* (1898), *Pragmatism* (1907) and *Talks for Teachers* (1899). In *Pragmatism* James argued that truths are made in the course of human experience – empirically verifiable and constructed for good purpose. James identified two types of thought, the tender minded and the tough minded, and a kind of dualism that might exist in a single individual. When James claimed that the individual 'wants facts; he wants science; but he also wants a religion', he might have had Deakin in mind.[33] Deakin would re-engage with James as part of an intense absorption in of the work of the French philosopher Henri Bergson in 1911–12 and whose notion of *élan vital*, summoning a vital spirit in both public life and private meditation, appealed to Deakin.[34]

Deakin had something approaching an obsession with French literature and the new ideas emanating from Paris. 'What demons at exposition these Frenchmen are!' Deakin enthused in a 1907 letter to his friend Walter Murdoch, a Melbourne University literature scholar. 'I shall always be grateful to you for putting me on to Faguet and the *Revue* [*Latine*]. There is always something luminous in it.'[35] Deakin was fluent in the language after refining, with characteristic dedication, his 'neglected schoolboy French' in the late 1880s.[36] In 1907 Deakin read five works by the leading intellectual and critic Emile Faguet, four in rapid succession in the early months of the year, including *Voltaire* (1895) and *La Liberalisme* (1903). Over the same few months Deakin read three works by the Symbolist writer Remy de Gourmont, including *Le Livre des Masques* (1896), in which Gourmont acknowledged that while imprecise, Symbolism may mean 'idealism, disdain for social anecdote, antinaturalism, the tendency to take from life only the characteristic detail, to pay attention only to the act by which a man distinguishes himself from other men'. Symbolism reflected 'a new truth . . . liberating and rejuvenating . . . the principle of the ideality of the world . . . the world (all that is exterior to the self) exists only as the idea formed of it.'[37] While drawn to the metaphysical, Deakin's reading was fed by an intense curiosity and engagement with the world, and even his reading of Symbolists reflected this imperative. In Maurice Maeterlinck's essay *L'Intelligence des Fleurs* (1906), the famed Belgian Symbolist playwright expressed sympathy with socialist ideas. An interest in French politics was reflected in Raymond Poincaré's *Idées Contemporaines* (1906), in which the future French president outlined his conservative vision of France.

On his way to London in April and on the return to Australia in late May, Deakin and his wife spent a few nights in the 'lovely city' of Paris, as he scribbled in his diary, briefly savouring engagements with French culture and politics that were otherwise only available in texts. With Pattie he visited the Louvre in April and strolled the Luxemburg Gardens; in May they visited the Salon, the exhibition sponsored by the Society of Artists and which provided an imprimatur of taste that by 1907 was fragmenting under the challenge of modernism. 'Splendid show', Deakin recorded. On 21 May he called on the French premier Georges Clemenceau in the Chamber of Deputies. Clemenceau led a government of progressive liberals, 'republican, radical and resolutely anti-clerical', multiple impulses and demands familiar to Deakin. In 1907 Clemenceau was committed to maintaining the entente cordiale negotiated three years earlier with Britain to counter their mutual German rival and creating a more efficient 'citizen army', developments that would have interested Deakin, although he left no account of their conversation in his diary. On their last evening in Paris before taking the train to Marseille, the Deakins attended a performance of Wagner's *Tannhauser* at the Opera; Deakin thought it a 'great success'. Boarding the steamer *Orontes* on 24 May he wistfully inscribed, 'Goodbye France'.[38]

Deakin's fascination with France was shared with a number of contemporary Australians, stimulated by contact with a vibrant expatriate community that in the period published its own French language weekly newspaper from 1892, *Le Courrier Australien*. The early 1890s also saw the establishment of the Alliance Française in Melbourne and Sydney, promoting the study of French language and culture.[39] Deakin's physician Marcel Crivelli was a leading figure in Melbourne's French community, a number of whom inhabited the same middle-class suburbs in which the prime minister's family lived. The Crivellis were well connected in the city's social and political circles.[40] A range of journals shaping middle-class taste and values reflected French-influenced fashions embraced by 'fair Australian women', whose portraits, adorned in the latest Parisian hat and dress designs, were wreathed in Art Nouveau scrolls in *The Red Funnel* and in the French-style black-and-white art that illustrated *Henslowe's Annual*.[41] The Francophile publisher and former *Bulletin* founder and editor Jules François Archibald ostensibly launched *Lone Hand* in 1907 to promote a distinctive Australian culture, although from the outset the journal amplified the obsession that had led John Feltham Archibald to invent a French genealogy for himself.[42] The graphic design and illustrations of *Lone Hand* provided a showcase of Art Nouveau style. The strong, swirling black-and-white contrasts of resident illustrator D. H. Souter's 'The Skirt Dancer' provided an exuberant tribute to the internationally famous Loïe Fuller, who excited Parisians with her diaphanous fan performances, a dramatically lit 'miracle of endless metamorphosis' that represented 'the embodiment of Art Nouveau'.[43] Archibald appointed Frank Fox as editor, and Deakin's Liberal Protectionist ally ensured that *Lone Hand* shared Deakin's politics as well as his cultural interests: in his inaugural editorial, Fox declared that '*Lone Hand* has for its political platform an Honest, Clean, White Australia'. Fox also noted that *Lone Hand* had retained 'the exclusive services of two of the best Parisian journalists to keep it informed of literary and art movements'.[44] Deakin was impressed with the new journal, not least its 'first-class' French critics, although he complained to Fox of the absence of Faguet.[45] Editions in 1907 were replete with vicarious dispatches of 'French Literature Today' and 'Literary Life in Paris', provided by *Lone Hand*'s special correspondents. Henri Verne declared that the Symbolists had triumphed over naturalism and 'vindicated the rights of dreamland'. Verne also reported that the leading dramatists presided at the *Café Anglais*; the most modern salons could be found in the exclusive homes of

Figure 13 Many Australians shared Deakin's fascination with France. D. H. Souter's 'The Skirt Dancer' provided an exuberant Art Nouveau tribute to the internationally famous Parisian entertainer, Loïe Fuller. *Lone Hand*, July 1907. National Library of Australia.

the *rive droite haute bourgeoisie* near the Parc Monceau.[46] By contrast cartoons of 'The Paris Poor' reprinted from *L'Assiette au Beurre* included a gaunt beggar inquiring of a gendarme: 'Excuse me, constable, could you perhaps run me in?' (Figure 13).[47]

Lone Hand's Parisian correspondents reported unsettling divisions that filtered into Deakin's reading. In 'The Clerical Crisis in France' Louis Blin outlined the controversial disestablishment of the Catholic Church initiated in 1905 and the removal of clergy from the education system by the Radical government of Premier Emile Combes. Despite denials it was 'anti-religious', one of Combes ministers declared that the government had 'put out the lights in Heaven'.[48] The clerical crisis – the impulse to overturn stifling tradition and embrace a modern, rational world – was only one of the disturbances shaking *fin de siècle* France and which Deakin seemed curious to understand in 1907, reading Emile Faguet's *L'Anticléricalisme* (1906). Faguet argued that the French bring 'to religious sentiment souls endowed with the spirit of contradiction', being both 'essentially irreligious' and 'essentially religious'.[49] Deakin would have appreciated Faguet's claim to bring an impartial, liberal mind to reflecting on the 'passion' of anticlericalism and the ambiguity of a conflict between spiritual feeling while required to govern a secular domain; in 1898 Deakin and his fellow Federal Convention delegates had prudently averted enflaming religious sectarianism by prohibiting the capacity to make laws for religion in the constitution of the new Australian Commonwealth.[50] In France, religious tension burst into the open with the Dreyfus Affair that had divided the nation from the 1890s and into the new century, and which had set the ultramontane Catholic values of many anti-Dreyfusards against Republican and Dreyfusard secularism.[51] Faguet regretted the 'fanaticism' of the affair, from which in 1906 the nation still reeled.[52] The unjust accusations of spying for Germany brought against Alfred Dreyfus, a French Army colonel of Jewish faith, had exposed a seething anti-Semitism.[53] The unresolved tension flowing from humiliation in the Franco-Prussian War of 1870–1 festered in the Dreyfus Affair and righteously contesting intolerance. As Faguet observed, 'as long as we are devoured by anti-clericalism, we will not be able to wage war, even when attacked.'[54] The entente cordiale cleared a path out of the divisions of anti-clericalism and the affair to fulfil the ominous ambition of *revanche*.[55] In his December Defence Statement Deakin regretted that it could no longer be imagined that 'Australia was outside the area of the world's conflicts'. A perception growing in his mind as he passed through Paris and consulted the Imperial ministers in London, as the web of alliance between Britain, France and Russia was drawn together, sealed with the Anglo-Russian Convention in August which established the Triple Entente.[56]

Deakin's literary selections absorbed *fin de siècle* anxiety over the future; he was drawn to stories that explored new forms of troubling identity and that probed the brittle façade of the conventions sustaining Western society. As the year closed Deakin read a work, only just published, by one of his favourite novelists: Joseph Conrad's *The Secret Agent* (1907), a mordant exploration of the seedy underworld of espionage and foiled terror in late Victorian London. The novel presented a 'weird compound' of motives, ideologies and identities, played out in the shadow realm of London's Soho district, where subversive foreign influences infiltrated the Imperial metropolis: at the end the manipulative professor, with 'no future', passed on in the Soho crowd, 'unsuspected and deadly, like a pest in the street full of men'.[57] In Deakin's reading the threat and potential of the outside mingle together, insinuating into inner consciousness. Gabriel Tarde's dystopian fantasy novel *Underground Man* (1896) dramatized the consequences of the extinction of the sun, driving humanity underground: 'the stiff supports of civilization' disappear, 'like bubbles pricked'.[58] Deakin also read George Bernard Shaw's *The Quintessence of Ibsen* (1891). Shaw was a favourite author of Deakin's, and the Irish dramatist's defence of the famed and controversial Norwegian playwright Henrik Ibsen attack on social hypocrisy must have resonated: Deakin promptly read Ibsen's dissection of the corruption of the rich, *The Pillars of Society* (1877).[59]

Deakin's September selection, Henry James's *The American Scene* (1907), provided an ironic lament at modern progress, degrading James's cherished memories of old Boston and New York.[60] The famed novelist (and brother of the philosopher, William) cultivated a dim view of the impact of the 'pecuniary power' of business on American life, 'its brutal short cuts and aggressive acts'. While researching the book, Henry James met with US president Theodore Roosevelt as his Progressive administration acted to restrain the juggernaut 'Trusts', the corporations of unprecedented scale that dominated US business from the late nineteenth century.[61] The increasing global hegemony of US trusts and corporations had already produced a legislative reaction from Deakin's government in 1906; as the end of 1907 approached, Deakin hoped that his programme of New Protection would provide, through tariff protection of Australian businesses and increased wages for workers, an 'industrial defence against the whole world', and not least the powerful American 'combines'.[62]

One of the few books with an Australian connection that Deakin read that year was the Tasmanian Anglican Bishop Edward Mercer's *The Soul of Progress* (1907). A controversial social reformer, Mercer was dubbed 'the socialist Bishop' for his support of workers' rights and trade unions. Mercer's appeal for Deakin may be indicated by a lecture that Mercer delivered in St Paul's Anglican Cathedral in Melbourne in March 1907 which outlined the book's themes.

> Dr. Mercer will deal with many questions which are exercising the minds of men at the present time. He will, for instance, speak on the doctrines of evolution, materialism and socialism in its various aspects. His utterances on Socialism will be awaited with considerable interest, for Dr. Mercer has an established reputation as an advanced liberal, with leanings towards what might be termed Socialism, tempered by ethical methods.[63]

Deakin's interest in new ideas and forms of identity was reflected in his engagement with the literature of the emerging New Woman. He had twice previously read Olive Schreiner's *Story of an African Farm* (1883), most recently in 1906; Schreiner's novel 'helped to establish both the intellectual basis and the rhetorical tropes of turn-of-the-century feminism'.[64] In 1907 Marcelle Tinayre's *La Rebelle* (1905) provided a 'romance of the New Woman', including a confrontingly 'direct' treatment of abortion and capturing a sense of 'the anxieties about women's changing attitudes towards their own procreative capacity troubling *fin de siècle* France'.[65] Elizabeth von Arnim's romantic novel *Fraulein Schmidt and Mr Anstruther* (1907) presented a young woman assertive of her desires. Deakin explored the identity of the New Woman even as his liberal politics struggled to accommodate women – offering the vote on the one hand while discouraging their active participation and candidature for office on the other.

Deakin explored the realm of alternative religions, spiritualism and the occult, inspired by his search for a satisfying and meaningful spiritual identity. Like a number of contemporaries in Australia and overseas, Deakin had dabbled with Theosophy, and he had read several works by its leading adherents – Madame Blavatsky's *The Secret Doctrine* (1888), Charles Leadbeater's *Some Glimpses of Occultism* (1903) and Annie Besant's *The Self and Its Sheaths* (1903). Deakin had attended spiritualist sessions, and although he had formally dispensed with these and Theosophy by the late nineteenth century, his interest in the occult and Eastern religion lingered. In 1907 Annie Besant became the president of the Theosophical Society, and Deakin would attend a lecture by her in Melbourne in June 1908.[66] In 1907 he read Arthur Waite's *Studies in Mysticism and Certain Aspects of the Secret Tradition* (1906) and *Steps to the Crown* (1907). A mystic and self-styled historian of the occult, Waite was a member of the Hermetic Order of the Golden Dawn based in Britain, 'the most well known magical group of the *fin de siècle*' and which in the 1890s attracted Maud Gonne, William Butler Yeats and Aleister Crowley.[67] Deakin also read William James's *Some Varieties of Religious Experience*, and its reflections on the occult, spiritualism and 'mystical experiences', and Michael Sage's *Mrs. Piper and Psychical Research* (1904), in which the author explored the claims of the American medium Leonora Piper on behalf of the Society for Psychical Research.[68] Established by scientists at Cambridge University in 1882, the society investigated 'the mass of obscure phenomena' that constituted the 'Spiritualistic'.[69] William James had attended a number of Piper's sessions and had concluded that she possessed 'supernormal powers'. Not usually a 'credulous person', James welcomed exposure of fraudulent mediums and the bogus claims of Madame Blavatsky. James, according to his biographer, 'was actually threading a middle way, rejecting the slipslop visions and bland assurances of Blavatsky', on the one hand, and 'rigid rationalism' on the other.[70] In exploring Theosophy, and Michael Sage's 'impartial investigation' of Piper's mediumship, Deakin seemed also to be seeking a middle way and may have taken some heart from Sage's inconclusive findings about Piper.

Deakin's search for a middle way reflected the oscillations of *fin de siècle* double consciousness, of apparent oppositions 'found to be coterminous, existing in tense equilibrium'.[71] Deakin accommodated the occult and spiritualism, anti-clericalism and secularism, dissenting Christianity. For a time in the late 1890s Deakin had been an adherent of Charles Strong's Australian Church, whose appeal lay in its mix of intelligent, ethical dissent from orthodox Christianity and in Strong's advocacy of social reform – not unlike the causes taken up by Edward Mercer.[72] Deakin's 'Clues' notebooks span a period from the 1880s to 1913 and reflect a restless search for knowledge and solace that apparently had to be maintained in disciplined practice. Deakin's entries also capture an imagination brooding over the tension between the appeal of the spiritual realm and the requirements of earthly responsibilities. On 13 July 1907, in the grip of crisis at Ballara, Deakin opened his 'Clues' notebook to observe the relationship between theology and drama by reference to French criticism. 'Dramatic criticism itself especially among the French is a fine art . . . the play itself is judged by its relation to actuality – to life as we see it – and to our ideals.' The 'acutest modern literature', Deakin wrote, is engaged with 'the life of the world of man of the universe the never beginning never ending drama of the deity in which we play our parts'. On 12 July Deakin expressed his desire to understand God and 'the world in which we live', and the need to 'interpret the particulars of our existence on this planet & to make us aware of its values opportunities and fruits. . . . But what a Kosmic grasp sublime ethical elevation of power insight and enormous experience we must possess to pray.'[73]

Prayer was a demanding discipline he imposed upon himself. The 'Clues' entries were followed by another fervent prayer written into the back of his 1907 diary over 3–4 August; 3 August was Deakin's fifty-first birthday. Physically and emotionally wracked across the deep of night that Deakin endured 'Aug 3-4', Deakin tried to work his way towards 'a light' that resolved into a prayer for deeper family intimacy, and a yearning for a harmony that seemed to elude him, even as he plaintively underscored his need of 'quietness' and 'peace', 'patience' and 'calmness' in order to be 'one's true self'. He contrasted these desirable states with his own recent experience: 'fever' and in London 'a frenzy', and the 'vanity of vanities' which had pursued – and in so many ways realized – in a triumphant moment of his public career, and which had left him spent and desolate amid the ringing accolades.[74] 'If you will give us Mr. Deakin, you may have all our leaders', one admiring English politician observed of the Australian prime minister and his eloquent command of principle and policy.[75] The London *Times* praised the 'extraordinary intellectual energy' Deakin displayed at the Imperial Conference.

'He has been undoubtedly the most conspicuous exponent of the ideas which the Colonial Premiers came here to advocate': principally, greater Imperial unity in trade and defence. Lord Alfred Milner, himself an energetic Imperialist who, as Governor of the Cape Colony, had done much to stimulate the Boer War to further British ambitions, regarded 'Mr Deakin's capacity for work with blank amazement'.[76] Flattery echoed in the Australian press. The pro free trade *Argus*, often a harsh judge of Deakin, observed that his 'temporary breakdown was no doubt in a considerable measure due to his excessive devotion to duty in London'.[77] 'Palpitations' and 'Exhausted' were entries Deakin marked in his diary from 31 July to 6 August.

Self-watching was exercised in public scrutiny. As Deakin arrived back in Melbourne on 26 June, the *Age* outlined Deakin's immediate future for him: 'so many matters of importance will engage the attention of the Prime Minister between now and the opening of the Federal Parliament on Wednesday of next week, and so many Cabinet meetings will have to be held, that Mr. Deakin will have little time to attend social or any other kind of functions.'[78] Character sketches, reports of receptions and public speeches outlined the demands that Deakin was now expected to satisfy on his return; he was observed as an articulate machine, able to continually generate useful energy, and who could translate compelling narrative into action. 'He is always in a hurry, but never going fast. Happy in the possession of a remarkable vocabulary, he commands a ready flow of language, pregnant with meaning, pointed and explicit.'[79] Deakin embodied the carefully geared accelerations of *fin de siècle* industrial modernity, an internal combustion engine fed on deep knowledge. Even as new technologies altered the patterns and processes of industry, landscape and consciousness, 'human labour power remained vitally important' and not only for the mass production line. Individual human labour power was also subject to entropy.[80]

In late July Deakin's private suffering was punctuated by public exposure of his vulnerable state. On 29 July Deakin was urgently required to abandon his Ballara convalescence and return to Parliament House to try to forestall the resignation of Treasurer John Forrest from cabinet. Forrest had long been unhappy with the government's reliance on Labor support in Parliament; Forrest had urged Deakin to instead combine with other non-Labor MPs – effectively, to follow the political logic of a two-party system fractiously evolving since Federation.[81] Labor support did not manifest in respect for the pompous Forrest. 'On several occasions during the present session he smarted so severely under the taunts and gibes of Labor members that he had walked out of the Chamber.'[82] In Deakin's absence, the government was led by the dour William Lyne, who struggled to prevail in parliamentary debate. Lyne enjoyed a poisonous relationship with Forrest.[83] Sitting on the crossbench, Forrest would further expose the weakened state of the government. There were also reports that Deakin's poor health might compel him to retire. It was 'incontestable', *The West Australian* observed, 'that Mr. Deakin is seriously unwell, and that there is no immediate prospect of his return to duty'.[84]

A reporter from the Adelaide *Register* tracked Deakin's movements from his arrival in Melbourne on the morning of 29 July, offering readers a mordant commentary on Deakin's deterioration. Deakin sought to downplay the nature of the political crisis as he strove to persuade Forrest to remain in the ministry.

> Mr. Deakin landed from the steamer a bright, cheery man. He looked a little worn, perhaps, but happy and hopeful. By the time luncheon was over the same harassed look that he wore when he was last in the House was beginning to return. It was plain that the burden of holding an Executive Council meeting about nothing was worrying him.

By 3.00 pm Deakin emerged from another meeting with his colleagues, 'tired and worried. "No, I am not well," he said. "I feel very bad, indeed."'[85] On 30 July Forrest tended his resignation.[86] Yet Deakin was plainly unable to return and restore the government's fortunes. During the day Deakin had consulted with Dr Crivelli, 'who, although he found nothing organically wrong with the patient, absolutely forbade him to appear in Parliament for some weeks to come'. The *Age* recorded Deakin's return to Point Lonsdale by train.[87] The *Register* reporter concluded that 'his absence strengthens the forces at present making for disintegration'.[88]

On 16 August Deakin left Melbourne for a 'health tour'. 'Friends and medical advisors urged him to go away, suggesting North Queensland as a suitable place for a winter visit.' Deakin was 'particularly desirous of travelling quietly and without fuss or any kind'.[89] Deakin neither escaped responsibility nor surveillance: he seemed to seek out attention and distraction. The press tracked Deakin in Bundaberg, as he visited sugar mills; he enquired into 'the sugarfields labour question' and 'sub-tropical cultivation problems'. In Bingera he was 'greatly impressed' with the irrigation system. He exchanged telegrams with Lyne over government business.[90] The Sydney *Bulletin* mocked his escape from 'the strenuous life':

> He began to take complete rest by travelling 8000 miles in trains, boats, coaches, launches, 'buses, buggies, and motors – in short, in every moving vehicle except wheelbarrows. He completely rested his mind by Re-reading Gibbon's 'Decline and Fall.' in six volumes; Mommsen's 'History of Rome,' in five; Grote's 'History

of Greece,' in twelve; Bruce Smith's 'Liberty and Liberalism,' (a short opuscule in one volume of 965 pages); J. C. Neild's 'Report of Old Age Pensions,' and the same gentleman's verses. To vary his resting, so that it might not become monotonous, he just ran through 335 Australian newspapers, sent after him every day, to see what was going on. . . . By this time, having got thoroughly rested, he threw off further fatigue by inquiring into the inwardness of black labor in Queensland, and the prospects of tropical culture.[91]

Old habits persisted. On 27 August he noted in his diary, 'in Queensland, reading Faguet' (almost certainly, following to the numbered system of Deakin's reading list, the light reading of *L'Anticléricalisme*). A busy schedule did not disguise the condition that had driven him north. The *Townsville Daily Bulletin* took Deakin's visit as an opportunity to consider 'Australia's Prime Minister' and the 'neurasthenia' that troubled him, and which he evidently sought to obscure from public view. 'The history of the illness which has withdrawn him from his work was of a kind which suggests some reticence as to its character for fear of complicating the political position.' Yet the *Daily Bulletin* editorialized in support of a leader which 'Australia could ill afford to lose'. Deakin must be restored to productive purpose, fit 'to again take up on his return from North Queensland the very strenuous work of his office'. Deakin seemed willing to conform with this requirement, assuring reporters of his improving health 'and having put on flesh' during his travels in the north.[92]

Deakin's disturbances continued on his return to Melbourne in early September. In that month the hyperactive and sharp-witted federal Labor MP, William Morris Hughes, bluntly diagnosed: 'Deakin is a very sick man: Nervous breakdown: he ought to go away for a trip where the wire stretches not nor does the phone tintinabulate [*sic*]: But he dodges about like a fly near the paper which to him spells death but smells life: It is the Universal law!!'[93] Through technology, modern life pursued the individual, encouraging feverish activism. Deakin's diary entries in September and October recorded sleepless nights, dizzy spells and lack of appetite, skipping breakfast for weeks at a time. Since July Deakin had recorded the fluctuations of his weight, which by early in the month had collapsed to 11s 10lb, although it was roughly restored from late July to the end of December, dipping and rising between 12s 3lb and 12s 6lb across the months.[94] It was reported in late September that Deakin was 'anxious to get back in active grips with politics again' although medical orders forbade it.[95] The scrutiny of 'Mr. Deakin's illness' led not so much to concern at his physical state – 'he looks well', as 'the fact the prolonged worry acting upon a nervous and restless temperament unfits him for close and exciting and continuous labour'.⁹⁶

Even a sympathetic profile in *Lone Hand* noted Australians 'regard their Prime Minister as a rather unstable character'. Deakin's 'inability to think in the same current with the great mass of the public has often brought him dislike and contumely'. Deakin 'alternately delights his friends by his greatness and vexes them by his Quixotic aberrations'. That awareness of the private Deakin slipped into the public sphere was evident in *Lone Hand*'s speculation of an alternative Deakin, if he 'escaped politics': 'a University Professor, lecturing eagerly on the fine *nuances* of French literature . . . or even perhaps a divine, preaching like a Chrysostom.'⁹⁷ In October the acerbic muckraking *Truth* put it pungently: Deakin, 'formerly a devout Spookite', went to England 'under the influence of a "spirit". . . . But when Deakin returned to Australia the "influence" ceased and Alfred broke up or broke down.'⁹⁸ The press was increasingly critical of the drift of the government. 'Sir William Lyne's leadership promises to lead the Commonwealth from confusion to despair', the *Sydney Morning Herald* tartly assessed. 'If Mr. Deakin's illness is to make all the difference between progress and stagnation then the outlook is desperate indeed.'⁹⁹ The *Examiner* claimed that 'Everybody thinks that a change ought to come. . . . The Deakin Lyne combination in its many evolutions has been too long in control. It is time for somebody else to get a show.'¹⁰⁰ Even the anonymous Australian correspondent of the London *Morning Post* observed the 'paralysed' state of the government in a piece penned on 15 July, as Parliament squabbled over tariff policy. 'Nothing is certain except uncertainty', and the odds, the correspondent observed, favoured an imminent change of government. No mention was made of Mr Deakin's absence.¹⁰¹

Preparing a defence policy and a new naval agreement with Britain had been left too long unresolved. 'Mr. Deakin has hitherto been prevented by circumstances which we all deplore from making his long-desired statement on this most important of questions.'¹⁰² The defence of a white Australia had long been a national preoccupation. Contesting his first election as prime minister in 1903, Deakin reminded Australians that while 'the principle of a white Australia' reached 'down to the roots of our national life', the population was small, the birth rate was low and the continent was vast. 'We only occupy a fraction, and of which we as yet use but a minute fraction.' Deakin's conception of Australian space omitted the Indigenous, 'a dying race' whom white Australians were 'dispossessing . . . and entering into their heritage'. To 'defend every part of our continent' required the development of an effective army and navy, rather than rely on the distant and perhaps tardy support of Britain.¹⁰³

The 'global-scale economic and political struggles' of the *fin de siècle* 'produced intensified racial practices' and 'activism predicated on racialized categories', including 'illiberal' reactions and 'fabricated national identities'.[104] In Australia, reactions against exposure to accelerations of imperial and national rivalries (evident in arms build-up and trade), unprecedented population transfers and a perceived vulnerability to the proximity of the Asia Pacific region manifested in white nationalism, the immigration restriction of non-white peoples and the marginalization of the Indigenous, and compulsory military training. These reactions were also driven by 'the subjectivity of the "white man", whose sense of self was felt to be so powerfully threatened'.[105] Introducing Australia's immigration restriction system in Parliament in 1901, Deakin said the legislation responded to 'an instinct of self-preservation . . . the national manhood, the national character . . . are at stake' (Figure 14).[106]

The Labor Party's federal leader John Christian Watson believed CMT was a vital measure in defence of a white Australia, threatened by alien races who 'were clever and warlike', like 'the sleeping giant', China. 'Peace could only be

Figure 14 The 'lone hand' responds to the call to arms. The Australian National Defence League endorsed Deakin's 'great' Defence Statement of December 1907. Norman Lindsay, cover illustration, *The Call*, February 1908. State Library of New South Wales. Copyright A., C. and H. Glad.

secured by being prepared for war – by having every male trained and ready to take up arms in defence of his native land.'[107] Deakin shared a fear of Australia's proximity to 'peoples', as he delicately noted in his Defence Statement, whose interests were 'antagonistic to our own'.[108] In 1905, the Australian National Defence League had been established to campaign for its introduction, drawing on cross-party and community support. By 1907, Deakin had decided to publicly endorse the proposal in London at an address delivered before 'a crowded and enthusiastic' audience in the Queens Hall in May, and conducted following the conclusion of the Imperial Conference. The address was sponsored by the British National Defence League, which campaigned for the adoption of universal military service and the establishment of a 'national reserve'. A major concert venue, the Queens Hall had an audience capacity of 2,500. On 16 May it was decorated behind the stage with a large banner of the League's motto, 'Lest We Forget'. Banners displayed in the hall were inscribed with 'The Briton's First Duty', 'A Nation Under Arms' and 'Hands Across the Sea'. The meeting was chaired by League president Field Marshall Lord Roberts, an embodiment of a martial spirit that subjugated resistance to empire: the decorated veteran of the 1857 Indian Rebellion, and field commander of the British Army during the Second Afghan War (1878–80) and the Boer War (1900–2).[109]

Greeted with 'loud and prolonged cheering', Deakin presented Compulsory Military Training (CMT) as not 'a menace of war, but a necessary duty of citizenship'. He predicted that compulsory 'universal service' would be adopted in Australia with 'little delay', in recognition of a belief that 'a community should discharge the duties of its own defence'. Deakin outlined CMT as a mild programme of drill and training in small arms. Just once Deakin summoned a vivid word picture, imagining young men preoccupied with the 'tasks of daily life', and only occasionally 'when across the background of their vision far away from them there shot suddenly to the heavens the red meteor-star of war, that they were alive to the fact that some day it might possibly descend, if not upon them, upon those dear to them, upon those united to them, upon their common country and their common flag'.[110] In the repeated cadence of threatened family, community and nation Deakin conjured an image that might have been drawn from the abundant fantasy literature of war and sudden, unexpected invasion that was so popular among readers in Britain and in Australia. 'Invasion narratives' were often sourced in a racial threat. In the English novelist Matthew Phipps Shiel's *The Yellow Danger* (1898), a young British hero thwarted an invasion by Asian 'hordes'. *The Yellow Danger* dramatized 'the double helix of *fin de siècle* representations of Empire . . . the promise of continued expansion . . . [and]

the fear of collapse, degeneration'.[111] To fulfil their duty to defend the nation, Australia required 'able-bodied youth' inculcated with 'the *habit of discipline and cohesion*'. In November 1907 the artist Norman Lindsay illustrated 'before and after universal service' for *The Call*, the journal of the Australian National Defence League: 'the raw material' was lazy larrikin propped against a fence post. 'The finished article' was the same young man transformed into an erect, square-shouldered figure in uniform, standing to attention with his rifle. Here was the 'double helix' rendered in two figures on the same page.[112]

War was evidently on Alfred Deakin's mind on the return voyage to Australia. Deakin's diary entries record Richard Haldane's *Pathway to Reality* on 4 June and Leo Tolstoy's *War and Peace* on the 6th. A reference to a 'ship talk' on the *Bhagavad Gita* was noted on the 13th, although a notation to reading it follows a little later in his list; whether or not Deakin delivered the talk, he was evidently present.[113] *War and Peace* and the *Bhagavad Gita* provided contrasting interpretations of the ethical imperatives and conduct of war. Tolstoy's depiction of the battle of Borodino, the military climax of Napoleon's 1812 invasion of Russia, famously presents confused battlefield mayhem driven by vainglorious delusion, futile orders and misinformation passed between adjutants and staff officers, unable to penetrate 'the fog of war' – quite literally, the dense cannon and small arms smoke that choked the cauldron of mutual massacre. Half the Russian forces of 100,000 were rendered casualties; a third of the French fell. Not until the first day of the Somme offensive in 1916 did more men die on a European battlefield. Tolstoy scathingly dismissed the false histories of the battle that extolled victory for either side; 'the actions of Kutuzov and Napoleon in offering and accepting battle at Borodino were involuntary and meaningless.'[114]

Deakin may have felt some relief in turning to the measured poetic dialogue that forms part of the ancient Hindu epic, the *Mahabharata*, a work at the centre of *fin de siècle* fascination with Eastern mysticism.[115] The *Bhagavad Gita* 'is about a decision to go to war'. Arjuna takes the counsel of Krishna, his 'confidant and charioteer', whom Arjuna realizes is a 'manifestation of God'. Their dialogue follows the form of a *samvada*, 'in which the options for action are explored, the meanings of those potential actions weighed carefully and teachings given. The *Gita* is a conversation in which Arjuna's very being is transformed by his encounter with Krishna.'[116] Returning to an absorption in Hindu texts that stretched back into the 1880s, Deakin likely read the recently published translation by Annie Besant, who argued in her introduction that the *Bhagavad Gita* demonstrated 'that union with the divine life may be achieved and maintained in the midst of worldly affairs'.[117] It is not hard to understand why the *Gita* appealed to Deakin:

'its contents include simple and moving poetry, dense philosophy, moral musing and an explosive description of God. . . . It has become a literary "site" which decision makers turn to to understand their dilemmas.' Arjuna is a warrior, 'a member of the *kshatriya varna*, the class of people whose duty it is to protect the kingdom and its citizens. . . . Arjuna knows when to fight and when to refrain from fighting; indeed, restraint, self-control and non-violence were essential to the warrior code.'[118] Restrained self-control reflected both Deakin's liberal politics and the persona he projected in the public sphere. 'Stirred by intense patriotism', Deakin's 'capacity for subordinating – indeed one might go further, and say excluding – personal interests has always constituted one of the political stumbling blocks in Australia'.[119] Deakin's 'simplicity . . . refuses all reward. . . . It is utterly divorced from every idea of pose.'[120]

It was the familiar pursuit of disciplined and transcendent self-knowledge, sourced in an engagement with the world, which led Deakin to Richard Haldane's *The Pathway to Reality*. Originally delivered as the prestigious Gifford lectures on theology in 1902–3, Haldane sought to explain 'how thinking of one's own limits leads to transcendence and ultimately to an understanding of the absolute mind and the nature of God'. Haldane also argued that the individuality of a human being is contingent and 'boundless', and 'incapable of resolution into any single aspect'.[121] Haldane probed the elusive relationship between being in the world and spiritual transcendence, which preoccupied Deakin's sleepless Ballara vigils. Individual contingency might manifest as a duality that seemed to recreate the spirit of Arjuna in Haldane: the Idealist philosopher was also the secretary of state for war in Campbell Bannerman's government and a minister on friendly terms with Deakin, who otherwise had tended to clash with the likes of the chancellor of the Exchequer, Herbert Asquith, and the president of the Board of Trade, David Lloyd George. In championing imperial preference, Deakin challenged a pro free trade government that had defeated its protectionist Conservative and Unionist political opponents at the 1906 general elections.[122] The proceedings of the Imperial Conference record tense exchanges between Deakin and these senior ministers over trade and relations between Whitehall and the Dominions. As Lloyd George charged: 'you are asking us to tax necessaries of either life or livelihood, which we cannot produce ourselves and of which you cannot for many a long year supply us with a sufficiency?'[123]

Deakin enjoyed a more convivial relationship with Haldane, lunching together in London's National Gallery on 20 April.[124] In 1906–7 Haldane was the architect of reforms designed to more efficiently prepare the British Army for conflict. Haldane established the British Expeditionary Force to be committed to the European continent in the event of war and also created the Territorial Army, a force of reserve regiments.[125] As Haldane reformed the army, his fellow 'liberal imperialist', Foreign Secretary Edward Grey, had established closer alliance with Russia and France in the Triple Entente in 1907, thus 'inventing' Germany as the enemy, as Christopher Clark observes, although not necessarily preordaining the disastrous conflict that broke out in 1914.[126]

Deakin returned to Australia focused on addressing defence policy. Illness disrupted intention until December, as Deakin gradually resumed his responsibilities and tentatively returned to Parliament from 25 September.[127] At the end of the year, and on the last sitting day of the parliamentary session that had commenced on 3 July, the turbulence of Deakin's progress towards resolving key policy initiatives unintentionally climaxed.

> Tired – Age attacks New Protection – Breakfast Ivy – Office – Parlt Tariff Bill passed Excise Procedure bill – lunch Got vote £5000 Shackleton expedition Gratuities bill – Beales report – commenced Defence speech 6 pm dinner – resumed 7.45 finished 9.45 House closed – celebration upstairs – Home midnight – exhausted.[128]

Deakin's diary entry for 13 December reflected how experience and perception accelerated and collided at the *fin de siècle*. The jumbled variety of these references obscures powerful motivations uniting and driving reports, legislation and exploration: the control of space and population, at a time when the world was more interconnected than ever before. In an editorial published on 14 December the Melbourne *Argus* registered its awe at 'how tremendous a shifting of the world's population is taking place. In all the grand migratory movements which history records ... there was no fusion or supplanting of peoples comparable to that which is being affected today.' The 'great crucible' of the United States took up to two million European immigrants a year, where they were 'fused into a new nation'.[129] Yet in California the Japanese and Korean Exclusion League of San Francisco was seeking one million signatures to a petition urging Congress to secure 'the exclusion of Asiatics from the United States' (Figure 15).[130]

By the early twentieth century, globalization had generated anxieties over unprecedented population shifts and intensifying rivalries between nations and empires. 'The easier it appeared to overcome distance, the broader was the horizon that needed to be scanned for possible enemies and competitors.'[131] New Protection was a programme enacted to ensure Australian workers shared the benefits of the tariff production of Australian industry against outside competition, which Deakin characterized in Parliament as a threat of 'foreign

'Some Disquieting Symptoms'   131

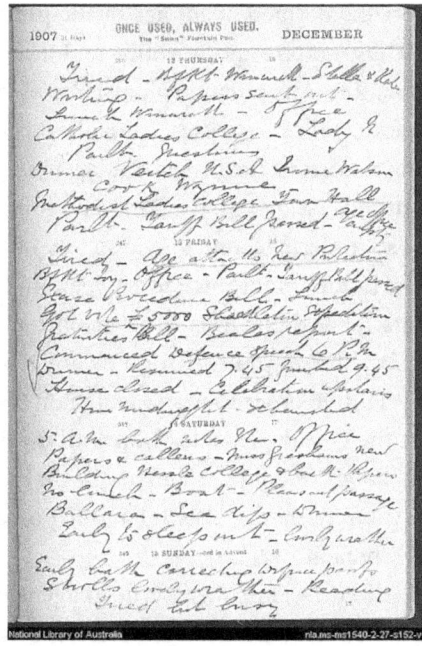

Figure 15 'Tired . . . exhausted.' Deakin's diary entry for 13 December 1907. National Library of Australia.

invaders'.[132] An important element of the New Protection legislation, the Excise Procedure bill, was passed by the House on the 13th, despite scorn expressed in the debate for 'the millennium which the Prime Minister intends to usher in', by securing higher wages for workers and which would in turn apparently realize 'the spiritual regeneration of the race'.[133] In his Defence Statement Deakin announced the government's intention to introduce compulsory military training, establish an Australian Naval Squadron and develop the industrial capacity to manufacture weapons within Australia. Deakin insisted that Australia 'must keep step' with the 'feverish haste' with which the world's 'leading nations are arming'.[134]

New Protection and the Defence Statement responded to the arms race and the acquisitive ambitions of empire and trade that had accelerated international tensions. Threats to a productive and healthy population could also insidiously emerge within the Australian population. Parliament briefly discussed arrangements for the publication of the Beale report into the use of patent medicines in Australia.[135] The report evolved from an earlier inquiry into the decline of the birth rate and focused on the illegal use of bogus and dangerous 'medicines' in abortions, a practice that Beale warned would lead to 'race suicide' and generated alarmed headlines in the press.[136] The exploration of the South Pole was fed by empire and scientific ambitions, and the possibility of acquisitive possession. The Australian geologist Professor Edgeworth David successfully appealed for financial support from the Federal Government to secure the final funding necessary for Ernest Shackleton's polar expedition. As well as conducting scientific research on the Antarctic continent, the expedition vessel *Nimrod* would also undertake a magnetic survey of the Southern Ocean: 'such knowledge is of extreme importance to navigation', for both commercial and naval requirements. Shackleton was a naval officer, and the expedition was supported by the British Admiralty. King Edward VII and the queen had travelled to the Isle of Wight 'in order to wish Lieutenant Shackleton God-speed before his departure ... the Queen presented him with the British flag for him to carry to the South Pole'.[137] Deakin told Parliament that 'if there are any economic possibilities in these Antarctic lands, Australia will probably be the country which will most directly benefit'.[138]

As prime minister, Alfred Deakin was a crucial agent in the negotiation of time and space, keeping step with the arms race, forestalling foreign powers and excluding alien populations, addressing the anxiety of race suicide, securing the space of the Australian continent and potentially the riches buried beneath a polar ice cap – demands that required the enervating displacement of energy by a leader of 'fervid advocacy', for whom 'no exertion is too exacting, no sacrifice too great'.[139] We know this lavish praise to be true, for Alfred Deakin bestowed an archive of his labours to the nation he served and whose pages tracked his journey towards 'exhaustion' by midnight 13 December 1907. Surveillance of Deakin that day began with his diary entries for the morning and the brief respite of breakfast with his eldest daughter Ivy, who lived next door to Llanarth with her husband Herbert Brookes and their children.[140] In Parliament Deakin was pursued by the press reporters and the rigorous process of the parliamentary stenographers who registered, minute by minute from 11.00 am, Deakin's requirement to field questions about the order of business, of which Deakin confessed he was not entirely sure, and taunts about *Age* criticism of New Protection. Deakin noted its 'attack' in his diary and it must have stung: while most of the major daily press across the Commonwealth favoured free trade, the *Age* was usually one of Deakin's few press supporters.[141] At approximately 12.25 pm, he was disparaged as a mere rhetorical 'cloud artist', a master at conjuring a 'golden haze of generalities', by an ambitious rival for leadership of Parliament's liberals, William Irvine, in the debate on the Excise Procedure bill.[142] At 4.00 pm Deakin recommended Parliament's support of the Antarctic expedition and finally began to address the house on defence policy from 6.00 pm, pausing for a dinner break, and then for two solid hours from 7.45 to 9.45 pm urged Australians to accept the burden of responsibility of a 'free people', to protect 'hearth and homes', and the 'great unoccupied parts of this immense continent'.[143] There was an acknowledgement of his skill and the energy expended. At the conclusion of the Defence Statement, Deakin was congratulated by the Labor Party leader, Andrew Fisher. 'The subject is a big one, and I do not think I have ever heard the honourable member to greater advantage.'[144] A brief celebration marked the rising of the House for the Christmas recess, followed by exhaustion.

Deakin's experience across 1907 reflected the dilemmas of the way of action. Both in public policy and in his private writings he undertook a dialogue with himself in the hope of a transformed perception. A quest for transformation was an active stimulus in Deakin's imagination that he transferred into public policy. In the ringing peroration of his Defence Statement Deakin invoked 'the motive power of every-day working patriotism', a force of energy immanent in the potential citizen soldier and which 'bids them to do more than work for themselves'. The 'great disciplinary power' of compulsory military training represented 'a potent factor in fostering that national spirit on which we rely'.[145] Yet disciplined potency was summoned to try to subdue threats from a world seemingly spinning out of control, of 'armed nations' steeped in 'cut-throat competition' and which posed an existential threat: 'the obliteration of our race and nationality can not be compassed by the imagination.' The fact that such a threat colonized the imagination was confirmed in the delivery of the Defence Statement, the cultivation of invasion narratives and immigration restriction, a truly potent fear, as Deakin reminded the House, of 'alien rule'.[146] Reading the Defence Statement it is easy to nod over his iteration of estimates; they constituted the vital empirical verification of the insinuating logic of naval construction, militia training and arms manufacture, reaching into every home and sustained by the 'will of the men of our country, the heart of our women', and to become as natural for the male recruit as 'breadwinning for his family or fathering his children'.[147]

Order and purpose, illness and mayhem: the stresses of *fin de siècle* double consciousness reflected the accelerating forces of modernity that intensified turbulent subjectivities, stirred in the incessant tintinnabulations of the telephone and the furious absorption of *The Pathway to Reality*, *War and Peace* and the *Bhagavad Gita*, even as gathering illness stalked him. The ethical and philosophical merged into the chaos of war and contingent human experience; it all might have a profound meaning or it all might be 'involuntary and meaningless'. By December 1907 Deakin had sufficiently struggled out of breakdown to muster the energy required to prepare and deliver the Defence Statement, although he had 'driven himself too far and too fast. There was something damaged, and it could not be repaired.' He was never the same after 1907, ever conscious of decline and fragmenting memory.[148]

At Portsmouth in May 1907 Deakin witnessed one of the great spectacles of the *fin de siècle*, staged at the climax of empire: the Naval Review, the salute of the fleet before the monarch at Spithead.[149] Deakin toured HMS *Dreadnought*, then the most innovative of battleships, and watched as a new, 'potent form of weapon', a submarine, 'curious, porpoise-like vessels', slide mysteriously beneath the surface of the Solent; itself a spectacle, as he observed, both wondrous and demoralizing, as he imagined the anxious reaction of 'those in charge of battle-ships and cruisers', realizing that this unseen threat lay in wait. Deakin was fascinated with these vessels, 'modern structures of enormous interior complexity', and acknowledged the strain that the unprecedented requirements of 'expert knowledge and training' placed on the men who served in them. Deakin described a submarine 'gradually submerging until nothing but the periscopes appeared above the surface, these, too, disappearing and leaving no trace of their movements'.[150]

6

David Unaipon, 'the super-aborigine'

Unaipon shows great intelligence. Those who know him say he is a genius. He was educated at a mission school and is said to have shown extraordinary capacity to absorb knowledge. Now he is best described as a scientist, anthropologist, inventor and public speaker. He is the super-aborigine.[1]

In April 1907 the Adelaide *Advertiser* drew its readers' attention to 'an ingenious Aboriginal'. David Unaipon was visiting the South Australian capital 'on a remarkable errand'. Unaipon 'brought with him a neatly-drawn design of a piece of mechanism which, he claims, can be attached to machinery and facilitate the attainment of perpetual motion, which science has declared to be impossible'. Unaipon explained to the reporter that

> the forces by which he proposed to bring about the results he had in view were gravitation and momentum, and he had come to Adelaide to seek the assistance of the Aborigines Department in procuring certain mechanical parts in the shape of four bevelled wheels, a spindle, a tube, and so on. He is confident that when he has got these requisites he can put together a machine which will bring perpetual motion appreciably nearer.

The author marvelled that the 34-year-old Unaipon 'speaks excellent English' and represented a 'startling exception to the rule' that 'the native mind is not apt to stray from the narrow and beaten paths that have been formed by generations of habit.... People who are inclined to deprecate all efforts to educate the natives as being unprofitable, will do well to remember that Uniapon is a full blooded native.' The *Advertiser* also noted that Mr Unaipon, 'like many a white man who has a mathematical tendency, is fond of music, and he plays the organ in the Point McLeay Mission Church'.[2]

David Unaipon was born in the Point McLeay mission in 1872. The mission had been established in 1859 by the Congregational Church-run Aborigines

Friends Association to provide a reserve on the traditional land of the Ngarrindjeri people. Unaipon had a strong, lifelong Christian faith; his father, James Ngunaitponi, had been a church deacon.[3] The Point McLeay mission (since 1982 the Ngarrindjeri community of Raukkan) was located on the shores of Lake Alexandrina, the freshwater lake that the Murray River filled before its waters mixed in the Southern Ocean at the Coorong. Established to provide its inhabitants with a self-sustaining community, the mission struggled to develop as a productive entity, largely due to poor soil and the encroachment of neighbouring white farms. 'Ngarrindjeri' is a general term, which means 'belonging to people', that had achieved currency as a European descriptor of a 'constellation of clans'. Ngarrindjeri is used by Aborigines today 'who recognize a common descent from original inhabitants of the region'.[4] Although confined in an enclave of their formerly extensive lands, the reserve may have at least provided some protection for the Ngarrindjeri, 'a breathing space', as Ronald Berndt observed, 'without which the disintegration of their traditional lifestyle would have been much more rapid and their chances for re-adaptation slender'.[5] Elsewhere in the South Australian colony in the mid-nineteenth century, the mounted police enforced the expansion of white pastoral settlement into Indigenous tribal lands, an appropriation prosecuted in acts of violence and expulsion, and 'indicative of a culture of frontier policing which did not easily regard Aboriginal people as equal British subjects deserving of protection'.[6]

By the beginning of the twentieth century, expulsion and confinement in reserves meant that few Aborigines could be found living in or even passing through the major cities and white settlements of South Australia. Although Point McLeay was only 80 kilometres (50 miles) south-east of Adelaide, the *Advertiser* presented Unaipon's 1907 visit to the state capital as the unusual arrival of an alien. Indeed, Unaipon entered a city where only months before 'incorrigible Aborigines' had been driven from it. 'Every possible effort should be taken to prevent the aborigines begging about the city, and staying week after week about Adelaide and suburbs. Several Aboriginal women just out of gaol are now staying on in Adelaide, and should be compelled to go to their own districts at once.' The police attempted to drive them away, although several persistently returned. It was suggested that they could be sent to 'some island where they could not get away'. Some of these 'incorrigibles' came from the Point McLeay mission.[7]

David Unaipon sought acknowledgement of his innovative mind and to assert the rights of his people within the developing Australian Commonwealth. In the post-Federation period Unaipon confronted triumphalist white nationalism.

The leader of the Australian Labor Party, John Christian Watson expressed the widespread satisfaction of white Australians that the numerically 'negligible' 'Aboriginal natives' had been cleared from 'this land we have made our own'; Australia should advance on the basis of white 'racial purity'.[8] The cultural forms of the Australian *fin de siècle* were enlisted to insidiously reinforce the fiction of Indigenous disappearance: in the illustrated pages of the *Sydney Mail*, Waratah flowers rendered in stylized Art Nouveau design celebrated white progress, wreathed around a photograph of a young white boy, slightly built yet able to lead a three-horse plough.[9] In D. H. Souter's *Lone Hand* (1908) pen drawing, youthful white men and women languidly posed on the sands of a Sydney beach, enjoying an untroubled possession that represented 'the growth of culture in Australia' – presumably, none had preceded white settlement.[10] A 'pleasure-loving' white race flourished in 'Australia Felix', where 'there was neither an effective savage, nor a civilized and hostile neighbor to cope with'. This *Lone Hand* article concluded with an illustration of an innocently smiling European maiden surrounded by elongated, Art Nouveau-styled mangrove grass stems waving in the air, a pair of armorial Brolgas supplicant before her figure gracefully swaying in a bed of flowers.[11] By contrast the Aborigine was represented in *Lone Hand* as a redundant exotic of the landscape; even the 'black tracker' of legendary skill is 'becoming scarcer, and the date of his total extinction is not far ahead' (Figure 16).[12]

Figure 16 A 'pleasure-loving' white race flourished in 'Australia Felix', where 'there was neither an effective savage, nor a civilized and hostile neighbour to cope with'. *Lone Hand*, December 1907. National Library of Australia.

In 1907 David Unaipon reflected 'that there are possibilities of no mean order with regard to the intellectual development of the Australian natives', disturbing the prevailing assumption that Australia's Aborigines constituted a dying race.[13] Unaipon looked to a brighter future. He wanted to be part of the unprecedented possibilities generated by the second industrial revolution and its accompanying technological innovations, which seemed to manifest in rapid succession as the new century began. Inspired by the Point McLeay school teacher, Unaipon embraced the rich diversity of ideas generated at the *fin de siècle*.

> My teacher talked about the wonderful progress made during the 19th century – progress in science, art, and commerce . . . and mentioned also the three problems which had puzzled science – the philosopher's stone, the elixir of life, and perpetual motion. The latter problem attracted me. About 15 years ago I took up the study of mechanics and read all the books of philosophy I could get. I studied the laws of gravity and motion on an inclined plane, and directed my attention principally to the centre of gravity of moving bodies.[14]

Unaipon engaged with physics, the exploration of perpetual motion, manned flight and gravitation, and polarization of light; in the years between 1907 and 1914 Unaipon explored these vexed problems, proposing solutions and inventions and seeking patents for them. The 'New Physics' of the *fin de siècle* witnessed a transformation of the discipline, as diverse theories and claims proliferated.[15] Unaipon's experiments and patents reflected the tension between established science and innovation that characterized *fin de siècle* physics and which at times pulled in a spiritualist and non-rational directions.

Unaipon's profile as a 'genius' and his contributions to public debate provided a focus on eugenics, social Darwinism and degeneration. Sally Ledger and Roger Luckhurst argued that at the *fin de siècle* 'notions of developmental progress or degenerative and entropic decline insistently inform discussions of the individual, the city, and the nation-state'. Scientific 'ideologists' stirred fear of racial decline in the public sphere in Britain and Australia.[16] Herbert Spencer, Francis Galton and Edwin Ray Lankester were among the scientific ideologists whom Unaipon invoked in his talks. Rather than accept the apparently fatal judgement that evolutionary theory posed for Aborigines, Unaipon sought to adapt it to champion the viability and creative potential of his people.

It has been argued that historians must resist claims that 'autonomous Indigenous spaces within a settler colonial society cannot exist'.[17] The inhabitants of the Point McLeay mission in the period between Federation and the First World War struggled to assert autonomy. Yet the mission provided the space for David

Unaipon to establish his identity and his aspirations, and as a representative of his people. Unaipon negotiated the intensification of state surveillance and control that was imposed upon Aborigines in the early twentieth century, as governments extended their authority over Aboriginal mission stations. He spoke out against the discrimination suffered by Aboriginal people, and the lack of educational opportunities afforded them, although he was at times compelled to collaborate in the construction of this prejudice. In 1910, he and a party of his fellow Ngarrindjeri performed in a pageant that validated the future of white nationhood by presenting an elaborate fiction of European exploration and colonization.

Isolated as an exception to otherwise 'despised Aboriginals', Unaipon was presented as 'an Aboriginal Genius', 'a contradiction in human terms, an Australian native, who is a philosopher, inventor, and musician, and who devotes any spare time he may have to the study of evolution; a full-blooded aboriginal who can quote Newton, Huxley, Darwin, and other evolutionists and philosophers.'[18] The press cultivated a formulaic identity of the 'Aboriginal genius', presented as a flattering mimicry of white inventiveness and intellectual culture. Philip Jones has observed that 'in 1914 [Unaipon's] repetition of predictions by others about the development of polarized light and helicopter flight were publicized, building his reputation as a "black genius"'.[19] Unaipon gave the white press what they wanted, although he adapted this narrative to his own purposes, on behalf of his own self-realization and his people: Unaipon's chief innovation was as a highly skilled narrator of ideas and aspirations. Diverse and contradictory stories pass through the identity presented in the public sphere as David Unaipon poised between white and Black worlds at a moment of unstable and accelerating change.

By 1914, Unaipon had achieved widespread recognition for a series of inventions and patents, news of which had even reached the London press.[20] 'He has invented the curvilineal motion or getting a straight line or motion from a circular motion. He has been successful in getting a provincial patent . . . [and] applied it to the well-known Moffat Virtue – shearing machine.' The report also noted that Unaipon 'thinks that the dream of scientists (perpetual motion) will soon be an accomplished fact through the discovery of this new motion'.[21] Indeed, Unaipon believed that 'the application of the principle . . . can be extended almost indefinitely. It is, however, such a big scientific invention as to be almost before its time. The inventor has no doubt that it will be quite possible to produce motion traversing a square, a triangle, a circle, and indeed any geometrical form desired.'[22] Other inventions and patents associated with Unaipon included a centrifugal motor, a multiradial wheel and a mechanical

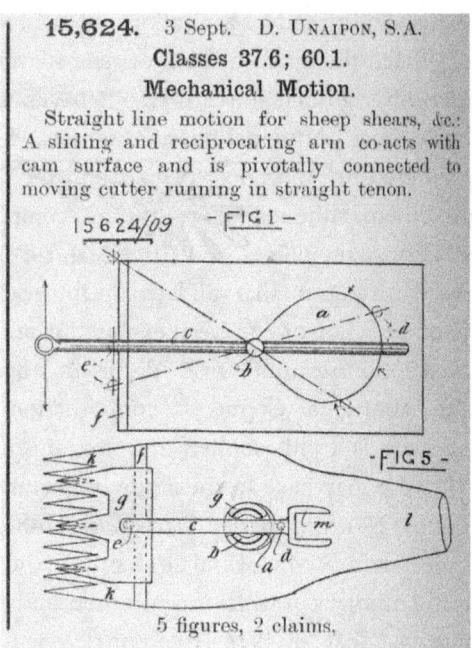

Figure 17 David Unaipon's 1909 patent for a shearing tool. 'I lost financially any material gain arising from this discovery'. State Library of South Australia.

propulsion device. Unaipon, however, did not benefit from his innovations, lacking the funds or support to develop them commercially.[23] Although he had obtained a patent for his shearing machine in 1909, 'I lost financially any material gain arising from this discovery, as this was passed to others who made use of my invention without giving me any compensation (Figure 17).'[24]

Unaipon imagined a limitless future of modernity.

> Perpetual motion has offered to him a fountain of thought which has occupied his mind for years, and his regret that scientists are not giving more time to the study of this problem, which he believes is capable of solution. . . . Surely this is something great for an aborigine, largely self taught, to accomplish. His achievements stamp him as a man of remarkable natural attainments.

The Sydney *Sun* also observed that 'another complex problem that has claimed his attention is the polarisation of light, and the concentration of light at a given point. "These would be the greatest weapons in future warfare," prophesied Unaipon. "We are gradually coming to the age when we might expect to be able to hurl electricity, like Nature does, for instance, in the shape of lightning."'[25] Unaipon also claims to have invented a contrivance by means of which aeroplanes can rise vertically from the ground without first running a long distance in order to gain impetus; How he accomplished this, and the devices he intends to use to raise the machine, Unaipon will not disclose at the present moment. He is applying for patent rights; but when the manufacture of some special appliances has been completed he says that he will be prepared to demonstrate.[26]

Unaipon invoked a legend of Aboriginal mystery in the promotion of his innovation in the public sphere. 'Speaking of the science of flying, he claimed to have restored "the lost art" of making the boomerang hover over his head like a bird and return to the point of despatch.' The principle of the boomerang can be applied to the aeroplane, he asserted. 'An aeroplane can be manufactured that will rise straight into the air from the ground by the application of the boomerang principle. The boomerang is shaped to rise in the air according to the velocity with which it is propelled, and so can an aeroplane. This class of flying machine can be carried on board ship, the immense advantages of which are obvious.'[27]

Unaipon was not unique in pursuing the search for a solution to perpetual motion or revealing the secrets of gravitation, scientific breakthroughs that might change consciousness or lead to a boundless future. There were a number of 'Perpetual Motion Seekers' in the period, amateurs and professional scientists who sought to invent a perpetual motion device with unlimited productive and commercial applications.[28] In 1903 the Adelaide press reported that a Transylvanian schoolmaster claimed to have solved the problem of perpetual motion by inventing a motor 'which works by the influence of the force of the earth's attraction'.[29] Mr R. W. O. Kestel of Port Adelaide had experimented for many years to support his hypothesis 'concerning the existence of a repelling force in the universe in addition to a great attractive force'. In 1901 he provided a demonstration to local members of the Astronomical Section of the Royal Society of a model 'apparatus' to illustrate the forces of repulsion at work in the universe but which could not prove 'the existence of an unaccepted force in nature'.[30]

'The Gospel of Energy' was a key element of the New Physics of the *fin de siècle*, and Unaipon embraced its spirit. Energy was seen as 'more fundamental than matter, and thermodynamics more fundamental than mechanics', challenging Newtonian conceptions of a mechanical universe. 'Energetics', as it was dubbed, reflected an 'element of utopianism' that could be found 'in other sciences at the turn of the century'.[31] After 1895 'physicists were forced to recognize that their discipline was potentially open-ended to fundamental novelty in both experiment and theory'.[32] The transfer of energy included an element of mystery, a potential revelation of unseen forces. In 1907, it was claimed that it was possible to photograph the invisible – the 'luminous' imprint of dots and dashes evident on photographic plates, although undetectable to the human eye, as they streamed from Marconi's wireless station in England. The transmission of transatlantic telegrams reflected 'important advances of scientific knowledge' that revealed 'hitherto unknown electrical emanations, such as the X rays'. The novelty of extraordinary innovations left play for the imagination. Marconi's wireless technology had only been patented in 1897 and successfully demonstrated in 1901. The Adelaide *Register* speculated that 'possibly the camera may yet be utilized as a means of elucidating some of the mysterious psychological phenomena which have baffled investigation'. A Paris doctor claimed to have a series of 'mental images' of a patient progressing from delusions to restored health; another image apparently captured 'a column of prayer ascending from the summit of the Eiffel Tower', taken 'while a band of devout persons were engaged in devotional exercises'.[33]

The mystical and the scientific blurred in speculation over human origins. In 1914 a white anthropologist, Herbert Basedow, linked these realms to David Unaipon, the 'Aboriginal genius' whom Basedow championed. 'Volatile, idealistic and impatient', Basedow had won a reputation as a defender and pioneering researcher of Indigenous tribal life in northern Australia.[34] In 1911 he had briefly been appointed by the Commonwealth Government as Chief Protector of Aborigines in the Northern Territory, although he had abruptly resigned over what he claimed was interference in his authority – Basedow proposed to incise a physical mark or scar on the bodies of Aborigines to facilitate identification and control of the population. Fortunately, Commonwealth officials demurred.[35] In an interview conducted in Adelaide in 1914, and during which Unaipon was present, Basedow asserted that the Aborigine was 'the first man' who had originated in the vast super continent of Lemuria, located, Basedow claimed, to the north-west of Australia. 'All lines of migration are traceable from that portion of the earth.' In the Australian Aboriginal, Basedow asserted, 'you have a type of the original man – one who was, so to speak, isolated from the rest of the world.' Competition between populations who migrated north from Lemuria reflected the ruthless requirements of 'the survival of the fittest' and led to 'present day Europeans'. Finding a 'happy hunting ground' in Australia, there was no need for the Aborigine 'to fight for existence, hence no call for any special display of ability'. Although 'modern science' had demonstrated that the Aboriginal brain was smaller than that of the white man, nonetheless 'all the natural instincts are present in the aboriginal brain ... and you will find that a native will rise to the occasion every time. You have an example before you in Unaipon.' The *Daily Herald* reporter concurred. Unaipon was 'a wonderful example of the degree of perfection to which the aboriginal brain could attain'. The reporter presented a summary of Unaipon's interests in intellectual ideas, inventions and theories. Unaipon's skill as an organist was often observed in the press, and the reporter listened to a brief recital of Unaipon's rendering of 'difficult variations ... with precision and correctness'.[36]

Basedow presented Unaipon as a scientific specimen, as much as an exhibit in support of his claims about Lemuria as recognition of Unaipon's individuality and attainments. Basedow persisted with his claims about Lemuria, which at the turn of the century accorded with interest and speculation about this apparently lost Eden, 'disappeared beneath the waves', as the Adelaide *Express* claimed in 1906, and wondering if Adam and Eve had been 'black folks'.[37] Stories about the 'fabled' and ancient continents of Lemuria and Atlantis were regularly rehearsed in the press and adopted by enthusiasts of Theosophy and the occult, and taken up as the subject of popular *fin de siècle* fantasy novels, notably C. J. Cutcliffe Hyne's *The Lost Continent* (1900).[38] Unaipon did not seem to explicitly embrace the Lemurian myth, although at times he referred to a traditional story of the migration of the Ngarrindjeri from north-west Australia until they settled by the shores of Lake Alexandrina – as he recounted in the 1914 interview and at which point Basedow interjected: 'And tradition is correct in this instance'. Basedow did not outline scientific evidence that supported his confirmation of Unaipon's story.[39]

In other ways Unaipon represented himself as a link between the spiritual and the scientific realms. 'Hypnotism, clairvoyancy, mental telepathy and other of the occult sciences were – if David Unaipon is to be believed, and his remarks certainly bear the brand of truth and genuineness – well known and practiced by the Australian aborigines long before the advent of the White people to the shores of Terra Australis.' By 1914 Unaipon enjoyed a substantial profile in the press, both as an inventor and as a skilled narrator capable of articulating Aboriginal culture and beliefs for a white audience. Unaipon travelled interstate giving lectures on his inventions and Aboriginal customs and traditions. In July 1914 he spoke in Ballarat's City Hall, in regional Victoria.

> David asserted that hypnotism used to be practiced extensively amongst the Australian aborigines; and that witchcraft killed more of them than did the drink. Then he spoke of the smoke signals, about which so many travellers theorised, and said that they used to communicate to each other by means of mental telepathy and the smoke was merely to attract the attention of the person with whom it was desired to get into touch.

Unaipon claimed that 'clairvoyance was also practiced by the Australian Blacks. They went off into a trance, and said their spirit travelled to see where their friends were.' Concerned to reassure his audience, Unaipon added that 'he had not practiced that sort of thing himself'. Unaipon outlined mystical skills that had practical and therapeutic applications, cultivated by a people worthy of respect and inclusion. 'I want you to take a deeper interest in my people, so that they may become Christians and useful citizens of our Commonwealth.'[40]

Unaipon's enthusiasm for innovation, science and progress ran simultaneously with the new science and regimes of governance that rationalized the expected extinction of his people. In Australia, Russell McGregor describes how evolutionary theory was enlisted in service to 'Doomed Race Theory': 'the natural law of survival of the fittest replacing Divine providence as the corner-stone of the doomed race idea'.[41] In 1899 the anthropologist Walter Baldwin Spencer and his co-author F. J. Gillen published *The Native Tribes of Central Australia* that helped to provide an apparently robust empirical basis to the theory. As McGregor observes, 'like other evolutionary anthropologists, Spencer persistently depicted human history as a series of collisions between discrete racial entities, from each of which one race emerged victorious both physically and culturally'. Scientists, government officials and philanthropists such as A. W. Howitt and Daisy Bates propagated the view that for Indigenous people, 'contact with the white race is fatal'. Promoting her own ad hoc welfare initiatives among remote Indigenous communities, Bates declared in 1907 that 'all that can be done is to render their passing easier'.[42] Bates reflected the influential argument advanced by the British eugenicist Karl Pearson in 1901 that the struggle between races 'is the fiery crucible out of which comes the finer metal'.[43] These views were replicated in the Australian press. In September 1914, as Unaipon visited Melbourne and a number of Victorian towns to promote his ideas and the rights of his people, the Adelaide *Advertiser* editorialized that 'in the more settled portions of Australia the aboriginal question has solved itself by the death of nearly all the blacks'. Governments had tried to 'acquit themselves of their duty to a weak and dispossessed people'; however, 'there is no withstanding a law that seems almost universal. As white settlement waxes the native numbers wane. The degenerate savage cannot breathe the air of civilization and survive through more than a few generations.'[44]

A month later, Unaipon invoked eugenics to assert the durability of his people. The 'distinguished Aboriginal scientist and inventor' gave an address to the Geelong Presbyterian Guild in which he identified the common beliefs and aspirations of white Europeans and Australian Aborigines.

> Mr. Unaipon spoke of the marriage laws of the people, and showed that in some ways they have enforced laws and codes that civilisation has aspired to but not yet reached. The doctrine of eugenics has been practically applied for many years and the result has been that it is a rare thing to see an aboriginal with physical defects. Great care is taken that a suitable wife in disposition and otherwise is selected.[45]

John Burrow has suggested why individuals such as Unaipon could find in evolutionary theory support for their aims. In the decades following the publication of *The Origin of Species* in 1859, 'Contemporaries inevitably assimilated Darwinian evolution to their own contexts of thought and emotional response: defensive, embattled, optimistic, hubristic, polemically materialist, latently or explicitly pantheistic'.[46] An unsettled heterogeneity of new ideas could arouse fears of racial decline or offer the possibility of renewal.

In a parish hall in the Melbourne suburb of Malvern, Unaipon gave 'a stirring and excellently delivered address', appealing to his 'fellow Australians on behalf of his own people'. Quoting the leading British Darwinist and zoologist Edwin Ray Lankester, Unaipon said that

> for a race there were three possibilities open – balance, evolution or degeneration. Mr. Unaipon maintained that for the Australian aboriginal there were huge possibilities of mental and moral development if he were given the opportunity: he is on the balance. Environment is a stronger force than heredity, and the aborigine can be educated if he is given the chance. Eloquently, Mr. Unaipon pleaded that the white people enjoyed pride of place in the world, and that it was in their power to raise and help us to become useful citizens of the Commonwealth.[47]

In the Victorian town of Daylesford, Unaipon, 'with easy naturalness', invoked 'the names and theories of great scientists living and dead . . . Huxley, Spencer, Haeckel, Drummond, Wallace, Ray Lancaster [sic], were each mentioned in turn as great evolutionists, with something to say of interest regarding the Australian aborigine.'[48] A number of these scientific ideologists, as identified by Sally Ledger and Roger Luckhurst, functioned from an assumption of the inferiority of non-white races. Herbert Spencer and Lankester feared that increasing complexity could lead to retrogression and degeneration, with 'an ominous lesson for "the white races of Europe"', as Lankester observed in *Degeneration: A Chapter in Darwinism* (1880).[49] Others, such as Henry Drummond, sought through evolutionary theory to reconcile science and evangelical Christianity.[50] Ernst Haeckel found in nature a form of pantheism, a harmonious 'world soul'.[51]

Unaipon was attracted to the search for harmony. He subverted the ingrained assumptions of inferiority that evolutionary theory seemed to impose, by turning its precepts in service to the 'huge possibilities' of advancing his people and ensuring its survival in a Commonwealth in which white and Black were reconciled. It was not lost on commentators that Unaipon embodied these possibilities. As the *Daylesford Advocate*'s correspondent noted, Unaipon had managed on the basis of his reputation as a 'remarkable man' to draw together a rare assembly of 'Methodists, Presbyterians, Salvationists, Baptists, and Nondescripts' to fill every pew; and 'by sheer force of talent and personality' could 'rise up and rebuke the conceit of learned savants . . . and stand at least as an equal in the midst of a people proud of its achievements'. Emerging from his own people, who seemed to be 'fast passing into oblivion', Unaipon represented 'the operation of a law as old as the planet itself . . . the survival of the fittest'. And if, as Unaipon claimed, he was only one of a number of his people who responded to the opportunities of education, then 'surely we who have dispossessed the aborigine owe an obligation to the remnant of the race, which cannot be discharged without giving them the amplest opportunity to develop their latent powers'.[52] The *fin de siècle* had provided David Unaipon the opportunity to cultivate this transformative message to the tormentors of his people, as they reflected on their hegemony and refined their systems of control.

Post-Federation Australian nation building seemed to require complex and interwoven enclosures of space, in the regulated and gendered demarcations of the workplace, women often relegated in the home: in zones of immigration restriction and Aboriginal protection. The rule of freedom in liberal governance seemed to require compulsion and restriction.[53] No Australian population was more scrutinized and controlled than the Aboriginal population. Maria Nugent has observed that 'between 1905 and 1911, almost all Australian states introduced new legislation that covered Aboriginal people as a separate category and subjected them to a suite of restrictions, regulations and rules'.[54] These interventions were driven by anxiety at the growth of mixed race populations, and determination to corral and separate the Indigenous outside the Australian nation. The new federal state simply assumed that Aborigines did not exist; the Commonwealth of Australia created in 1901 was prohibited from making laws on their behalf or of counting them in the Commonwealth census. As Helen Irving observed of the process of framing the terms of the Australian Constitution in the 1890s, '[a] reader may search the records of [Federal]

Convention debates, and find barely a mention of the Aboriginal people.'⁵⁵ The protection of Aborigines was left to the individual states, although a Chief Protector of Aborigines was appointed to the Commonwealth domain of the Northern Territory in 1911, bringing 'increased intrusion into, and control over, their lives'.⁵⁶

In South Australia, Aborigines were confined to mission stations like Point McLeay. In December 1906 the South Australian Protector of Aborigines reported that there were 3,900 Aborigines in the state (not including the Northern Territory, then still under South Australian control). Aborigines were not included in the Commonwealth Statistician's estimate of a South Australian population, in 1906, of 383,829. The Protector observed that 'the natives are apparently slowing dying out, the decrease in numbers during the last five years being about 160'. In particular 'the true-blooded blackfellow is dying off'. At the Point McLeay Mission Station there were 254 Aborigines and 122 children: births 15, deaths 17.⁵⁷ By 1913 a new South Australian Chief Protector, William Garnet South, believed that the decline of the Aboriginal population was not only a reflection of evolutionary theory: 'the principal reason why the natives were dying out, said the Protector, was that they were herded in places like Point McLeay.'⁵⁸ Yet an assumption of inevitable full blood decline governed South's assessment of the Aborigines under his control. Only a government takeover of the missions could arrest the decline of the 'half caste' and 'quadroon' population to the level of the full blood Aborigines who were 'rapidly dying out'. South wanted to encourage a culture of industrial work to reduce a dependency on charity. 'If the half-castes are given a fair chance I have great hopes of them; but so long as they are reared as hitherto, there is no hope of their rising much above the level of the ordinary aboriginal.'⁵⁹ The difficulty of moving Aborigines from dependency and integrating them into the community was indicated in an exchange at the hearings of the Royal Commission on the Aborigines established in 1913 by the South Australian government. In response to South's suggestion that the government workshops should be opened to Indigenous employment, commissioner John Verran observed that 'the question of throwing open the Islington workshops to them is a somewhat awkward one. It would be difficult to put the natives in over the heads of the white men.'⁶⁰ In 1911 the South Australian Parliament passed a new law lifting restrictions on Aboriginal employment, although Verran's discouragement indicated the difficulty of enforcing good intentions.⁶¹

Press reports entrenched the prejudice against the 'poor workers' at Point McLeay who lacked 'that dogged determination which has placed the Caucasian race in the forefront of the world's peoples', as the Adelaide *Daily Herald* maligned the inhabitants of the mission in May 1911. The mission had been established fifty-two years previously by the Aborigines Friends Association, whose leader, the schoolmaster George Taplin, 'undertook the preaching of the gospel to the benighted heathen of the lakes'. When Taplin arrived there were a thousand Ngarrindjeri warriors; 'today they could not muster 100 men, women and children (that is, full-blooded natives).' There were also 'over 200 half-castes and quadroons'. The Ngarrindjeri 'cannot understand the idea of thrift' and were sustained by 'the coddling method' of handouts of supplies, which reduced them to the 'begging' dependency of 'a spineless mendicant'. Sympathy was expressed with the efforts of the Aborigines Friends Association, but 'a much better plan of government and industrial education is required if any further advancement is to be achieved'.[62]

David Unaipon was the first witness to present evidence before the Royal Commissioners on behalf of the community. In hearings conducted at the mission in March 1913, Unaipon explained that he had spent part of his youth as an apprentice machinist in the settlement's boot shop, but he could not abide the gas burning in the shop: 'being a child of nature gas did not agree with me. It was something foreign to me. I have done nothing in particular since then – just odds and ends about the mission station, nothing very important.' In more recent years there was much less work available at Point McLeay. Asked if there was any 'great discontent among the natives here', Unaipon replied that the only dissatisfaction was the lack of work. Unaipon believed that the South Australian government should assume control of the mission, which would provide better funding and support for obtaining employment.

Unaipon recommended that 'when the children leave school they should be . . . educated to some trade', so that they could become 'independent and self-supporting'. Asked at what age 'the children should be taken away', Unaipon suggested at age nine or ten. Seeking to raise the educational and work opportunities available to the mission's children, Unaipon did not endorse permanent child removal. As a later witness, Matthew Kropinyerie, clarified at the end of the Point McLeay hearings:

> In regard to the taking of our children in hand by the State to learn trades, &c, our people would gladly embrace the opportunity of betterment for our children; but to be subjected to complete alienation from our children is to say the least an unequalled act of injustice, and no parent worthy of the name would either yield to or urge such a measure.[63]

The South Australian government assumed control of the settlement in 1916, fulfilling the Royal Commission's recommendation in October 1913.[64] The commissioners also recommended that 'half castes' be separated from 'full-bloods' and resettled in a separate 'sub station' in 'new undeveloped country' near the Murray River. It was also recommended that children be removed 'at the age of 10 years whose environment is not conducive to their welfare, and, at the desire of the parents, of any other children, and place them where the Board deems best in the interests of the children'. No mention was made of facilitating contact between parents and children following removal.[65]

The description and distribution of Aboriginal lives in space conceived by the Royal Commission reflect 'emplacements' that have 'the curious property of being connected to all the other emplacements' in society but are suspended from them.[66] Heterotopias, as Michel Foucault described this spatial phenomenon, 'are sites where the ordinary emplacements of society are simultaneously represented, contested and reversed. They are localized, but also outside all other places.'[67] Heterotopias may function as emplacements of 'deviation', 'in which individuals are put whose behaviour is deviant' in relation to 'the required norm'. In the Point McLeay mission the Ngarrindjeri were forced to mirror the culture, forms and spatial structure of the society which had subsumed them: a settlement occupying 3,000 acres of 'sandy country' and consisting of thirty to forty small cottages, 'a fine church', a store and a post office. In May 1911, a prominent illustrated feature in the *Daily Herald* presented the Point McLeay mission to its readers, signalled by the emphatic banner headline 'Among the Natives', scrolled in a central semicircle between a grid of photographs of young inmates neatly posed in the dining room of the children's home, the ration store, the native school children with their teachers, the flowering garden of the Jubilee Reserve; the confident ensemble of the white school headmaster P. W. Francis seated in the circle of his adult sons, who were also teachers; and 'Mr. W. G. South, Protector of Aborigines, visiting the camp', standing formally posed with a party of Indigenous women by a humpy. None of the Aborigines in the photographs were identified by name. Point McLeay might have appeared to be similar to other small South Australian communities, except for its 'deviant' population, held apart yet connected by systems of control and representation with white society and governed by white agents, although the author of the article asserted that the Ngarrindjeri were themselves entirely to blame for their 'indolence, their carelessness of the future'. 'Among the Natives' was written by P. W. Francis, the Point McLeay schoolmaster.

The Ngarrindjeri's struggle to eke out a living at the mission was a task rendered virtually impossible given the poor condition of the marginal land that constituted its space, and the lack of funds and resources available to the Aborigines Friends Association. Considerable effort was made to promote the mission as a commercial attraction and to highlight special events. An excursion from Adelaide to the 'popular' mission was advertised for Christmas Day 1909. 'The Natives will give a Musical and Literary Entertainment in the Church' demonstrating how Aborigines may be educated 'under efficient management'. An exhibition of boomerang throwing was promised, and 'native weapons and curios' would be available for purchase.[68] In May 1909 the jubilee celebration for the fiftieth anniversary of the founding of the mission was held in the packed church (Figure 18). 'Magic lantern scenes of the life of Christ were thrown on a sheet.' David Unaipon provided an overture on the church organ. There were recitations from Matthew Kropinyerie and songs and 'dialogue' from other mission residents. It is not clear how many of these performances were traditional or conducted in the Ngarrindjeri language; one 'address' was identified as 'native dialect'. Two elderly residents recalled the arrival of George Taplin, 'the first white man who tried to uplift the natives'. Great progress had been made in teaching the English language, 'and now the natives have schools for the children the same as whites'.[69]

Figure 18 Point McLeay fiftieth anniversary, 1909. Seated at the organ, David Unaipon was artfully posed in a transition between Indigenous tradition and Western Christian modernity. National Gallery of Australia.

Heterotopias are not only permanent emplacements; they may function as festivals, 'transitory and precarious', where the culture of political rule is validated in dramatic display.[70] In 1910 a party of Ngarrindjeri from Point McLeay were enlisted into a celebration of European nation building. Led by South, the Protector of Aborigines, and David Unaipon, identified as 'an organist, and something of a genius', the nine men and three women were invited as guests of the Tasmanian government to participate in events at the inaugural Hobart Carnival conducted over two weeks from 21 February. A highlight of the carnival was a historical pageant focusing on the exploration and settlement of Tasmania, or Van Dieman's Land, as the former colony was known until 1855. The ambitious and elaborately staged historical pageant 'was the first of its kind in Australasia'. The Ngarrindjeri men and women were expected to 'play, sing, and recite, while some of the males will give an exhibition of boomerang throwing. They might, too, be able to give the semblance of a corroboree.' The fact that it was felt necessary to draft Aboriginal men and women from South Australia was also acknowledged. 'The aborigines of Tasmania have long since been extinct, so the little contingent of natives from South Australia will be quite a novelty at the celebrations.'[71]

The participation of the Ngarrindjeri was crucial to the elaborately constructed artifice. On an 'intensely hot' Saturday a crowd of over 10,000 assembled for the opening ceremony at the Hobart showground, as the Ngarrindjeri, recast as Tasmanians arising from nature, were enlisted in sanctioning all that would follow by greeting the state governor at the commencement of the pageant.

> The party of South Australian aborigines then entered the lawn, and greeted His Excellency and Lady Barron in the native style. They wore the aborigines' costume, consisting of one garment, called the merri, being an opossum skin rug, hung from one shoulder, leaving the other bare, and extended from the neck to below the knees. Their bare legs and the sides of their heads were festooned with leaf sprigs of gum bushes and ferns. They certainly looked a swarthy, savage, dark-skinned group. Then Mr. South, who was in charge of the party, was introduced to His Excellency, the blacks salaamed, displaying their white teeth, and retired, amid the plaudits of the crowd.

The Ngarrindjeri represented the apparently extinguished Aboriginal Tasmanians, the last of whom, Truganini, was said to have died in 1876, reflecting, in the eyes of her white contemporaries, 'the failure of an inferior race to thrive in the presence of a civilized people'. As Lyndall Ryan has observed, 'Truganini was not in fact the last "full-blood", let alone the last of her people', who continued to survive in small communities, particularly in the Bass Strait islands.[72] The theatrical resurrection and welcome by the Tasmanian Aborigine was essential for a reassurance that the brutality of dispossession could be smoothly suppressed in entertainment. An apparently natural evolution from Dutch exploration to British settlement was enacted by 300 amateur performers participating in a 'striking and unique' spectacle of 'historic and patriotic' scenes; 'the ladies and gentlemen of the Dutch and Javanese Court looked quite imposing in their stately robes and regalia. . . . It was a quaint mixture of civilized and barbaric people, serving to illustrate a story of historic episodes, and to conjure up the strange adventurous times of long ago.' The climatic drama was a recreation of the arrival of the Dutch explorer Abel Tasman's ships in 1642.

> The next scene represented the coast of Tasmania, then a terra incognita. Screens were drawn across the arena to represent the sea. A number of natives appeared on the beach, armed with spears and boomerangs, and executed a War dance. Suddenly, in dumb show, they became intensely interested in something out at sea, and Tasman's two ships, the Heemskerk and Zeehan, appeared in the distance, beating up towards the shore. The natives, in excellent pantomime, displayed their terror and astonishment at the 'two enormous birds with dark bodies and white wings,' as they gradually loomed larger and larger, and when guns were fired from the ships they rushed about in frantic terror, and lit fires to bring the news of the strange arrivals to their companions, finally scampering off in alarm.[73]

Through historical pageant the crowd could again arrive at the present and find reassurance for their colonization of imagined incognita, and as overlords of a primitive and deferential race that had given way to progress. The pageant created 'a different space . . . as perfect, as meticulous, as well arranged as ours is disorganized, badly arranged, and muddled'.[74] Not all the arrangements were meticulously executed: the caterers had vastly underestimated the numbers attending the pageant, and 'a crowd simply roared at the attendants for a cup of tea and cakes', and made for a 'not too pleasing sight'.

The Ngarrindjeri provided boomerang demonstrations, astonishing onlookers who had never seen such a display: 'The dusky thrower, in his native garb, ran a few yards, and hurled the boomerang forward into the air. It travelled about 60 yards, gradually rising, and gyrated like a wheel, then stopped in its flight, and commenced to return in an elliptical route, and fell . . . close to the thrower's feet.'[75] This fascinating sight may also have presented a fiction: there is no surviving evidence to establish that Indigenous Tasmanians used boomerangs.[76]

Over the following days pageant performances celebrated the triumphs of the British Empire. An attack by 'dervishes' on a British Army encampment was beaten off to the strains of 'Rule Britannia'. While it was felt that the dervishes – members of the Hobart garrison artillery and cadets – did not come close enough to the showground grandstand for easy viewing, an impressive verisimilitude was achieved. 'In the light of the red fire they looked exactly like the savage warriors which the British forces had to encounter in the Soudan, according to the illustrated papers.' This performance was followed by an enactment of a corroboree by the Ngarrindjeri, although by early evening 'there was hardly enough light to enable the onlookers to see it properly'.[77] The Ngarrindjeri also enacted a 'friendly parley' that claimed to represent Captain James Cook's landing at Bruny Island's Adventure Bay in January 1777. As he recorded in his journal, Cook met Aborigines (from the Nuenonne clan), who with calm dignity and good humour exhibited 'the least mark of fear and the greatest confidence imaginable', and who 'received every thing we gave them without the least appearance of satisfaction'.[78] Items of clothing were not among the proffered gifts, although in the Hobart showground the actor portraying Cook 'presented the natives with a quantity of European shirts and trousers, and other articles of civilised attire, which they put on in the most grotesque manner. It fairly convulsed the onlookers to see a brawny native putting his legs through the sleeves of a shirt, while a dark beauty paraded round with a pair of trousers round her neck'.[79] The performances were not designed to celebrate the past: they historicized the future, enacting the fiction of a new beginning by feeding the foundation legends of a young nation, in which an imagined primitive culture was enlisted. The performances required caricature to dramatize an intensification of the white imperial and nationalist projects at the *fin de siècle*, displaying the 'deepened discursive and ideological distinctions between colonizers and colonized'.[80]

On Sunday, 27 February, the Ngarrindjeri conducted a 'very bright and hearty' evening service in the Congregational Church in Richmond, just outside of Hobart. 'The church was very uncomfortably packed, doubtless many attending from curiosity.' Three of the party delivered 'very earnest addresses'. The native choir rendered well the sacred Christian songs, 'while the solo by a lady member, "Say are you ready", was a revelation to many of those present.' Unaipon provided the organ accompaniment.[81] Christianity was vitally important to Unaipon. 'Love the Bible!' He declared in an interview in 1911. The Bible, Unaipon believed, 'is the book for the whole family of man. My people had only dim gropings after the truth, but this book shows me clearly the way of salvation.' Unaipon never went on a journey 'without a Testament in my pocket'. Unaipon added that 'sixty or seventy years ago my people were wandering about with spears and boomerangs, living their wild and savage life; but the coming of the Gospel has changed all this'.[82]

Unaipon's advocacy of his inventions and his scientific interests, and his urging of justice for his people, found expression through Protestant Christianity. Most of the public addresses that Unaipon gave in the period were delivered in churches and church halls. It was in the pulpit that Unaipon developed a compelling speaking style and which the white press presented through the frame of race.

> At first sight, therefore, there appeared something strangely incongruous in the presence of this dusty figure, with round head and lank hair, flat cheeks, spread nostrils, and small gleaming eyes, in the pulpit of a church so anciently identified with the great seats of learning in our modern civilisation. But the incongruity faded away as the sermon proceeded. This man could speak the white man's tongue more fluently than many a highly educated white man. There was no wild gesticulation to suggest the corroboree. With well chosen language and clear, musical voice, possessing at times a singing undertone, reminding one of his native speech, the preacher proceeded with his message.[83]

Unaipon strove to transform perceptions made of him. In turn, this prompted a revision of assessments of Aborigines that Unaipon transmitted into the public sphere, in talks, sermons and through the press. 'Who could resist the noble pathos of the simple plea of this man on behalf of his people?' Resistance evidently persisted: Unaipon rejected as 'bunkum' assumptions that the shape of the Indigenous skull left them 'incapable of soaking in... knowledge'. It was possible, he insisted, 'to educate up' Aborigines 'to the highest standard of present-day civilized perfection'.[84] Unaipon's dismissal of a 'wild and savage life' was expressed in the context of demanding respect for a people capable of the kind of transformation he had made of himself. That survival, if not transformation, apparently had to be won at the expense of a traditional way of life reflected the degrading and too often brutal circumstances Unaipon and his Indigenous contemporaries faced in nineteenth- and early-twentieth-century Australia. 'Striving to gain recognition for his race', Unaipon promiscuously drew from the intellectual resources available to him, from Darwinism to Aboriginal lore and the Bible. Accommodating a ruthless logic of adaptation was the lesson that David Unaipon, 'the super-Aborigine', had distilled from the turmoil of prejudice, innovation and tradition that characterized the Australian *fin de siècle*.[85]

7

John Dwyer's family stories

I cannot ask you to remember me in your prayers, but I remember you in mine.
Daniel Dwyer to his father.

One perfect day in 1910 Daniel Dwyer sat on a hill outside Grenfell, in the central west of New South Wales, and wrote a letter to his father.[1] It was a beautiful scene, he told John. In the distance the line of the Weddin Ranges dissolved in the haze of the sun. A vast belt of golden wheat, 40 miles long, stretched away to his right; to his left, there was an endless run of well-fenced paddocks, filled with grazing sheep. Only the ring of a woodcutter's axe and the occasional bark of a dog broke the silence. Dan wondered how his family was coping in the 'jangling discord' of Sydney, 'where there seems to be no time to be kind and where selfish greed and ambition seem to be the dominating force'. He was glad to have escaped the city. 'I think a person can best realise themselves in solitude. The greatness of the bush here puts me in mind of the greatness of God.'

Twenty-nine years old, Dan had been a Methodist Home Missionary since 1905. He spent three years in the Sydney Central Methodist Mission and later among the bush communities of New South Wales as a 'Circuit Evangelist'.[2] 'It does seem a difference to worship in a little country church, to the great congregations of the city. All that is best and truest and noblest in one's character seems to be drawn out and the feeling of peaceful, restful quiet that steals over one appeals to me so much.' Country worship and solitude brought peace and a chance to reflect. 'I often think of the strange contradictions some of us are, good and bad, but there is comfort in the thought that some-time some-where all these contradictions will be harmonised.' God was harmony and release from the tangled web of life. 'I feel that I could not live without Him and be the man that I ought to be, and the man I want to be, but with Him to watch over and guide and love, all must be well.' Then he directly addressed his father. 'You must not think I forget you Dad. Although at times I think that you have not taught me to love you, as I would wish, perhaps the fault was mine.' Nonetheless, he said his father's good influence would always remain with him, as 'a benediction'. Nor could he forget his mother Annie's unselfishness and love: 'she is a brave little woman.' He would never return to the Central Mission and the work among the city poor. 'I'm not physically fit [and] the country air is making up for a few years of my life of sickness.' He closed 'affectionately': 'I cannot ask you to remember me in your prayers, but I remember you in mine.'

In Dan's gently devastating indictment John Dwyer was presented with the consequences of the struggles he had put his family through – the years of hard living in Sydney, and the strain that had placed on his relationship with his family and their well-being – Annie's self-sacrifice and Dan's health. John would not have failed to notice that Dan's reverie on the pastoral universe of a harmonious and loving God was subtly turned upon him, the urban apostate who believed that traditional religion placed 'cobwebs in the minds of the young' and who had mounted a soapbox in Sydney's Domain to advocate a 'Rational Sunday'.[3] Daniel feared his father's contradictions would never be soothed by the love of God. All the Dwyer children – Elizabeth, Daniel, Henry and Timm – seemed to embrace their mother's Methodism. John Dwyer was sensitive to the spiritual divide between himself and his own wife and children: in 1912 he recorded in his family history that his mother's grandfather, John Cook, 'had no religion, often said he would died [sic] without any – like his father, he did so die'.[4] Dwyer clung to the comforting memory of a conviction resolutely held in the face of death. That Dwyer had to cast back to the distant precedent of his great-grandfather was also a reminder of the lonely path he trod.

John Dwyer's archive provides unusually detailed and poignant insights into how the pursuit of *fin de siècle* dreams impacted on a working-class family. Twenty-one boxes of correspondence, manuscripts, minutes, handbills, tracts and newspaper clippings – plus several other volumes and an assortment of loose papers – document the life of a working-class political radical and spiritualist. The papers also reveal that his struggle to transform society was always a struggle to change and comprehend himself. Dwyer laboured to constitute a meaningful sense of self through his reading and translated into his notebooks. Dwyer's influences ranged from radical politics to literature and science, Theosophy and the occult. Dwyer's dialogue of interpretation and experience was maintained from the 1880s, as he started to gather his papers – itself an act of reflection – until the First World War. In 1916, at the age of sixty, Dwyer deposited the accrued evidence of his life with the State Library of New South Wales.[5] Dwyer was acutely conscious of his mortality, and the need to transcend Christian notions of a single life of suffering also drove this elaborate metaphor of self-preservation, as he recorded in his occult writings. 'Shall all the force and all the energy generated by man during a whole lifetime (if only one), all the force and energy, as represented by those experiences or impressions, be not conserved? Shall they be lost?'[6]

The years 1890–1914 were a period of intense ideological ferment, when new ideas in politics, theology and science aggressively challenged the old certainties. At the *fin de siècle*

> the life of the 'spirit' or the 'soul' came to be regarded as an antidote to the material pursuits of science, and the active adoption of such spiritual alternatives came to be construed as a political act . . . it is necessary to consider several different manifestations of the reaction against positivism in the late nineteenth century: spiritualism; dream psychology; new religious sects, such as the Theosophical Society.[7]

By the mid-1890s Dwyer had fallen under the spell of Theosophy, patching it with his radical politics in a search for a better life, in this world and beyond. Jill Roe observed that Theosophy required 'study, practice and moral discipline, by which the tyranny of our sensuous nature is overcome'. Responsibility lay with the individual to overcome the limits of the self.[8] Seeking transformation of self and circumstance, John Dwyer immersed in these complex and demanding narratives in *fin de siècle* Sydney. Dwyer's family was drawn into the consequences of his quest: Annie and the two eldest children, Elizabeth and Daniel, were uprooted from a settled London life and found themselves in a small town in a distant colony, followed by a debt-driven flight to the capital. In Sydney two more sons, Henry and Timm, were born, as the family spent years in a shiftless existence among the city's dejected unemployed.

John Dwyer was born in London's Whitechapel district in 1856 into an impoverished working-class community divided by long-established enmity between Irish Catholics and English Protestants.[9] Dwyer's father was an emigrant Irish cabinet maker who died young in a workplace accident; his mother was an English Protestant who did not have her son baptized in the Catholic faith until he was around age ten. From age fifteen to thirty-two Dwyer was employed by the London and St Katherine Docks Company, working for a decade as a foreman at the company's Shadwell Basin dock. He was an active supporter of the Temperance cause in the East End. By the early 1880s, Dwyer also fell under the influence of the National Secular Society and its leading militants, Annie Besant and Charles Bradlaugh, in their drive to separate church from state, a cause which led many workers to a broader critical perspective on society. Dwyer also joined the Social Democratic Federation, formed in 1884, to provide an autonomous and socialist political voice for the working class.[10]

While Dwyer strove to break free of his religious and class inheritance, some patterns were repeated. John Dwyer married Annie Bennett on Christmas Day 1879 in Stepney Parish Church.[11] Annie was born in the East End on 12 August 1857, a Methodist and a firm supporter of temperance.[12] They had possibly met through common membership of the Independent Order of Good Templars. The IOGT took its anti-drink crusade to the working class in Britain and Australia, and it was a cause the Dwyers consistently supported.[13] John's marriage to a Methodist, and the fact that his children would be raised as Methodists, suggests that he had already abandoned the Catholicism belatedly imposed upon him as a child. In 1888 Dwyer emigrated to Australia from London, searching for work and greater security for a young family after leaving the Docks Company and unsuccessfully attempting to establish as an East End shopkeeper; he may have fled London to escape creditors.

In New South Wales Dwyer soon failed in an attempt to settle as a small-scale market gardener in the rural town of Mittagong, south-west of Sydney. Driven to the metropolis, Dwyer joined a small group of radicals constituted as the Active Service Brigade, which agitated for the rights of the unemployed during the economic depression conditions of the 1890s and which reached a peak of intensity just as Dwyer arrived in the colonial metropole. As many as 25 per cent of the workforce were rendered unemployed. The Brigade ran a 'barracks' for unemployed men in the working district of Sydney's lower Castlereagh Street, providing cheap accommodation and encouraging political mobilization. In 1894 the Brigade split as a result of a criminal libel charge brought over the publication in the ASB's journal, *Justice*, of a salacious accusation of impropriety concerning Thomas Slattery, the justice minister in Premier George Dibbs Protectionist government. The ASB leaders were convicted and imprisoned.[14] In 1895 Dwyer took the ASB under his own control, although the barracks ideal had been reduced to a succession of boarding houses, providing the Dwyer family with a threadbare income for the next twenty years.

As Dwyer struggled to revive the ASB he also became involved in the Theosophical Society. These activities were expressions of Dwyer's imaginative struggle with 'Babylon the Great', his notebook indictment of an insidious network of state and capital power.

And the Kings of Babylon are strong,
Their dungeons dark and deep,
and the rich rejoice in a reign of wrong
And the priesthood joins in the robbers song,
While the workers die or weep.[15]

Political mobilization provided one potential path out this fate; when that seemed to fail as the 1890s unfolded into a new century, Dwyer turned to the elusive promise that seemed to be offered in the spiritual and fantasy texts that he read and transcribed, including the Australian spiritualist Rosa Campbell Praed's 1886 novel, *The Brother of the Shadow*:

> There exists in nature . . . a force more powerful than the ordinary electricity, by the help of which, a single man able to grasp and direct it, might change the face of the world.[16]

Theosophy was an attempt to achieve 'divine revelation'.[17] Adherents hoped that the study of Eastern religions and philosophies, and the investigation of 'the mystic powers of life and matter', would serve the establishment of 'the brotherhood of man'.[18] It was not enough to act as an agitator on behalf of others: to change the face of the world, Dwyer had to change himself. Personal transformation began in the mind, another lesson that Dwyer took from Praed's novel:

> Concentrate your vital energies, and direct the fluid, while you mentally conjure the larvae in the form of evocation. Beware of faltering – the great impetus once given, and the astral potencies set in motion, they will accomplish their aim, but if arrested, the force will rebound upon yourself.[19]

A theosophical tract Dwyer collected warned that the key notions of karma and reincarnation that Theosophy borrowed from Eastern mysticism were 'entirely a doctrine of free will . . . it is true that Karma is destiny . . . but it is destiny of man's own making; and it is destiny which he is making and modifying every day'.[20] Dwyer sought to master fate and the forces of the universe, to win through to that 'grand occult life, the acquirement of power and knowledge'.[21] Only the dedicated acolyte could find the right road. *Winged Seed*, an extract from Madame Blavatsky's *The Key to Theosophy* (1889) that Dwyer preserved, defined Theosophy as 'the quintessence of duty'.

> To drink to the last drop, without a murmur, whatever contents the cup of life may have in store for us; to pluck the roses of life only for the fragrance they may shed on others, and to be ourselves content but with the thorns.[22]

A Ukrainian mystic, Helena Petrovna Blavatsky provided the ideological framework of Theosophy in *Isis Unveiled* (1877), *The Secret Doctrine* (1889) and *The Key to Theosophy*.[23] The appeal of *The Key to Theosophy* for Dwyer was evident in its aims, satisfying 'the quest for secret knowledge, the achievement of self-improvement, and humanitarianism'. Theosophy was 'aggressively anti-materialist' and appealed to socialists, and not least seeking a way out of the hard grind of impoverishment.[24] Dwyer and his family had suffered the consequences of economic depression since their arrival in Australia. By 1893 the need of a living income had literally pulled John and Annie apart. Failing to set up a market garden business or find secure employment in Mittagong, John travelled to Sydney in January 1893. He found work as a sculleryman on the SS *Monowai*, which did a regular run between Sydney and San Francisco.[25] The two return voyages he completed kept him away from his family until late June, save for brief visit home between trips. Annie remained in Mittagong with the three children – a second son, Henry, was born in the local School of Arts on 15 February 1891.[26]

In July 1893 Annie wrote to John, almost a month after his return from the second voyage; he had remained in Sydney. Annie had just received his letter; she had been anxious to hear from him and had already been expecting his return to Mittagong. 'I suppose you will come when you can.' Annie's letter perhaps indicates why John would not return again – bound, as she was, in daily family difficulties and the intractable financial problems generated by debts, including unpaid rent on their home. Two-year-old Teddy (Henry was always known in the family by this shorthand version of his second name, Edward) had an abscess on his face that had broken a few days earlier. 'He has had five fits I suppose it is all his teeth I was going to take him to the Doctor but I could not borrow any cash.' The crisis had passed; he was eating again.[27] In another letter she told him that she was keeping thirteen-year-old Lizzie home from school for good. 'Going to school hungry was more than she could bear you know her age and I must be careful of her for a little while I had to get her some medicine' (possibly an allusion to menstruation). She considered asking a Mr Jones to take Dan on, but Jones refused. Dan was still at school, and as such his availability for work was severely limited. Jones claimed that 'he can get the state [orphaned] children and 5/- with them'.[28]

Motherhood, as Ellen Ross has observed, 'was all encompassing' for a working-class woman raised in the traditional social roles of nineteenth-century London. She had the responsibility to provide all the basic caring services on behalf of the children. Her love for them 'was expressed in work', and it was part of her function to supplement her husband's usually inadequate income by extracting work from the children, thus 'insuring household survival'.[29] In Mittagong, Annie found her social role breaking down before the fact of poverty – she could not provide sufficient care; she could not send Dan or Lizzie out to work to bring in an income nor painfully pass them on to a stranger's care to reduce the family financial burden. She was in despair: 'I have been all over town trying to get work I might just as well stay at home.' Annie wanted to get out of Mittagong as soon as possible; she thought she might try to find work 'in service' in Sydney. She wanted to get out of Australia. She asked John to pass on her regards to a family friend 'and tell him to keep single as long as he stays in Australia for a man can't keep himself here without having a family tell him I have had to beg for bread to keep life in the children'. She had sold John's overcoat to raise five shillings, a meagre and symbolic compensation for his failure to provide. 'Don't keep promising to send money when you know you can't.' Only a few weeks after her July letter, Annie realized John would not return to Mittagong. John was supposed to contact Edward Larkin, their landlord. 'You told me you would write to him and explain things to him so I have keep out of his way until he heard from you but I might have known you would take no more trouble when you was out of this yourself.'[30] By December 1893 the bailiffs were knocking at the door, seeking unpaid rates and taxes. 'Larkin says I had better let them come the money must be paid. Just such a Christmas Box as I got last year.'[31]

In December 1893 Annie and the children finally joined John in Sydney. She sent Dan on ahead with some of their possessions, worrying over his safety on the train. Lizzie, Teddy and herself would follow on 'the first cheap train'.[32] She had been trying to raise the price of the fares since August. Annie was glad to escape the humiliating problems that had oppressed her in Mittagong – she once wrote that she had not seen Larkin for two weeks: 'I think we are wearing him out like everybody else.'[33] Annie did not want John to return to sea, as he had apparently planned to do in July. 'You can't live on the wind no more than we can', she warned him. She understood his urge to escape the conditions that held them down, the restlessness triggered by leaving the London and St Katherine Docks Company, his desperation to keep alive the immigrant dream. She had an instinct for the dangers that might flow from John staying in Sydney, a choice she feared even more than his life at sea. 'I should like you to be here or on ship anywhere out of Sydney.'[34]

Dwyer was poised between an old life and the reinvention that had failed in Mittagong. Annie was glad to hear that John was keeping away from strikers; 'they would only lead you into trouble.'[35] John's correspondence to Annie in

Mittagong has not survived, but he was obviously sending her reports of the life he was making for himself and the new friends he had found. By December, Annie was trying to adjust to the idea of John taking part in the management of a boarding house for unemployed men run by the Active Service Brigade, the radical political group that John had recently joined. 'I hope the place will prosper it will be good for the working man but how will the managers make it pay it seems such a small amount to charge for bed and breakfast.'[36] John had apparently told her of the ASB's intention to charge the unemployed only a few pennies a night, but he did not tell her everything. He withheld the knowledge that might have prompted her to veto his unfulfilled ambitions, his need to overcome marginality. 'I hope you do not mix up with the Tommy Dodd set Mr. Larkins [sic] says he thinks they will get in trouble if they are not very careful.'

It was the Tommy Dodd set, the Active Service Brigade, to whom John had been magnetically drawn. Led by the radical stirrer Dodd, the Brigade seemed to offer Dwyer another chance of renewal; it proved disastrous. From its Castlereagh Street barracks the ASB roused society's unemployed fringe dwellers into provocative public protest. The unemployed and the 'agitators' who moved among them provoked a fear among colonial authorities as they crowded around the Labour Bureau or gathered in parks and stalked the streets. The Slattery criminal libel case provided an efficient instrument for suppressing the ASB and its leaders, including Dwyer. At the June 1894 trial, Justice Long-Innes said that 'it was not desirable to stir up class hatreds in the community', although the charge had been brought over an attack on the NSW justice minister's character. Dwyer railed in the courtroom at the injustice imposed upon him, denying any knowledge of the libel prior to its publication in *Justice* and lamenting his fate as an anonymous drone. 'I am very sorry I was connected with the paper. I was head cook and bottle washer at the barracks. I worked 24 hours a day over and over again. I cleaned up and managed the place. I did all I could for the men. There were 300 hungry men there. They got three meals a day.'[37] Defiantly, he added that 'he would be an agitator so long as the system prevailed that caused the libel to be put in the paper, and placed him in the position he was'.[38] Dwyer was sentenced to six months' imprisonment in Maitland Gaol, over 100 miles north of Sydney and distant from his family.[39]

While Dwyer languished in gaol, Annie doggedly campaigned to secure her husband's release, even approaching the libelled minister and other members of the NSW Parliament.

> I know I must do something soon it is to much for me this afternoon I went to Mr. Slattery wated from 1/4 to 3 till 1/4 to 5 O'Clock but he was away at a Cabnet

meeting I am going again in the morning at 1/2 past 9 I hope he will do what I want if not I will ask Mr. Widdon M.P. the boot maker and Black to do what they can.'[40]

Annie may have felt that George Whiddon, an MP in the new Free Trade government led by Premier George Reid, might 'do what I want' – presumably, arrange John's early release. There is no evidence that either Whiddon or the Labor MP George Black intervened with Reid (governing in alliance with Labor).

Annie was anxiously distracted by her need to care for the children and run a new boarding house at 491 Elizabeth Street, opened only weeks before Dwyer's imprisonment in the wake of the ASB's collapse. Work was her overwhelming constraint: managing the boarding house from 6.00 am until midnight, she rarely had time to leave. 'I must attend this place here or else I shall be without a home.'[41] Labour-intensive housework was a daily demand – washing and ironing, mending, cleaning, preparing meals – except on a larger scale than the average working-class home. Lizzie helped her run the boarding house. 'I do not know what I should have done without her.' Dan was kept at school, while Teddy, 'poor little chappie he looks a bit neglected'.[42] The boarders were all men, mostly unemployed and all certainly poor. Annie had trouble keeping the place full, and she was always short of money; many of the unemployed could not afford the board. 'Poverty is still very great in Sydney and people are sleeping in the parks.'[43]

Some of the lodgers tried to take advantage of Annie, alone, as she complained, with no man to help her manage them. There were '3 troubling strangers' who rarely went out; others refused to pay, playing 'mean dirty tricks' on her, going up to bed without first paying or alleging that John had allowed them a week's free accommodation a month for 'good conduct'. The pipe in the bathroom had broken, and the water had been cut off; she had stopped paying the rent until it was fixed. She refused admittance to drunks. 'It is strange what a low beast the drink makes a man . . . I wish every man that drinks to keep a thousand miles from me.'[44]

Annie's opinion of several of Dwyer's friends was little better. The anarchist John Arthur Andrews had helped her deal with the men, but, as noted further, he soon followed Dwyer into prison. Annie disliked and distrusted Arthur Desmond (the model for Henry Lawson's dying anarchist): 'one of those people that does all the nice talk and takes all the honour and glory and gets other people to do all the work and take all the responsibility.' She believed that John had allowed Desmond and another man, O'Reilly, to make a 'cat's paw' of him.[45]

O'Reilly was believed to be the anonymous author of the Slattery libel published in *Justice*. 'You know what I always said about him', Annie reminded John, mindful of the prison censors. 'He does not trouble himself about anybody – his own big self first pig.' O'Reilly occasionally came around to Elizabeth Street, 'sneering' that the ASB was 'done'; 'I told him they were not done.'[46] Only Tommy Dodd, of the ASB leaders, tried to help her and the children, arranging from gaol promissory notes for his share of the old ASB barracks income to be transferred to her, but apparently the notes were invalid.[47]

Annie was upset that despite her struggles, John seemed to think she kept him in the dark. 'I tell you everything I positively can if I was to tell you more you would not get the letter.' She tried to reassure him: 'we are going along all wright just now so don't fidget about things', but he could not help fretting, so far from his family.[48] Dwyer received two letters from 'your loving daughter', Lizzie, writing to let him know 'I have not forgot you', and carefully printing out twenty-six 'kisses' at the foot of one.[49] Dwyer and his family were paying a high price for his association with the ASB.

Following his release from prison Dwyer maintained a fitful political activism while pursuing his commitment to Theosophy. In 1896 Dwyer was the president of the Isis Lodge of the Theosophical Society in Australasia, a small, splinter group of dissidents who left the mainstream Australian Theosophical Society in 1895.[50] In the Isis Lodge Dwyer's most loyal theosophical adherent was his friend, the anarchist Andrews, another refugee from the consequences of confronting the state. Public repudiation of violence had not prevented Andrews' imprisonment in 1894 over a technical failure to identify the publisher of a melodramatic pamphlet, *A Handbook of Anarchy*, which roused fears of anarchist attacks at a time when these 'outrages' in Europe attracted sensational attention in the Australian press. Andrews was caught up in the suppression of radicalism by the NSW government that had swept away the ASB. Like Dwyer, Andrews drifted in the late 1890s between political causes and idiosyncratic enthusiasms. Together, they crafted their protests in crude woodblock illustrated pamphlets and hand-written manuscripts which Dwyer preserved, his name characteristically stamped on the pages: the demands for the abolition of the state and resentment at the oppressions of the law provided the themes extolled on soapboxes in Sydney's public Domain.[51] Both Andrews and Dwyer sought alternative spiritual nourishment to traditional Christianity; they were drawn to the myths of ancient Egypt, Lemuria and Atlantis. Theosophists believed that ancient societies had solved the riddle of 'whence came man', a solution that modern humanity might regain through the tantalizing myth of Lemuria, a vast prehistoric continent said to have stretched across what is now the Indian Ocean, South-East Asia and the South Pacific.[52]

Dwyer drafted 'the Book of Notes and Observations on the Occult Subjects' in 1897 as a basis for Theosophical Society talks. The text expressed sympathy for those persecuted for their opposition to traditional religion – ecclesiastical authority backed by 'the axe and the burning stake'. He hoped that the advances made by evolutionists, new scientific breakthroughs by Edison and Marconi, and Röntgen's discovery of X-ray, opened further paths to discovering invisible worlds; he noted that only a few years ago these pioneers would have been regarded as 'madmen and fools'.[53] Dwyer expresses his 'deep gratitude' to over twenty thinkers who aided his 'pursuit of enlightenment'.[54] A list heavily populated with Darwinists and rationalists, including the evolutionists Thomas Huxley and Herbert Spencer, whose *Principles of Biology* (1864) applied Darwin's natural selection to human society. Spencer's assertion of the ruthless principle, 'the survival of the fittest', opened the door to the logic of eugenics and purging the unfit from society.[55] Dwyer acknowledged a debt to Dr John Draper, author of the *History of the Conflict between Religion and Science*, and the pioneer psychiatrist Henry Maudsley, a Darwinian who in *Pathology of Mind* (1895) was troubled by a suspicion that humanity revealed a greater tendency to degeneration than development.[56]

Dwyer continued his agitation on behalf of the unemployed, organizing protests and meetings through the ASB, which remained a small sect, hovering on the fringe of the labour movement under his own control as a self-described 'Master Worker', a claim of superior status that nonetheless tied his identity to the prevailing regime of industrial work that he sought to contest. He fashioned an ASB logo that featured on the large red field of a banner: two interlocking pyramids, borrowed from the Theosophical Society and symbolizing Theosophy's link between heaven and earth, and, for Dwyer, between the realms of radical politics and mystical belief.[57] At times he lashed out the 'fittest' 'sharks and hypocrites' who flourished in a corrupt society, and against 'the Chow and the Kanaka' who he claimed took advantage of women while 'white men' were reduced to penury (Figure 19).[58]

As the century closed and Dwyer railed and struggled to maintain a meagre livelihood, his children began to find their own way in the world. In 1903 Dwyer provided a snapshot of his family life in a diary he briefly kept. On 20 April 'Lizzie left home to go to work for strangers'.[59] Elizabeth, his 23-year-old daughter and eldest child, presumably took work as a live-in domestic, asserting a degree of independence while responding to an economic need. There was no

Figure 19 John Dwyer (left) and John Arthur Andrews unfurl the Active Service Brigade's banner. On a red field two interlocking pyramids symbolized theosophy's link between heaven and earth, and the realms of radical politics and mystical belief. Dwyer holds his son Teddy's hand. *c.* 1895. State Library of New South Wales.

reason for her to leave, John insisted in his diary. 'Without doubt in my mind the act of deliberate opposition to my wishes. I refused to consent to her going', although she still left. Economic need seemed real enough: on 29 April a bailiff turned up seeking unpaid rent for 372 Sussex Street, one of the two unemployed shelters Dwyer operated in 1903; the other was a little further along the street. The Dwyers appeared to be living at 'the large and roomy building' at no. 296.[60] The nearby public school between Bathurst and Liverpool streets may have provided an education for Henry or Timm, the only Dwyer children still of school age in the early 1900s. Life in Sussex Street must have incited memories of Shadwell Basin, dominated by the bustle of the wharves that ran its length along the eastern edge of Darling Harbour, and the adjacent railway goods yards. Sussex Street was congested with overburdened drays serving the warehouses and ships, and the boisterous life of its working-class community – wharfies and draymen, domestic servants, rail workers and factory hands. A street adorned with a necklace of pubs, drawing out the intemperate and the lonely from narrow terraces and unemployed shelters.

While the children were young, the gulf between John's anti-Christianity and Theosophy, and Annie's Methodism, may not have reared as a sharp divide.

As the children grew, they each seemed to embrace a conventional blend of Methodism and temperance. Elizabeth was a committed temperance activist. In 1906 she travelled to Hobart with a young woman's temperance group. Elizabeth told her father that she attended five lodging meetings and had visited a local fair, and enjoyed the amusements and the food, although 'I am very sorry to say there were 3 tent-hotels there too'.[61] In 1914 Elizabeth married Hubert Belhatchet, and their wedding was described as a 'Good Templar Wedding' in a clipping proudly kept by John from the *Australian Temperance World*, the journal of the Independent Order of Good Templars. 'Two well known metropolitan Good Templar workers', Brother Belhatchet and Sister Dwyer, 'both old members of the Prince Edward of Wales Lodge', were married at the Parramatta Congregational Church on 2 February.[62]

Henry was already making his own way in the world. In 1909 John recorded that eighteen-year-old 'Ted' started work as a telegraph messenger at the GPO in Sydney and in 1910 successfully completed the Post Master General's Department Junior Fitter's exam.[63] Timm was still at school. Daniel's letters urged his father to allow Timm to visit and gain some relief from inner-city life. Daniel's instinct was acute: in October 1910 Timm spent several weeks with Dan at Nundle, a little to the south of Tamworth. Timm told his father, 'I am so healthy that I have generally 4 meals a day.' Dan was apparently staying at a local farm, 'Happy Valley', and Timm was initiated into the rituals of bush life. He learnt to ride Dan's horse, Barney; he watched a lame cow shot and skinned and helped drag its carcass to the pit. He visited the White Horse Gold Mine and found a small nugget. Every evening he had 'a nice run' helping to bring the cows into the inner paddock. He was nearly frightened out of his wits, he said, by two 'wallaroos' that bounded up from behind and passed him.[64] There are cards and letters from Elizabeth, Timm and Henry recording excursions outside Sydney but none from Dan before he took up his mission posts in 1908. Childhood travels outside the city may have been experiences he missed; he certainly seemed determined that Timm would not.

John had the physical resources to cope with the impoverished conditions of working-class Sydney in the 1890s; his son Dan seemed sensitive to its privations. Dan was only eight when he arrived in Sydney after the family's extraordinary journey across half the globe. It was understandable that Dan might have felt adrift in the world, given that the family had spent so many of the following years shifting about Sydney, never able to scrape together more than a basic income. Dan brooded on his role in life, the conditions and expectations placed on the individual by society, and the fate of his wilful and dissatisfied father.

Uncertainty, and a sense of isolation, seemed to run like a tremor through the life of his eldest son, Dan, as he made plain in a poem he composed and sent to his father.

> Driftwood
> Men say I drift with any way-ward tide
> They liken me to driftwood on the sea
> And murmur passing with averted face
> They see no use in floating planks like me
> But planks will float where staunchest ships go down
> I drifted by a shipwrecked life at sea
> Clinging to me, it safely reached the shore
> God sees some use in floating planks like me.[65]

Dan was the child most like his father, although perhaps the similarities were not apparent to either of them. There is little record of Elizabeth, Henry or Timm following in his father's footsteps. Daniel followed John into several projects – singing at a Theosophical Society function in 1897, briefly running the lodging house in 1903. Dan's work among the poor as an evangelist also reflected a sense of social justice that his father might have encouraged. Yet the relationship between John and Dan seems to have been the most difficult within the family.

Dan cannot have been too morbidly withdrawn, for he would never have survived the rigours of the training regime provided by the Central Methodist Mission for its future evangelists. Dan enrolled in the mission's Evangelists Training Home in Sydney in 1905. One of the mission's principal ministers, the Reverend P. J. Stephen, said the trainees wanted were men of 'personality, force of character, grit, with a thorough consecration of life to Jesus Christ'. The mission hoped that trainees might contribute something towards their maintenance, possibly the precondition Dan felt most unable to satisfy. The home was 'no place for the weak': evangelists 'come here with an earnest purpose to work; they live in an atmosphere of work; and when they lose the relish for work they have to go home'.[66] The home had places for a dozen trainees, although there were usually only half that number enrolled.[67]

The year-long training regime consisted of instruction in English History, English and Arithmetic, Theology and Practical Evangelism. The day began with devotional reading at 6.00 am, a morning of study and afternoon of work in the 'slums' and hospitals, and finally an evening of evangelism in the streets and mission halls, finishing at 10.00 pm.[68] Dan escaped this exhausting routine in 1908, the work he told his father in his 1910 Grenfell letter that he had not the strength to resume. In Hargraves (a small town north of Hill End in central west New South Wales) in September 1908 Dan gave an evening lecture, 'Light and Shadows', or 'three years in the slums of Sydney, being a little of my experience whilst in the Central Methodist Mission'.[69]

As a circuit missionary, Dan was poised on the fringe of the communities he served. Driftwood had its uses, but it was a lonely social utility, and it was probably just as physically demanding as the city work he had abandoned. As Richard Broome observed of the isolated life of the circuit missionary, 'like all bush people, the cleric had to confront an unpitying environment and ultimately himself . . . the bulk of the bush clergy travelled up to 6,000 miles a year on horseback, pushbike or buggy'.[70] Dan needed to cultivate resilience; he told his father that the preacher is 'the butt of general criticism . . . one is forced to wonder if people think the "poor parson" is something more than human'. A sense of alienation is reflected in Dan's descriptions of Harden and the surrounding country of southern New South Wales. The reverie of a Grenfell hilltop was not the life of a country town in 1910. From Harden, Dan wrote that he was 'over-awed' by the Australian bush – its high temperatures, grasshopper plagues, bushfires; 'it takes a person with a bit of grit to be a "sunny optimist" through it all.' Harden was a railway town, surrounded by some of the best pastoral and wheat country in New South Wales. There was a busy trade in poisoning the rabbits that competed with the grass reserved for the pastoralists' sheep. The 'stench' of the rotting carcasses stacked in the rabbiter's carts hung in the town air and was 'simply unbearable'. Harden was a society dominated by its pragmatic economics. The 'wretched boarding house keepers are veritable shylocks, they grab and fleece, right and left, everything is awfully expensive'. Dan had exchanged one kind of boarding house life for another, although his experience did not seem to increase his sympathy for other travellers. Dan was struck by the human 'flotsam and jetsam' that passed through the town: men carrying the swag, going nowhere in particular, who had opted out of the country economy, and as such 'they are as bad as the rabbits . . . if you ask some to cut a little wood they simply curse you . . . some absolutely refuse to work for the farmers at harvesting time'. Dan enjoyed reporting to his father that when introduced to a local man, he was asked if he knew 'Dwyer the socialist'. The Harden man gave a hostile report of this socialist's Domain harangues, which Dan found 'deadly funny'. When Dan revealed the family connection the embarrassed local started to 'enumerate' John's virtues. 'So you are well known even in the heart of the Australian bush. Don't you feel flattered?'[71]

Daniel's restless progress continued after his stint in Harden. He transferred in 1912 to Queensland, working as a Home Missionary near Ipswich and spent most of 1913 in South Australia.[72] In November Dan consulted Arthur Gault, a leading medical specialist in Adelaide, and as a result of the consultation Gault immediately wrote to John.[73] Dan had 'well marked' tuberculosis, covering 'a good area' of his left lung: 'This requires immediate attention.' Gault strongly advised sanatorium treatment. Essentially a regime of rest in a clean, well-ventilated nursing home, sanatoria represented the most advanced treatment then available for tuberculosis sufferers and a treatment upon which Gault was an acknowledged authority.[74] Gault added, 'I understand that he has not been told on account of his nervousness.' Gault also noted a report from the colleague who had referred Dan, a Dr Gibson, who said that Dan also suffered from epilepsy. Gault could not confirm this diagnosis, although he was certain of tuberculosis: 'Act promptly it is his only chance.'

In 1909 one of Australia's chief public health officials described the tuberculosis bacilli as 'the greatest enemy with which man has had to struggle for his life. It has slain more human beings than have fallen by the hand of man in all the wars of history.'[75] The rate of death from tuberculosis had been steadily falling since the middle of the nineteenth century, although it still accounted for approximately one-fifth of all deaths in Australia in the early twentieth century.[76] Tuberculosis struck hardest among men and women aged twenty to forty-five, particularly among 'mercantile' and industrial workers, according to a 1916 Commonwealth Government report.[77] The slow onset of tuberculosis was 'frequently overlooked', dismissed as little more than an irritating cough or chill.[78] McIntyre Sinclair, the chief medical superintendent of a NSW sanatorium, told a 1905 Australasian Medical Congress that new research revealed that the tuberculosis bacilli was found in every living human being by the age of forty. 'No-one reaches old age without having a focus of tuberculosis somewhere', although a majority of men and women 'possess sufficient powers of resistance to cope sufficiently with the bacillus'.[79]

Treatment of 'the terrible scourge' of the 'white plague' was also complicated by attitudes that associated tuberculosis with degeneracy. In 1911 Dr Frank Antill Pockley delivered the presidential address at the Australasian Medical Congress held in Sydney. Pockley outlined the claims of eugenics made by its leading British advocates, Francis Galton and Karl Pearson: the idea of 'selection for parenthood, based on the facts of heredity', and a dilemma the medical profession must face: caring for the 'individual degenerate, or transmitter of disease', while preventing 'such individuals from multiplying'. The international popularity of eugenics spread rapidly among medical professionals and scientists at the *fin de siècle* and not least in Australia. Applying Darwin's principles of natural selection to human society, Galton believed eugenics promised 'racial enrichment and physical regeneration'; Karl Pearson believed the alternative to eugenics was 'race suicide'.[80] Yet as Pockley observed, elimination of degenerates seemed a step too far for 'the present state of public sentiment'. Pockley noted that 'many philosophers, poets, scientists, economists, historians, and heroes have been tubercular, alcoholic, or insane, or degenerate. It would appear that it would have been better to have let Nature manage this business in her own way', although 'we are driven to the adoption of some measures to limit the undue multiplication of the unfit'. Pockley did not identify what might constitute these measures, although sterilization and separation from the wider community were considered alternatives to radical elimination.[81]

In Australia, it was the working class that was identified as a disturbing and potentially large-scale source of the dangerously unfit. In March 1914 a report on efforts to treat tuberculosis noted the environmental and class context: 'most of the cases treated are from amongst the working classes.' In working-class neighbourhoods the white plague thrived as a consequence of poor diet and inadequate standards of ventilation, hygiene and sanitation.[82] Sanitary inspectors' reports for lodging houses like those that Dwyer conducted describe conditions in which tuberculosis flourished. In 1912 Dr W. G. Armstrong, medical officer with the Metropolitan Board of Health, urged Sydney sanitary inspectors to conduct a war against slum landlords and badly run boarding houses. Good ventilation, plenty of light and dry walls were 'essential to the health of the occupants'.[83]

Blaming the Dwyers for the conditions they lived and worked in is like vilifying them for being born into the working class. The very conditions that John and Annie faced day to day – the quality of the buildings they leased, the struggle to make ends meet – guaranteed that apparently simple standards of cleanliness and hygiene were almost impossible to meet. A moral imperative may have demanded that owners adequately maintain properties leased to working-class tenants, but there was little financial incentive. Dan's letters indicate that his health had always been poor and that in moving to the bush he was trying to overcome 'a life of sickness', as he told his father in the Grenfell letter. Illness pursued Dan: in 1908 he had a nasty accident at Hill End, when he fainted and fell into an open fire and had to be dragged out.[84] Annie rushed to see him, travelling by train to Bathurst followed by a thirteen-hour coach ride over the rough road to Hill End. Annie told John that Dan had 'a fit', but epilepsy may not have been diagnosed, or Annie chose to doubt it. 'I do not think the Dr understands him as well as I do.' Dan made light of the episode, telling his father that he did not have much faith in the doctor's opinion; he felt like the 'redoubtable cat with nine lives' (Figure 20).[85]

Dan's condition rapidly deteriorated in early 1914. In February Dan was in Milthorpe in central west New South Wales, staying at a boarding house, probably having tried to carry on as circuit missionary. The boarding house manager wrote to Annie on the 18th; Dan was too ill to write, and certainly too ill to travel to the Waterfall tuberculosis sanatorium south of Sydney, established by the NSW government in 1909, and where a place had been found for him.[86] The manager urged Annie to come as soon as possible. 'We have him in ice packs, all his food has to be iced and he is not allowed anything solid or in the least warm.' The need to bring down a feverish temperature indicated that Dan's condition was well advanced. Soon after another note warned that Dan was weak after an attack of bleeding from the lungs.[87] Annie arrived on 21 February. Over the next week she wrote regularly to John, each day hoping that Dan would be well enough to survive the trip to Waterfall. Dan's left lung was 'gone', and the right was 'very bad', although the haemorrhaging slowed by 25 February.

Figure 20 Annie and Daniel Dwyer. 'She is a brave little woman', Daniel told the father he struggled to love and remembered in his prayers. Undated. Dwyer family.

Annie planned to travel with him, 'as I can keep him quieter than the others'. Dan became upset, she said, at 'the least excitement'. The doctor had told her that Dan 'is at a very catching stage' and had ordered people not to enter his room, although Annie must have done so.[88]

Annie held the family together, rushing to Dan's side to tend him. She felt the strain: she did not like being in a stranger's house, although they were very kind. Annie hoped to be home soon, she told John, 'and get a good rest'. The other children were rarely far from Annie's thoughts. 'Tell Ted to be good and Timm not to starve himself.'[89] Annie reminded John to feed the family pets, Boxer and Jacko; that John was disconnected from daily family life is also implied when she asks John to give Timm a couple of shillings, 'till I get back'.[90] The children probably found it easier to reciprocate their mother's easy affection and attention, confirming John as a distant paternal figure – a tension evident in Dan's Grenfell letter. Something of the children's more relaxed relationship with their mother is reflected in a 1910 cartoon of Annie by Timm. The cartoon is a mock advertisement for a bogus weight reduction formula. Annie is shown reading 'How to be happy though married'.[91]

John tried to help Dan deal with his illness: In January 1914 Dan followed his father's advice and wrote to Labor MLA Fred Flowers, presumably seeking access to a sanatorium. 'I could only ask him for a favourable consideration of my case.' John had also written to Flowers; both father and son were gripped by a sense of urgency, but Dan tried to play it down. 'I am feeling fairly well but need a couple of months skilled treatment at once, if possible.'[92] Flowers had a long interest in public health policy. Three months after Dan's letter to John, Flowers became the first minister for health commissioned in a New South Wales government.[93] Flowers may have helped: a Mr Lomas at the Health Department agreed to facilitate Dan's admission to the Waterfall sanatorium.[94] Dan was admitted on 6 March 1914.[95]

Two days later Dan wrote to his father from his bed in ward six, reporting the doctor's advice that he needed six months' total rest. Dan fretted over money, although the sanatorium's services were provided free of charge. 'Well, this spells, finance, I've had plenty of that lately in travelling fees, etc. Is it not possible to gain me a little stamp money under the "invalidity section" of the Pensions Act?' Other patients had received such a benefit; Dan would not hesitate to accept the same, if his father could help arrange it. Dan added that he had been put back on a light diet, owing to renewed bleeding.[96] Dan was appreciative of the sanatorium's care. On 25 June the *Daily Telegraph* printed a letter Dan had written to promote community awareness of the 'beautifully situated' Waterfall sanatorium, sheltering over 300 patients. 'From the poor man's standpoint this sanatorium offers the best and most modern treatment.' Patients could only be grateful for the 'courteous and instant' treatment provided by the medical and nursing staff, and the 'abundant' fresh food provided. The staff gave their dedicated 'skill and sympathy' to their work, as every day patients described the 'most distressing symptoms' of this 'scourge of the age'.[97] Testifying to the quality of the Waterfall sanatorium, Dan's letter was a testament to his character.

By the time the letter was published Dan was dead. His father cut the clipping out of the newspaper eight days after his son died in the Waterfall sanatorium on 18 June. Dan was thirty-one years old.[98] Dan's treatment, however kind and attentive, could not overcome the virulence of a disease for which there was no effective cure: advanced cases were invariably fatal. The tuberculosis bacillus was only identified in 1882, but doubt about the discovery, and how the disease spread, endured for many years afterwards.[99] Tuberculosis was not a notifiable disease in metropolitan Sydney until 1904 and in other parts of New South Wales until 1915.[100] The first free anti-tuberculosis dispensary to serve Sydney's poor was only established in 1912.[101] Gault conceded in 1905 that sanatorium treatment in Australia 'is still on trial', and the doubts seemed confirmed by the Commonwealth report of 1916, which challenged extravagant claims of cure in sanatoria. Returns from the Waterfall sanatorium for 1911 indicated that of 283 patients, 108 had died, and only 91 were cured or showed signs of significant improvement from a regime of disciplined rest (in the absence of an effective pharmaceutical or surgical remedy).[102]

The Commonwealth report could not precisely estimate the number of tuberculosis cases around Australia in 1916: its only sources of reliable data were the reports of deaths from the disease and the allocation of pensions, which were restricted to 'persons permanently incapable of earning their livelihood'. Tuberculosis was overwhelmingly a disease of the poor, and the poor were only offered financial aid when they were at death's door.[103] Daniel's condition was too advanced to survive the belated recognition of the authorities. Dan was one of 3,111 Australians who died of pulmonary tuberculosis in 1914 and one of 1,178 victims in New South Wales.[104]

Scientific discovery and public health reform not only contested with medical ignorance, bureaucratic lethargy and social injustice: there lurked within the Australian community a belief that tuberculosis 'discharges a useful function in weeding out the unfit'. To what degree was the fight against tuberculosis retarded by a belief that its selective culling fulfilled the perverse ambitions of social Darwinism and eugenics? It is difficult to measure an implicit state of mind, a mentality of dogged individualism that shrugged, in token of sympathy and with a trace of self-satisfaction, as some fell by the wayside. A mentality real enough for the 1916 report to confront as 'idle and mischievous': tuberculosis 'swept away' 'great numbers of the most promising young folk'.[105] Social Darwinist individualism was a pervasive instinct not confined to grim rationalizations about tuberculosis in *fin de siècle* Australia. Daniel's self-esteem had already been infected by his failure to adapt and prosper. Alienated by the getting and spending around him, Dan saw himself as driftwood, a poor plank of little economic value, of whom he hoped his God had found some use.

The only record of Daniel's death in his father's papers is the newspaper clipping, a slight testament to Dan's brave suffering. There is no record of any correspondence from John to Daniel; nothing is preserved of Annie's grief. The surviving letters from Dan to his father come in fitful bursts – 1908, 1910, 1914, a reflection of the gulf between father and son. Daniel once told his father, 'please don't think I'm mad because I'm writing you a letter.' Dan did not explain this cryptic plea, although he noted that 'there does not seem to be the same bond of kinship existing between us, that I observe in other fathers, and their sons. Still I suppose it's there somewhere, and only needs developing.'[106] We will never know if John responded to his son's tentative invitations to communicate. John's papers for 1914 record only his business. Even the diary John briefly kept is absorbed with the routine of his political agitation – save for a small note a month before Daniel's death. John records his wonder at a hydroplane flying over Sydney, as he watched it 'drop straight down also fly sideways and upside down'.[107] The brilliant turns of the hydroplane provided a brief glimpse of a carefree life, liberated from the conditions John Dwyer had known since he was a boy in Whitechapel.

John Dwyer pursued the politics of a restless soul, exalting 'the life of the spirit ... as an antidote to the material pursuits of science'.[108] He also embraced the social Darwinism expressed by Herbert Spencer and Henry Maudsley, a new form of 'scientific ideology' that rationalized the elimination of the unfit as a means of forestalling a wider degeneration of the race, a ruthless rationale that might have been applied to Daniel's fate.[109] John could not have foreseen that such cold abstractions might draw close to home. The erosion of traditional religious faith by the subversive forces of science and secularism at the *fin de siècle* had opened a space for rational positivism, and a range of spiritual and ideological alternatives, tantalizing vague or oppressively grim. The congested tension of these conflicting ideas is preserved in the unruly array of Dwyer's archive, together with the quiet indictment of the appeals for a bond of kinship directed by an anguished son to his distracted father.

Conclusion

Fin de siècle afterlife

In June 2006 the National Gallery of Australia (NGA) announced the acquisition of Charles Conder's painting, *Hot Wind*. It had disappeared from public view only a few years after being executed in 1889; for over a century its whereabouts were unknown. A black-and-white image was last reproduced in a work on Conder published in 1914.[1] Sent for auction in 2006 and acquired by the NGA, *Hot Wind* was lavishly praised by its new owner as 'a major nineteenth-century symbolist painting' and 'arguably the most important of Conder's group of allegorical paintings that will greatly strengthen the national collection'.[2] The British-born Conder left Australia in 1890, having spent only six years in the colonies; he never returned. His work was often spurned by his fellow colonists in the late 1880s, and he particularly felt that *Hot Wind* was unappreciated by Australians.[3] Conder took the painting with him when he sailed from Melbourne. The painting disappeared into private hands; Conder gravitated from London to Paris and a *belle époque* life among his louche Montmartre confrères Henri de Toulouse-Lautrec and Oscar Wilde, producing the delicate silk fan designs and watercolours of imagined eighteenth-century idylls, 'languorous and dreamful'. Conder became a defining personality of the legend of the 1890s, as Holbrook Jackson described in his classic 1913 study of the *fin de siècle*: 'Charles Conder represents . . . the peculiar artificial mood of the Nineties. His work has the indefinable hot-house atmosphere of the decadence.'[4]

Conder has been periodically summoned back to Australia. In 1927 it was announced that 'CONDER COMES HOME AGAIN'.[5] An exhibition championed the Heidelberg School artists, including Conder, as defining a conservative conception of national life and its material progress. In two magisterial volumes William Moore's 1934 *The Story of Australian Art* promoted the Heidelberg legend in dedicated chapters: 'Sydney in the Eighties and Nineties', 'The Camps Around Melbourne' and 'National Life'. Moore insisted that Australian art was a nation-building enterprise. 'We are inclined to regard art as something apart from national life; but in years to come it will be realized that art affects the life of the people like any other form of endeavour.'[6] In the interwar years Conder was represented as an emphatically Australian artist from which the ambiguities of *fin de siècle* symbolism were stripped and at a time, Conder's biographer John Rothenstein observed in 1938, when 'rigid orthodoxies' of politics were emerging, and a 'stricter conformity' in the arts, in a world 'shaken by universal war' and seeking to 'renounce a measure of personal liberty... in order that some larger entity, national, racial, or universal, may live more tolerably'.[7] There was scant tolerance of dreamy Symbolists. Oscar Wilde had been untroubled by Conder's enigma: 'it is absurd not to know the unknowable', Wilde observed in 1898, recommending Conder's friendship to the publisher Leonard Smithers. Conder died in 1909, stricken with syphilis and unknown to himself.[8]

Seeking the dead from out of the flux of the past, historians thread the archival remains of their subject's experience into narratives seamlessly plotted from beginning to end. Hayden White counselled that we will not understand what happened, and what is happening, until our histories acknowledge discontinuity, that the past throws up many meanings, many choices of interpretation and models of future action.[9]

For providing both a metaphor and the reality of disruption, it is hard to identify a more apt phenomenon than the overwhelming, chaotic sequence that contemporaries struggled to classify: so they called it 'The Great War'. From August 1914, Rothenstein's universal war consumed Australian society and reduced lives and ideals in service to its demands. Four years of unparalleled social distress and political division, repeatedly agitated by feeding the juggernaut toll of battlefield conflict, stirred impatience with elegant obscurities. In November 1918 the *Sydney Morning Herald* observed that Christopher Brennan's poetry had prior to the war exhibited a 'symbolism and an allusiveness which often left his readers groping in the dark behind him. But the war has moved him to greater directness.' In his recent collection, *The Chant of Doom*, Brennan was 'the prosecutor with a voice of thunder', in support of Australia's commitment to the war, whose verses 'breathe a patriotism which transcends the noisy platitudes of the street'.[10]

In the remote reaches of the long run, a tremor of the *fin de siècle* and its forestalled agenda of questioning tradition and demanding recognition of the marginalized, of alternatives to the logic of rational progress, travelled into the future. Meanwhile, the subjects of *The Fin de Siècle Imagination in Australia* were moulded by the logic of directness; some soon died in the post-war years, and their ideals and causes often failed before they passed away. The *fin de siècle* had witnessed extraordinary accelerations of vibrant ideas and energetic activism, and an intensive ferment generated by anxieties of class, gender and race. The post-war years saw a collapse into entropy for these subjects, in a shell-shocked time that reflected 'paradoxically conservative, stabilizing forces, blocking exploration and awareness of the troubling issues raised' at the *fin de siècle*.[11] A tendency to inward-looking insularity, a form of cultural protectionism, tightened its grip in interwar Australia.[12] Reckoning with the suspension in lateness of these once questing men and women does not neatly wrap up what happened next nor concludes; it probes further into the complicated ephemerality of aspiration and experience. Ends blur into beginnings – if not for these subjects, then perhaps in our response to their creative courage, a willingness to engage in political action and reform or reluctance to accept complacent perceptions that constituted the prevailing order of social reality.

The war imposed implacable polarizations. The many potential meanings of life were simplified, smothering activism and coarsening imaginative response; iconoclasts embraced the bond of patriotic conformity. In plain prose the thunderous prosecutor Chris Brennan railed against Daniel Mannix, the Catholic Archbishop of Melbourne, for opposing the conscription of Australian men to fight in the struggle to defend 'civilization'. Brennan urged Australians to vote 'yes' in the December 1917 conscription plebiscite and repudiate the comfort 'Mannixism' lent to Germany.[13] Alfred Deakin's 1907 proposal of compulsory military training evidently compelled a logic of compulsory military service for overseas duty; the 1917 vote was the second, stubborn attempt by the government of William Morris Hughes to attract majority public support for the introduction of conscription. The first 1916 plebiscite was narrowly defeated and the federal Labor government split, expelling pro-conscriptionists such as Hughes, who resorted to governing in coalition with his once trenchant political enemies.[14]

As one of the leaders of the small if boisterous company of the Women's Peace Army, Vida Goldstein campaigned across the country against conscription.[15] The political radicalism emerging in her outlook before the war had also assumed a logic of directness. In Hobart in December 1917, and just as the Bolsheviks had seized power in Russia, Goldstein told an anti-conscription meeting that although she did not want Australia to follow Russia into revolution, she did seek 'a social and industrial revolution brought about by the ballot box . . . capitalism was doomed', and 'the war was going to have very different results from the capitalists thought it would'.[16] The 'no' case was successful in the plebiscite, although Australia's participation in the war was maintained until the end in November 1918, exacting nearly another year of sacrifice from the fallen and their families. Capitalism survived.

As the world reeled out of disaster, in May 1919 the *Woman Voter* issued a public appeal for funds to send two representatives of the Women's Peace Army to attend the International Women's Peace Congress in Zurich. The Congress would follow the Peace Conference meeting in Paris to end the war. Vida Goldstein had been selected as one of the Women's Congress delegates. 'Whether social and industrial freedom are to be worked out by constitutional or revolutionary methods, the community cannot afford to ignore the views of women in Peace and Reconstruction, and Australian women have their contribution to offer to the world's thought about them.'[17] In the immediate post-war years Goldstein's loyalty to this conviction ebbed, as she increasingly withdrew from Australia and political activism. The *Woman Voter* ceased publication in 1919; Goldstein did not return from overseas until 1922. Arriving in June, she insisted that she would never again run for elected office. 'I have had my time in the hurly burly of politics, and now I think more is to be achieved by individual work.' In her three and a half years away, Goldstein had observed 'a reaction all over the world . . . people do not know which way to turn'. It was a 'new world', she said, 'and there is no use trying to reconstruct the world on pre-war lines'. Goldstein looked forward to an era of 'co-operation instead of cut-throat competition' and respect for the views of others. 'There should be no class antagonism any more than sex antagonism.' Goldstein welcomed what she described as the advent of the 'bachelor woman', single women able to exercise their agency, although an identity in a state of 'transition', as she asserted: 'They have yet to learn the difference between licence and liberty.'[18] Out of the shock of war and embittered political conflict Goldstein sought after harmony. Goldstein was in transition into a meditative life in Christian Science, into which she withdrew from the mid-1920s until her death on 15 August 1949.[19] The obituaries were brief; a correspondent regretted that her passing was 'almost unnoticed'.[20] The *Argus* cursorily recalled 'a pioneer in the fight for women's political rights', although it conceded that 'we should not forget our pioneers – men or women. After all we still have much pioneering to do.'[21]

Alfred Deakin retired from political life in 1913. In a rare post politics public statement on 19 December 1917, the day prior to the conduct of the second conscription plebiscite, a letter was published in the press in Deakin's name, urging a 'yes' vote. It was not certain that Deakin himself composed the appeal. By then, the effects of a degenerative condition inhibited communication and memory. Deakin died at Llanarth on 7 October 1919.[22] The obituaries for a man who had served as a Victorian government minister, federation architect and three times prime minister of Australia were muted; he was memorialized in the *Age* as little more than a compelling voice. Deakin was a 'great parliamentarian', rather than a great statesman, not remembered for 'any great legislative achievement, but as a superb orator'. He was possessed of a temperament 'more attuned to the philosopher, and more fitted to the meditations of the closet'.[23] The *Argus* also noted Deakin's 'exceptional gifts in oratory' but concluded that with the achievement of Federation in 1901, 'the work for which Mr. Deakin was best fitted was over'. Deakin's 'policy of giving ground encouraged the more turbulent elements', by which the conservative *Argus* presumably characterized the Labor Party. 'The world has moved with tragic rapidity since Mr. Deakin retired six years ago.'[24] On 20 January 1913 Deakin had attended his final party meeting as leader. Vacating the chair, Deakin sat on the balcony at one end of the room, unable to hear clearly the speech delivered by his successor, Joseph Cook. 'The blood has rushed to my head,' he recorded in his notebook. 'I take in the picture and dwell upon it as the last. . . . I see them as if far way and myself as an invisible onlooker.'[25] The post-Federation, nation-building policy initiatives associated with Deakin have been more fulsomely appreciated by historians; Deakin has been rated by historians and political scientists as one of Australia's three most outstanding prime ministers.[26] That such a prominent public figure should have so quietly vanished reflected the shadow that the war had cast over the society that had marched into it in 1914.

The governing wartime politicians exercised little tolerance for dissenting voices – not only specifically anti-war or anti-conscription protests, which became increasingly prohibited under the censorious terms of the War Precautions Act, but any social or political cause that did not conform with the requirements of military or industrial mobilization.[27] As the war broke out, John Dwyer's activism had largely reduced to urging the New South Wales Labor government to pursue legislation enshrining a 'right to work' and hence validate Dwyer's long agitation, in meetings, street protests and lobbying on behalf of the often disregarded interests of the unemployed.[28] Premier William Holman's government split over the conscription crisis in 1916, and the Right to Work legislation lapsed as Holman's pro-conscriptionists formed a coalition with the non-Labor parties in the NSW Parliament.²⁹ Dwyer's quarter century of activism seemed also to lapse. In 1916 and again in 1917 he deposited his papers with the State Library of New South Wales. Archiving his activism may not have necessarily ended it, yet there is little trace of Dwyer's agitation or spiritual speculations thereafter. Perhaps the impact of his son Daniel's death played a part in this withdrawal; perhaps it all just seemed too late, overwhelmed by radically changed circumstance.

Rose Cadogan, née Summerfield, died in Villa Rica, Paraguay, on 14 April 1922, four days before her fifty-eighth birthday. In 1908 the Cadogans, who by then had four children, left the failing New Australia settlement for life as shopkeepers in the nearby town of Yataity. With a husband taken to drink, Rose was left virtually singlehanded to run the shop and the family. By 1915 she pined for 'the scent of wattle', as she wrote plaintively in a poem, 'Australia', a longing denied in 1920, when the Cadogans lost their savings in a bank failure only months before finalizing arrangements to return to Australia.³⁰ An obituary in the Brisbane *Worker* recalled a presence from another world, 'Rose Summerfield', a pioneer of 'the nineties of the last century' and her 'brilliant addresses . . . a generation ago', and how 'her literary gifts and militant nature at once asserted themselves with her growth into womanhood, and her ready pen was placed at the service of any and all of the small band of valiant papers that were then battling for the cause of human betterment and intellectual enlightenment'. In the throes of birth, the labour movement 'found in Rose Summerfield a stalwart and an energetic helper'.³¹

Some pioneers lacked a memorial of any kind. On 16 June 1954, Annie Dwyer died of a cerebral haemorrhage. Annie was ninety-seven years old, and she had been in New South Wales sixty-five years.³² Annie Dwyer was laid to rest with her son Daniel in the Methodist section of Woronora cemetery at Sutherland, in Sydney's south. Annie and Dan have no headstone. Mulched leaves cover a patch of earth between two graves. Annie Dwyer had outlived her husband by twenty years. John Dwyer died in the State Hospital at Liverpool, south-west of Sydney, on 1 February 1934, aged seventy-seven.³³ The cause of death was recorded as 'carcinoma of the glands of neck', the secondary spread of a primary malignancy, presumably a melanoma, on his lower lip. Did Dwyer still believe, as he lay dying, that his death resulted from too much life? As we live, he wrote in 1897, the 'life waves' rush with increasing intensity through the body and 'a time comes when we are not able any longer to endure their power'. Dwyer had hoped that his astral light would endure beyond the death of his exhausted body.³⁴ He was buried in the Methodist section of Sydney's Rookwood Cemetery, after a Methodist service. Perhaps he had asked for the comfort of tradition; perhaps his mourning family reclaimed him for the Christianity he had rejected but which sustained them in their grief. Only the cemetery records indicate where Dwyer rests. No details of Dwyer's life, or the presence of his remains, are recorded on the gravestone.

By the time that Christopher Brennan's *Poems* were published in December 1914 he could hardly hope for popular appreciation of works of which 'the majority belong to the last century', although the *Sydney Morning Herald* registered a mark of respect for a 'formidable' work. 'In a review of Australian poetry Mr. Brennan's volume will rank among the most important landmarks', even if 'Mr. Brennan is so steeped in Symbolism that sometimes his meaning is almost impossible to follow'. There was some clear line of meaning: while yearning for 'days of azure', Brennan had seen the 'hideous' streets of cities that 'belch their sodden dream of Empire, lust, and blood'. It was, the reviewer observed, 'the old cry of the soul which, bruised and hardened by contact with the crude materialism of life, still regrets the pristine innocence which it can never recover'.³⁵ That *fin de siècle* dream had faded. It had represented literary expression and an identity that had proven difficult to live by; Brennan struggled to control his drinking or the consequences of that consumption. Brennan deteriorated after his lover Violet Singer was killed in a tram accident in 1925. As a result of subsequent divorce proceedings that brought the relationship to public attention, Brennan was removed from his position as Associate Professor of German and Comparative Literature at the University of Sydney that he had held since 1920.³⁶ He never recovered personally or professionally from these blows, his alcoholism intensified and he died on 5 October 1932.³⁷ He was recalled as a 'believer in old ideals', who scorned 'modern idols' of the post-war world such as James Joyce, who had merely laid bare, Brennan asserted, 'the cesspit' of the human mind. 'The literature of our time has no beauty. . . . All that was worthy in life and art died with Thomas Hardy. All that was worthy in psychology died with William James.'³⁸ His memorialists hoped that Brennan would be remembered for *Poems* rather than *The Chant of Doom*, described in the *Catholic Press* as 'versified vituperation', produced by 'war fever'.³⁹ *Poems*, 'his best book', had a 'grimness, melancholy and bitterness', although also 'full of beauties, craggy and tempestuous': literary attributes that reflected the man.⁴⁰

In the mid-1920s David Unaipon seemed on the cusp of recognition for his untiring efforts to assert the richness and legitimacy of Aboriginal culture and spiritualism, with the preparation in 1924–5 of a manuscript of Aboriginal legends.[41] He had made a name for himself in the post-war years through a series of press articles on these themes. Unaipon had also experienced frustration and appropriation in his attempts to develop the inventions that he had patented a decade earlier. In July 1914, as he was reported to be in Melbourne 'attending to the business of the invention of a new shearing machine made by him', a prescient warning appeared in the Brisbane *Worker*, a journal of the union that represented shearers: 'David Unaipon had better keep his weather eye open, else those capitalists or patent righters will rob him of his invention as they always rob labour, black and white, of the harvest of its toil.'[42] In the interwar years Unaipon suffered another misappropriation, with his manuscript of Aboriginal dreamtime stories published under the name of a white man. In 1930 the medical officer and 'amateur anthropologist' William Ramsay Smith was credited as the author of *Myths and Legends of the Australian Aboriginals*. David Unaipon's *Legendary Tales of the Australian Aborigines* was not published 'for the first time in their original form' until 2001.[43] David Unaipon died on 7 February 1967 aged ninety-five and 'without ever having seen the book published in his own name and with his genius remaining largely unrecognised and unappreciated', as the historian Jeanine Leane observed. David Unaipon was buried in the Point McLeay cemetery, his passing neglected by the white society that had consumed his legacy. Unaipon has since received recognition, with the inauguration in 1989 of the David Unaipon Award for an Unpublished Indigenous Writer.[44] In 1995 Unaipon was memorialized as a transaction between Australians: his portrait appeared in a new design of the Australian fifty-dollar note.[45]

By 1915, Henry Lawson was, like Christopher Brennan, keen to stake a claim in Anzac myth-making. Lawson's book of poems, *My Army, O, My Army!*, was published in August and included the 'Song of the Dardanelles', glorifying the Gallipoli landing on 25 April. In 1887, Lawson's first published poem, 'A Song of the Republic', drew inspiration from radical and republican politics. In the pages of the *Bulletin* Lawson declared that Australians, 'the sons of the South', had to 'arise' and choose between England and the hardships its rule imposed on the working class, and the urgent need to create a new society, a choice between 'The Land that belongs to the lord and Queen, And the Land that belongs to you'.[46] In 1915 Lawson's 'Song of the Dardanelles' celebrated that Australian manhood, 'The youngest and strongest of England's Brood', had proved themselves worthy in the empire's cause by storming ashore at Anzac Cove.[47]

The *Freeman's Journal* declared that Lawson's 'war songs' reflected how Australia had become 'a faithful daughter': Australia 'has identified herself heart and soul with the Mother Country', a cause 'well worth fighting and dying for'.[48] The war had stunned the young nation into a withdrawal within the familiar identity of empire. *My Army, O, My Army!* proved to be Lawson's last notable publication. Lawson's failure to secure a successful future as a writer in the early twentieth century, and his increasing dependence on alcohol, had by 1914 reduced his life to separation from his family and spells in gaol and asylum. By early 1922 he was living in a cottage in suburban Sydney, tended by a housekeeper. His writing days were behind him, although when he died on 2 September a notebook and pencil were found lying by the body.[49] Prime Minister Billy Hughes, who had known Lawson since the 1890s, eulogized 'the poet of Australia . . . the minstrel of the people'.[50]

Every ending is a beginning, and Lawson was on his way into legend. In July 1931 a statue of Henry Lawson was unveiled at Mrs Macquarie's Chair, in a harbourside setting adjacent to Sydney's public Domain. A Memorial Fund had financed its creation, the first 'of an Australian poet to be erected in the Commonwealth'. The statue proved to be the last work completed by the artist George Lambert prior to his death. The bronze ensemble depicted Lawson standing, in the company of a slumped bushman worrying his face with a distracted hand and a sheep dog keeping a sharp-eyed watch. NSW governor Sir Phillip Game officiated at the ceremony, daintily praising the ideal 'Mate-iness' that Lawson proclaimed in 'the simple dialect of the bush'.[51] Newspapers reporting the unveiling also headlined angry stories that Lawson would have recognized, of shuttered banks, distressed depositors and bitter political divisions, the consequences of another calamitous economic depression to rival the collapse that scarred lives in the last decade of the nineteenth century.[52] There was criticism that the statue's location 'shared the site with the unemployed'. The cast totems of Lawson, sheep dog and shepherd were nightly surrounded by 'sundowners' dossing in the parkland setting of the Domain and Mrs Macquarie's Chair: 'a friend to the poor', Lawson would not have minded. From tales of isolation Lawson had fashioned an imagined community. At the unveiling, Australians expectantly lifted their faces before the representation emerging from the awkwardly tugged shrouds – appropriately enough, a sober ceremony disrupted by comic relief. Lambert

Figure 21 Unveiling of the Henry Lawson Memorial, 1931. State Library of New South Wales.

rendered a pensive Lawson with a hesitantly lifted right hand, 'so as to see a distant hill or as if to recall far horizons of memory, a familiar gesture of the poet' (Figure 21).[53] Lawson appeals to the shades of spent lives and frayed dreams. The old bush undertaker might stir from his reverie and call: 'Five Bob! Fetch 'em back'.

Notes

Introduction

1 Mark Hearn, 'Originally French but Afterwards Cosmopolitan: Australians Interpret the *Fin de Siècle*', *Journal of Australian Studies*, 43, no. 3 (2019): 365–80. doi: 10.1080/14443058.2019.1643391.
2 Matthew Potolsky, 'Fin de Siècle', *Victorian Literature and Culture*, 46, no. 3–4 (2018): 697. doi: 10.1017/S1060150318000591 (accessed 11 June 2021).
3 Michael Saler (ed.), *The Fin de Siècle World* (London: Routledge, 2015), 4.
4 Alexis Bergantz, *French Connection: Australia's Cosmopolitan Ambitions* (Sydney: NewSouth Publishing, 2021), 14–17.
5 Paul Greenhalgh, 'The Cult of Nature', in Paul Greenhalgh (ed.), *Art Nouveau 1890–1914* (London: V&A Publications, 2000), 57.
6 'Australia Felix', *Lone Hand*, 2 December 1907, 117–20, National Library of Australia (NLA); Ron Radford, *Art Nouveau in Australia* (Canberra: Australia Council and Art Gallery Directors Council, 1980), 8, 10; Denise Mimmocchi, *Australian Symbolism: Art of Dreams* (Sydney: Art Gallery of NSW, 2012), 15, 110–11.
7 Norman Lindsay, cover illustration, *Lone Hand*, 1 May 1907, National Library of Australia. https://nla.gov.au:443/tarkine/nla.obj-408666105.
8 R. F. Foster, *Vivid Faces, The Revolutionary Generation in Ireland, 1890-1923* (London: Penguin, 2015), xvii–xviii.
9 Rachel Holmes, *Eleanor Marx* (London: Bloomsbury, 2014); Rachel Holmes, *Sylvia Pankhurst, Natural Born Rebel* (London: Bloomsbury, 2020); Sheila Rowbotham, *Edward Carpenter, A Life of Liberty and Love* (London: Verso, 2008); Sheila Rowbotham, *Rebel Crossings, New Women, Free Lovers, and Radicals in Britain and the United States* (London: Verso 2016).
10 Deaglan Ó Donghaile, *Oscar Wilde and the Radical Politics of the Fin De Siècle* (Edinburgh: Edinburgh University Press, 2020), 5; Jessica M. Dandona, *Nature and the Nation in Fin-de-Siècle France, The Art of Emile Gallé and the Ecole de Nancy* (London: Routledge, 2017).

11 Reinhart Koselleck, 'Does History Accelerate?', in Sean Franzel, and Stefan-Ludwig Hoffmann (eds), *Sediments of Time: On Possible Histories* (Stanford: Stanford University Press, 2018), 88.
12 Reinhart Koselleck, *The Practice of Conceptual History* (Stanford: Stanford University Press, 2002), 120.
13 Saler (ed.), *The Fin de Siècle World*; Mikulas Teich and Roy Porter (eds), *Fin de Siècle and Its Legacy* (Cambridge: Cambridge University Press, 1990), 3. The publication of two key works by Carl Schorske and Stephen Kern significantly stimulated historical research into the *fin de siècle* and the ideas and forces associated with it. Carl Schorske, *Fin de Siècle Vienna* (New York: Vintage Books, 1981); Stephen Kern, *The Culture of Time and Space 1880–1918* (Cambridge, MA: Harvard University Press, 1983); Elaine Showalter, *Sexual Anarchy: Gender and Culture at the Fin de Siècle* (London: Virago, 1992); Shearer West, *Fin de Siècle: Art and Society in an Age of Uncertainty* (London: Bloomsbury, 1993); Sally Ledger and Scott McCracken (eds), *Cultural Politics at the Fin de Siècle* (Cambridge: Cambridge University Press, 1995); Asa Briggs and Daniel Snowman (eds), *Fins de Siècle: How Centuries End, 1400–2000* (New Haven: Yale University Press, 1996); Sally Ledger and Roger Luckhurst, *The Fin de Siècle: A Reader in Cultural History* (Oxford: Oxford University Press, 2000); J. W. Burrow, *The Crisis of Reason: European Thought, 1848–1914* (New Haven: Yale University Press, 2000); Gail Marshall, ed., *The Cambridge Companion to the Fin de Siècle* (Cambridge: Cambridge University Press, 2007); Dandona, *Nature and the Nation in Fin-de-Siècle France, The Art of Emile Gallé and the Ecole de Nancy*; Ó Donghaile, *Oscar Wilde and the Radical Politics of the Fin De Siècle*.
14 Saler (ed.), *The Fin de Siècle World*, 5–7.
15 Christopher Bayly, *The Birth of the Modern World, 1780–1914* (Oxford: Blackwell Publishing, 2004), 451.
16 Michael Roe, *Nine Australian Progressives: Vitalism in Bourgeois Social Thought, 1890–1960* (St Lucia: University of Queensland Press, 1984); Jill Roe, *Beyond Belief: Theosophy in Australia, 1879–1939* (Kensington: University of New South Wales Press, 1986); John Docker, *The Nervous Nineties: Australian Cultural Life in the 1890s* (Melbourne: Oxford University Press, 1991); Al Gabay, *The Mystic Life of Alfred Deakin* (Melbourne: Cambridge University Press, 1992); Susan Magarey, Sue Rowley, and Susan Sheridan (eds), *Debutante Nation: Feminism Contests the 1890s* (St Leonards: Allen & Unwin, 1993); Bruce Scates, *A New Australia: Citizenship, Radicalism and the First Republic* (Melbourne: Cambridge University Press, 1997); David Walker, *Anxious Nation: Australia and the Rise of Asia, 1850–1939* (St Lucia: University of Queensland Press, 1999); Martin Crotty, *Making the Australian Male: Middle-Class Masculinity, 1870-1920* (Melbourne: Melbourne University Press, 2001); Susan Margarey, *Passions of the First Wave*

Feminists (Kensington: University of New South Wales Press, 2001); Frank Bongiorno, 'A Short History of New Thought in Australia, 1890-1914', *Australian Cultural History*, 23 (2004): 25-42; Marilyn Lake and Henry Reynolds, *Drawing the Global Colour Line, White Men's Countries and the Question of Racial Equality* (Melbourne: Melbourne University Press, 2008); Michelle Hetherington (ed.), *Glorious Days, Australia 1913* (Canberra: National Museum of Australia Press, 2013); Alan Atkinson, *The Europeans in Australia*, vol. 3: *Nation* (Sydney: NewSouth Publishing, 2014).

17 Melissa Bellanta, 'Rethinking the 1890s', in Alison Bashford and Stuart Macintyre (eds), *The Cambridge History of Australia*, vol. 1 (Melbourne: Cambridge University Press, 2013), 240.

18 Hearn, 'Originally French but Afterwards Cosmopolitan', 373.

19 Aleida Assmann, 'Transformations of the Modern Time Regime', in Berber Bevernage and Chris Lorenz (eds), *Breaking Up Time: Negotiating the Borders between Present, Past and Future* (Göttingen: Vandenhoeck & Ruprecht, 2013), 45.

20 Jill Roe, 'Leading the World? 1901-1914', in Jill Roe (ed.), *Social Policy in Australia* (Sydney: Cassell Australia, 1976); Marian Sawer, *The Ethical State? Social Liberalism in Australia* (Melbourne: Melbourne University Press, 2003); William Coleman (ed.), *Only in Australia, The History, Politics, and Economics of Australian Exceptionalism* (Melbourne: Oxford University Press, 2016).

21 'As Others See Us', *Mercury* (Hobart), 13 April 1909, 3.

22 Ibid., *Register* (Adelaide), 17 July 1909, 4.

23 Ibid., *Leader* (Orange), 2 March 1906, 2.

24 J. Ramsay MacDonald, *Labour and the Empire* (London: George Allen, 1907), 52, 62, 84-5.

25 'As Others See Us', *Maryborough Chronicle*, 14 January 1907.

26 John Jervis, 'The Modernity of the *Fin de Siècle*', in Michael Saler (ed.), *The Fin de Siècle World*, 60.

27 Ledger and Luckhurst, *The Fin de Siècle: A Reader in Cultural History*, 133-7.

28 Alison Bashford and Catie Gilchrist, 'The Colonial History of the 1905 Aliens Act', *The Journal of Imperial and Commonwealth History*, 40, no. 3 (2012): 423, 427. doi: 10.1080/03086534.2012.712380.

29 Marilyn Lake, *Progressive New World, How Settler Colonialism and Transpacific Exchange Shaped American Reform* (Cambridge, MA: Harvard University Press, 2019), 136-7.

30 Greg Melleuish, *Cultural Liberalism in Australia* (Cambridge: Cambridge University Press, 1995), 28, 39-40.

31 Helen Irving, *To Constitute a Nation, A Cultural History of Australia's Constitution* (Cambridge: Cambridge University Press, 1997), 112-14.

32 Alfred Chandler, '*Fin de Siècle* Industrial Transformation', in Teich and Porter (eds), *Fin de Siècle and Its Legacy*, 28-29.

33 Bayly, *The Birth of the Modern World, 1780–1914*, 1.
34 Lake and Reynolds, *Drawing the Global Colour Line*, 6.
35 Jürgen Osterhammel and Nick P. Petersson, *Globalization, A Short History* (Princeton: Princeton University Press, 2005), 81, 84.
36 'Lord Kelvin (1824-1907)', https://digital.nls.uk/scientists/biographies/lord-kelvin/ (accessed 23 February 2021).
37 Marshall, *The Cambridge Companion to the Fin de Siècle*, 2.
38 Patrick Joyce, *Democratic Subjects, The Self and the Social in Nineteenth Century England* (Cambridge: Cambridge University Press, 1994), 154.
39 Andreas Killen, 'The Second Industrial Revolution', in Michael Saler (ed.), *The Fin de Siècle World*, 46–8.
40 West, *Fin de Siècle*, 96–7.
41 Rowbotham, *Rebel Crossings*, 5.
42 Joyce, *Democratic Subjects*, 153.
43 Ledger and Luckhurst, *The Fin de Siècle: A Reader*, xiii.
44 Mimmocchi, *Australian Symbolism: Art of Dreams*, 14–15, 92.
45 Charles Conder, *While Daylight Lingers*, National Gallery of Victoria, https://www.ngv.vic.gov.au/explore/collection/work/5283/ (accessed 23 July 2021).
46 Henry Lawson, 'The Bush Undertaker', in Paul Eggert (ed.), *While the Billy Boils, the Original Newspaper Versions* (Sydney: Sydney University Press, 2013), 85.
47 Marshall, *The Cambridge Companion to the Fin de Siècle*, 4–5.
48 'About the New Woman', *Daily Telegraph*, 18 February 1895, 5.
49 'The Twentieth Century Woman', *Evening News*, 19 June 1895, 7.
50 'The New Woman', *Ovens and Murray Advertiser*, 14 November 1903, 1.
51 Christopher Brennan, 'Symbolism in Nineteenth Century Literature', in A. R. Chisholm and J. J. Quinn (eds), *The Prose of Christopher Brennan* (Sydney: Angus and Robertson, 1960), 87.
52 Edward Said, *On Late Style* (London: Bloomsbury, 2006), 14.
53 Christopher Brennan, 'The Wanderer', in A. R. Chisholm and J. J. Quinn (eds), *The Verse of Christopher Brennan* (Sydney: Angus and Robertson, 1960), 165.
54 Judith Brett, *The Enigmatic Mr. Deakin* (Melbourne: Text Publishing, 2017), 7. For Deakin's life and spiritualism, see also John La Nauze, *Alfred Deakin, A Biography* (Melbourne: Melbourne University Press, 1965); Gabay, *The Mystic Life of Alfred Deakin*.
55 David Unaipon, *Legendary Tales of the Australian Aborigines*, Stephen Muecke and Adam Shoemaker (eds) (Melbourne: Miegunyah Press, 2001); John Alexander, 'Following David Unaipon's Footsteps', *Journal of Australian Studies*, 21, no. 54–5 (1997): 22–29. doi: 10.1080/14443059709387333.
56 Tim Rowse, 'Indigenous Heterogeneity', *Australian Historical Studies*, 45, no. 3 (2014): 299–300. doi: 10.1080/1031461X.2014.946523. See also Shino Konishi, 'First Nations Scholars, Settler Colonial Studies, and Indigenous

History', *Australian Historical Studies*, 50, no. 3 (2019): 285–304, doi: 10.1080/1031461X.2019.162030
57 Ledger and Luckhurst, *The Fin de Siècle: A Reader*, 221–2.
58 See Roe, *Beyond Belief*.
59 Matthew Beaumont, 'Socialism and Occultism at the *Fin de Siècle*: Elective Affinities', *Victorian Review*, 36, no. 1 (Spring 2010): 219, 230.
60 West, *Fin de Siècle*, 138.
61 Mike Jay and Michael Neve, *1900: A Fin de Siècle Reader* (Harmondsworth: Penguin Books, 1999), xii–xvii.
62 T. S. Eliot, 'Little Gidding', in *Four Quartets* (London: Faber and Faber, 2001), 42.

Chapter 1

1 *Sydney Mail*, 25 June 1892, 1442.
2 Lawson, 'The Bush Undertaker', 85.
3 *Australian Town and Country Journal*, 5 March 1892, 42.
4 *ATCJ*, 5 March 1892, 43.
5 Ibid., 9 January 1892, 18.
6 *Sydney Morning Herald*, 17 November 1892, 7.
7 *SM*, 18 June 1892, 1399.
8 Eric Hobsbawm, *The Age of Empire* (London: Abacus Books 2002), 34–6.
9 *Bourke Shire Aboriginal Heritage Study* (Bourke: Bourke Shire Council, 2019), 43; D. W. A. Baker, *The Civilised Surveyor, Thomas Mitchell and the Australian Aborigines* (Melbourne: Melbourne University Press, 1997); *SM*, 18 June 1892, 1399.
10 Killen, 'The Second Industrial Revolution', 46–7; Bayly, *The Birth of the Modern World, 1780–1914*, 451. For the second industrial revolution and the theme of economic acceleration in the period, see also Chandler, '*Fin de Siècle* Industrial Transformation'; James Belich, *Replenishing the Earth: The Settler Revolution and the Rise of the Angloworld* (Oxford: Oxford University Press, 2009).
11 Stephen Kern, 'Changing Concepts and Experiences of Time and Space', in Michael Saler (ed.), *The Fin de Siècle World*, 85.
12 Jürgen Osterhammel, *The Transformation of the World, A Global History of the Nineteenth Century* (Princeton: Princeton University Press, 2014), 78, 322.
13 Colin Roderick, *Henry Lawson, A Life* (Sydney: Angus and Robertson, 1991), 88–9.
14 Mark Hearn, 'A Wild Awakening: The 1893 Banking Crisis and the Theatrical Narratives of the Castlereagh Street Radicals', *Labour History*, 85 (2003): 154.
15 Roderick, *Henry Lawson, A Life*, 29–32; see also Brian Matthews, *Louisa* (Melbourne: McPhee Gribble, 1987).

16 Henry Lawson, *A Camp-Fire Yarn, Complete Works 1885–1900* (Dingley: Redwood Editions 2000), 39, 48.
17 Sylvia Lawson, *The Archibald Paradox: A Strange Case of Authorship* (Melbourne: Allen Lane 1983), 190–4.
18 Roderick, *Henry Lawson, A Life*, ch. 6, passim.
19 West, *Fin de Siècle*, 33–4, 104.
20 William Leiss, 'Technology and Degeneration: The Sublime Machine', in J. Edward Chamberlin and Sander L. Gilman (eds), *Degeneration, The Dark Side of Progress* (New York: Columbia University Press, 1985), 156.
21 Lawson, 'The Bush Undertaker', 77, 85.
22 Lawson, 'The Drover's Wife', *While the Billy Boils*, 71.
23 Ibid., 61.
24 Lawson, 'On the Edge of a Plain', *While the Billy Boils*, 110.
25 Mimmocchi, *Australian Symbolism: Art of Dreams*, 14–15, 92. For Conder's life and work, see also Ann Galbally and Barry Pearce, *Charles Conder* (Sydney: Art Gallery of New South Wales, 2003).
26 Bernard Smith (ed.), *Documents on Art and Taste in Australia, 1770–1914* (Melbourne: Oxford University Press, 1990), 202; A. B. Paterson, 'In Defence of the Bush', in Leon Cantrell (ed.), *Writing of the Eighteen Nineties* (St Lucia: University of Queensland Press, 1977), 154. See also Mark Horgan and Michael Sharkey, 'Vision Splendid or Sandy Blight? The Paterson-Lawson Debate', in Ken Stewart (ed.), *The 1890s, Australian Literature and Literary Culture* (St Lucia: University of Queensland Press, 1996), 66–94.
27 Ann Galbally, *Charles Conder, The Last Bohemian* (Melbourne: Melbourne University Publishing, 2002), 58.
28 Conder, *While Daylight Lingers*; *While Daylight Lingers* was formerly known as *Yarding Sheep*. See Jane Clark and Bridget Whitelaw, *Golden Summers, Heidelberg and Beyond* (Melbourne: International Cultural Corporation of Australia Ltd., 1985), 111.
29 Russel Ward, *The Australian Legend* (Melbourne: Oxford University Press, 1978), 34–5, 130, 296; Richard Nile, 'Tell Them That Henry Lawson Is Dead', in Richard Nile (ed.), *The Australian Legend and Its Discontents* (St Lucia: Queensland University Press, 2000), 95. A. G. Stephens, 'Henry Lawson: An Australian Poet', *Bulletin*, 5 January 1895, reprinted in Colin Roderick (ed.), *Henry Lawson, Criticism 1894–1971* (Sydney: Angus and Robertson, 1972), 3.
30 Kay Schaffer, *Women and the Bush, Forces of Desire in the Australian Cultural Tradition* (Melbourne: Cambridge University Press, 1988), 118.
31 Michael Wilding, 'Henry Lawson's Socialist Vision', in Michael Wilding (ed.), *Studies in Classic Australian Fiction* (Sydney: Sydney Studies, 1997), 32; Vance Palmer, *The Legend of the Nineties* (Carlton: Melbourne University Press, 1954).

32 Christopher Lee, *City Bushman, Henry Lawson and the Australian Imagination* (Fremantle: Curtin University Books, 2004), 233–4.
33 Graeme Davison, 'Sydney and the Bush: An Urban Context for the Australian Legend', *Australian Historical Studies*, 18, no. 71 (1978): 191–209.
34 Of commentators on Lawson's work only Colin Roderick seriously considered the non-fiction in interpreting Lawson's aims and creative output. A number of Lawson's non-fiction articles from the period 1887–99 are anthologized as 'social and political comment' in Henry Lawson, *Autobiographical and Other Writings, 1887–1922*, Colin Roderick (ed.) (Sydney: Angus and Robertson Ltd., 1972).
35 Henry Lawson, *A Fantasy of Man, Complete Works 1901–1922* (Dingley: Redwood Editions 2000), 92.
36 *SM*, 9 July 1892, 103; Ian McLean, *Why Australia Prospered* (Princeton: Princeton University Press 2013), 126.
37 *SM*, 4 June 1892, 1263.
38 *ATCJ*, 5 March 1892, 41; *Western Herald*, 1 October 1892, 2.
39 *SM*, 18 June 1892, 1399.
40 Ibid., 25 June 1892, 1474; 9 July 1892, 103.
41 *Western Champion*, 11 October 1892, 7.
42 *SM*, 4 June 1892, 1263; Richard Waterhouse, *The Vision Splendid, A Social and Cultural History of Rural Australia* (Fremantle: Curtin University Books, 2005), 83–5.
43 *SM*, 10 September 1892, 571.
44 *SMH*, 7 November 1892, 6.
45 Killen, 'The Second Industrial Revolution', 49–50.
46 Belich, *Replenishing the Earth*, ch. 4, 4.
47 *Hummer*, 30 July 1892, 3.
48 Ibid., 21 May 1892, 1.
49 *Western Herald*, 21 September 1892, 2.
50 *SMH*, 12 September 1892, 5. R. J. Solomon (ed.), *The Richest Lode: Broken Hill 1883–1988* (Sydney: Hale & Iremonger, 1988).
51 *Worker*, 26 November 1892, 2.
52 Mark Hearn and Harry Knowles, *One Big Union, A History of the Australian Workers Union, 1886–1994* (Melbourne: Cambridge University Press, 1996), 70.
53 R. B. Walker, *The Newspaper Press in New South Wales, 1803–1920* (Sydney: Sydney University Press 1976), 135.
54 *Worker* (Sydney), 1 October 1892, 1.
55 Roderick, *Henry Lawson, A Life*, 123–4.
56 Paul Eggert, *Biography of a Book, Henry Lawson's While the Billy Boils* (Sydney: Sydney University Press, 2013), 65.

57 Henry Lawson, 'The New Religion', in Henry Lawson (ed.), *Autobiographical and Other Writings* (Sydney: Angus and Robertson, 1972), 17–18.
58 Lawson, *The Archibald Paradox*, 179.
59 Marilyn Lake, 'The Politics of Respectability: Identifying the Masculinist Context', *Historical Studies*, 22, no. 86 (1986): 121, 125–6.
60 *Worker*, 10 June 1893, 2.
61 Lawson, 'Baldy Thompson', *While the Billy Boils*, 278.
62 Lawson, 'Stragglers', *While the Billy Boils*, 115.
63 *Worker*, 13 October 1894, 2.
64 Lawson, 'In a Dry Season', *While the Billy Boils*, 91.
65 Ibid.
66 Ibid., 92–3.
67 *SM*, 18 June 1892, 1399.
68 Ibid., 18 June 1892, 1399.
69 *Australian Star*, 18 February 1892, 6.
70 *Evening Journal* (Adelaide), 3 June 1892, 2.
71 *Western Herald*, 26 November 1892, 2.
72 *Hummer*, 18 June 1892, 2.
73 *SM*, 23 July 1892, 184.
74 Roderick, *Henry Lawson, A Life*, 93.
75 Henry Lawson, *Letters 1890–1922*, Colin Roderick (ed.) (Sydney: Angus and Robertson Ltd., 1970), 50–1.
76 Robyn Burrows and Alan Barton, *Henry Lawson, A Stranger on the Darling* (Sydney: Angus and Robertson 1996), 113–14.
77 *Western Herald*, 23 November 1892, 2.
78 Lawson, 'The Union Buries Its Dead', *While the Billy Boils*, 101.
79 Ibid., 103.
80 Ibid., 105.
81 Zita Denholm, 'Tyson, James (1819–1898)', *Australian Dictionary of Biography*, National Centre of Biography, Australian National University, http://adb.anu.edu.au/biography/tyson-james-985/text7923, published first in hardcopy 1976 (accessed 14 December 2018).
82 Lawson, 'The Union Buries Its Dead', *While the Billy Boils*, 106.
83 Eggert, *Biography of a Book*, 62–3.
84 *Worker*, 6 October 1894, 1.
85 *Hummer*, 16 January 1892, 1.
86 *Worker*, 27 October 1894, 4.
87 Lawson, 'Stragglers', *While the Billy Boils*, 115–16.
88 Ibid., 116.
89 *SMH*, 14 January 1892, 4.

90 Lawson, 'Stragglers', *While the Billy Boils*, 116.
91 Ibid., 117.
92 Leiss, 'Technology and Degeneration: The Sublime Machine', 153.
93 Lawson, 'Stragglers', *While the Billy Boils*, 117–18.
94 Ibid., 118.
95 Burrows and Barton, *Henry Lawson, A Stranger on the Darling*, 116.
96 Lawson, 'Mitchell: A Character Sketch', *While the Billy Boils*, 98–9.
97 Ibid., and 'Mitchell Doesn't Believe in the Sack', *While the Billy Boils*, 96, 112.
98 West, *Fin de Siècle*, 33–5.
99 *Worker*, 10 June 1893, 2.
100 West, *Fin de Siècle*, 122.
101 Ignatius Donnelly, *Caesar's Column* (Chicago: F. L. Schulte & Co., 1890).
102 Scates, *A New Australia*, 69–71.
103 *Hummer*, 13 February 1892, 2.
104 Ibid., 12 March 1892, 3.
105 *Worker*, 26 November 1892, 2.
106 *Hummer*, 6 August 1892, 4; *SM*, 16 July 1892, 136; *SMH*, 19 August 1892, 6.
107 *Hummer*, 17 September 1892, 2.
108 *SMH*, 13 July 1892, 5.
109 Ibid., 7 April 1892, 5; 19 November 1892, 9; Mark Hearn, 'Struggle amongst Strangers: The Anarchist Andrews in *Fin de Siècle* Sydney', *Journal of Australian Colonial History*, 14 (2012); Roderick, *Henry Lawson, A Life*, 102.
110 *Argus*, 26 May 1894, 6.
111 *Evening News*, 14 September 1894, 7.
112 Roderick, *Henry Lawson, A Life*, 100–1, 118.
113 *Worker*, 15 September 1894, 1.
114 Lawson, 'The Union Buries Its Dead', *While the Billy Boils*, 101.
115 Lawson, 'The Bush Undertaker', 75.
116 Ibid., 76.
117 Ibid., 74.
118 Ibid., 78.
119 Lawson, 'Hungerford', *While the Billy Boils*, 234–6; Burrows and Barton, *Henry Lawson, A Stranger on the Darling*, 213.
120 Lawson, 'In a Wet Season', *While the Billy Boils*, 208; Roderick, *Henry Lawson, A Life*, 97–8.
121 Lawson, 'In a Wet Season', *While the Billy Boils*, 203.
122 Ibid., 205.
123 Roderick, *Henry Lawson, A Life*, 86.
124 Lawson, *Letters 1890–1922*, 53.

Chapter 2

1. Rose Summerfield, 'Master and Man', address for the Australian Socialist League, 17 July 1892, published as a pamphlet by *The Hummer*, Wagga, 1892, 3. Public Domain. Available as a PDF download from 'Rose Summerfield (1864–1922)', https://www.reasoninrevolt.net.au/biogs/E000072b.htm.
2. 'About the New Woman', 5; for the Australian Socialist League and Leigh House, see Verity Burgmann, *In Our Time, Socialism and the Rise of Labor, 1885-1905* (Sydney: George Allen & Unwin, 1985), 49–50, 54.
3. Ledger, 'The New Woman and Feminist Fictions', 156.
4. Hearn, 'A Wild Awakening'.
5. Mark Hearn, 'Rose Summerfield's Gospel of Discontent: A Narrative of Radical Identity in Late Nineteenth Century Australia', *Labour History*, 87 (2004): 68.
6. Katie Spearritt, 'New Dawns, First Wave Feminism 1880-1914', in Kay Saunders and Raymond Evans (eds), *Gender Relations in Australia* (Sydney: Harcourt Brace Jovanovich, 1992), 325–6.
7. Summerfield, 'Master and Man', 3–4.
8. Scates, *A New Australia*, 55–6.
9. 'About the New Woman', 5.
10. Margarey, *Passions of the First Wave Feminists*, 42–3.
11. Angelique Richardson, 'Who Was the "New Woman"?' in Laura Marcus, Michèle Mendelssohn, and Kirsten E. Shepherd-Barr (eds), *Late Victorian into Modern* (Oxford: Oxford University Press 2016), 162.
12. 'Princess Theatre – A Doll's House', *Age*, 16 September 1889, 6. William Greenslade, 'Socialism and Radicalism', in Gail Marshall (ed.), *Cambridge Companion to the Fin de Siècle*, 80; Rachel Holmes, *Eleanor Marx* (London: Bloomsbury, 2015), 253–6.
13. 'Mrs. Mannington Caffyn', *Express and Telegraph* (Adelaide), 12 May 1894, 5.
14. Geulah Solomon, 'Caffyn, Stephen Mannington (1850–1896)', Australian Dictionary of Biography, National Centre of Biography, Australian National University, http://adb.anu.edu.au/biography/caffyn-stephen-mannington-3137/text4677, published first in hardcopy 1969.
15. 'Mr. Conder's Latest Exhibit', *Table Talk*, 23 August 1889, 4.
16. Ursula Hoff, *Charles Conder* (Melbourne: Landsdowne Press, 1972), 39.
17. Mimmocchi, *Australian Symbolism: Art of Dreams*, 91.
18. Richardson, 'Who Was the "New Woman"?', 166.
19. Hearn, 'Originally French but Afterwards Cosmopolitan', 377–8.
20. 'The New Woman', *Australian Star*, 25 December 1895, 8.
21. 'About the New Woman', 5.
22. Grimshaw et al., *Creating a Nation*, 172–3, 185–6.

23 'The Woman's Vote Craze', *Sydney Morning Herald*, 24 November 1893, 6; Margarey, *Passions of the First Wave Feminists*, 49.
24 'The Woman's Vote Craze', 6.
25 'Protection of Young Girls', *Daily Telegraph*, 28 November 1893, 3.
26 'Deputations to Ministers', *Maitland Daily Mercury*, 6 September 1894, 3.
27 Judith Allen, *Rose Scott, Vision and Revision in Feminism* (Melbourne: Oxford University Press, 1994), see chapter 3.
28 'Miss Rose Scott', *Worker*, 6 January 1894, 1.
29 Jan Roberts, *Maybanke Anderson, Sex, Suffrage and Social Reform* (Sydney: Ruskin Rowe Press, 1997), 69–71.
30 'Demos', *Hummer*, 18 June 1892, 1.
31 'Women Compositors', *Worker*, 26 November 1892, 2.
32 'Here and There', *Worker*, 8 October 1892, 2.
33 *Western Herald*, 21 September 1892, 4.
34 'Our Sister's Column', *Worker*, 8 October 1892, 2.
35 *Worker*, 8 October 1892, 6.
36 'Mrs. Rose Summerfield', *Western Herald*, 5 October 1892, 2.
37 'Here and There', 2.
38 'Mrs. Rose Summerfield', 2.
39 Summerfield, 'Master and Man', 6.
40 'The Workers' Union of NSW', *Gundagai Times*, 11 November 1892, 2.
41 Killen, 'The Second Industrial Revolution', 53–4.
42 'Sister's Column', *Worker*, 8 October 1892, 2.
43 'The Workers' Union of NSW', *Gundagai Times*, 11 November 1892, 2.
44 'Country Notes', *Goulburn Evening Penny Post*, 19 November 1892, 7.
45 'Laundry Work', *Western Herald*, 29 October 1892, 2.
46 'Bourke Branch GLU', *Worker*, 10 June 1893, 1.
47 'The Eight Hour Demonstration', *Western Herald*, 4 October 1893, 2.
48 Hearn, 'Rose Summerfield's Gospel of Discontent', 77–8.
49 'The Politician', *Worker*, 29 January 1898, 7.
50 Sheila Rowbotham, *Dreamers of a New Day, Women Who Invented the Twentieth Century* (London: Verso, 2011), 4–5.
51 'The New Woman', *Barrier Miner*, 8 September 1894, 2.
52 'Mrs. Besant's Autobiography', *Daily Telegraph*, 4 November 1893, 4. Anne Taylor, *Annie Besant* (Oxford: Oxford University Press, 1992), 241–5.
53 Mark Hearn, 'The Spirit of Inquiry and Unrest Is Everywhere: John Dwyer's *Fin de Siècle* Narrative of Transformation', *Journal of Australian Colonial History*, 18 (2016): 154–7; Roe, *Beyond Belief*, 109–10.
54 'The New Woman', *Barrier Miner*, 8 September 1894, 2.
55 'A Few Hours in Sydney Streets', *Worker* (Brisbane), 7 September 1895, 1.

56 'Stray Notes', *Worker*, 4 February 1899, 6.
57 See various reports *Worker*, 29 January 1898 1, 3; January 28 1899, 5.
58 Summerfield, 'Master and Man', 3.
59 'Social Democratic Federation', *Australian Workman*, 12 October 1895, 3.
60 'A Social Democratic Federation', *Daily Telegraph*, 4 February 1895, 6; Scates, *A New Australia*, 113.
61 'The New Australia Movement', *Worker*, 8 October 1892, 6.
62 'The New Australia Settlement', *Sydney Morning Herald*, 12 May 1894, 9.
63 Editorial, *Sydney Morning Herald*, 12 March 1894, 4.
64 'New Australia', *Worker*, 9 June 1894, 2.
65 'An Ideal Realized', *Worker*, 20 November 1897, 8.
66 'A Message to Workers', *Worker*, 29 January 1898, 5.
67 'Mrs. Cadogan on Flowers', *Worker*, 25 February 1899, 4.
68 'Stray Notes', *Worker*, 4 March 1899, 2.
69 'Social to Mrs. Cadogan', *Worker*, 1 April 1899, 5.
70 Kern, 'Changing Concepts and Experiences of Time and Space', 76.
71 Shearer West, 'The Visual Arts', in Gail Marshall (ed.), *The Cambridge Companion to the Fin de Siècle*, 140.
72 'The Voice of Toil', *Worker*, 25 March 1899, 7.
73 'Here and Now', *Worker*, 22 January 1898, 1; Gavin Souter, *A Peculiar People, The Australians in Paraguay* (Sydney: Sydney University Press, 1981), 122.
74 *Worker*, 23 November 1901, 1.
75 'A Few Hours in Sydney Streets', *Worker* (Brisbane), 7 September 1895, 1.
76 'Stray Notes', 2.
77 'This Earth Is the Lords', *Worker*, 31 October 1896, 8.
78 Richardson, 'Who Was the "New Woman"?', 150.
79 'Stray Notes', 6.

Chapter 3

1 Christopher Brennan, 'Twilights of the Gods and the Folk', in A. R. Chisholm and J. J. Quinn (eds), *The Verse of Christopher Brennan* (Sydney: Angus and Robertson, 1960), 151.
2 'Impressions of Sydney', *Brighton Southern Cross*, 26 July 1902, 4; 2 August 1902, 2.
3 'Those Plague Rats', *Australian Star*, 21 July 1902, 7.
4 'Draining the City', *Sydney Morning Herald*, 8 July 1902, 4; 'New Pyrmont Bridge', *Australian Town and Country Journal*, 5 July 1902, 6.
5 'The Illuminations', *Australian Star*, 11 July 1902, 3.

6 'Fog at the Heads', *Evening News*, 1 July 1902, 5.
7 Brennan, 'The Wanderer', 159.
8 *Hermes*, University of Sydney Undergraduate Association, The Jubilee Number, 1902, 65. State Library of New South Wales.
9 Christopher Brennan, 'Philosophy and Art', in A. R. Chisholm and J. J. Quinn (eds), *The Prose of Christopher Brennan* (Sydney: Angus and Robertson, 1960), 42, 45.
10 Brennan, 'Symbolism in Nineteenth Century Literature', 87.
11 Christopher Brennan, 'Curriculum Vitae', in Terry Sturm (ed.), *Christopher Brennan* (St. Lucia: University of Queensland Press, 1984), 162, 172.
12 Wallace Kirsop, 'Christopher Brennan's Reading', *Southerly*, 68, no. 3 (Autumn 2008): 234–5.
13 Axel Clark, *Christopher Brennan, A Critical Biography* (Melbourne: Melbourne University Press, 1980), 53.
14 Brennan, 'Curriculum Vitae', 177.
15 Clark, *Christopher Brennan*, 33–5.
16 Christopher Brennan, *Poems* (Sydney: G. B. Philip and Son, 1914).
17 'Impressions of Sydney', 4.
18 Clark, *Christopher Brennan*, 163–4.
19 James McAuley, *C.J. Brennan* (Melbourne: Oxford University Press, 1963); A. R. Chisholm, *A Study of Christopher Brennan's The Forest of the Night* (Melbourne: Melbourne University Press, 1970); Terry Sturm, 'The Structure of Brennan's *The Wanderer*', in Leon Cantrell (ed.), *Bards, Bohemians, & Bookmen* (St Lucia: University of Queensland Press, 1976); Dorothy Green, 'Towards the Source', *Southerly*, 37, no. 4 (1977): 363–81; G. A. Wilkes, 'Interpreting Brennan's Poetry; or, "The I of My Verses Is Not Necessarily Me"', *Southerly*, 37, no. 4 (1977): 421–6; Terry Sturm (ed.), *Christopher Brennan* (St Lucia: University of Queensland Press, 1984); Katherine Barnes, 'Christopher Brennan and the Religion of Symbolism', in Colette Rayment and Mark Levon Byrne (eds), *Seeking the Centre: 2001 Australian International Religion, Literature and the Arts Conference Proceedings* (Sydney: RLA Press, 2002); Veronica Brady, 'The Wanderer on the Way to the Self: Christopher Brennan', in Colette Rayment and Mark Levon Byrne (eds), *Seeking the Centre: 2001 Australian International Religion, Literature and the Arts Conference Proceedings* (Sydney: RLA Press, 2002); Katherine Barnes, *The Higher Self in Christopher Brennan's Poems* (Leiden and Boston: Brill, 2006); Henry Weinfeld, '"Thinking Out Afresh the Whole Poetic Problem": Brennan's Presience; Mallarmé's Accomplishment', *Southerly*, 68, no. 3 (Autumn 2008): 10–26; G. A. Wilkes, 'False Starts and Winding Ways: Christopher Brennan's "Vigil"', *Southerly*, 68, no. 3 (Autumn 2008): 81–107; Kirsop, 'Christopher Brennan's Reading', 229–43.

20 Frank Kermode, 'The European View of Christopher Brennan', *Australian Letters*, 3, no. 3 (March 1961): 57–63; Peter Kirkpatrick, '"*The Wanderer* and the Flâneur": Christopher Brennan as Modernist', *Southerly*, 63, no. 2 (Summer 2003): 63–77; Katherine Barnes, 'Hearths and Windows: Christopher Brennan's Interlude Poems and the Question of Modernism', *Southerly*, 68, no. 3 (Autumn 2008): 39–55; Michael Buhagiar, 'The Erotic Secret Heart of Christopher Brennan's *Poems 1913*', *Sydney Studies in English*, 38 (2012): 110–30.
21 Saler (ed.), *The Fin de Siècle World*, 3.
22 Greg Melleuish, 'The Master and the Disciples: A. R. Chisholm, Randolph Hughes and Carl Kaeppel on Christopher Brennan', *Journal of Australian Studies*, 32, no. 1 (March 2008): 112.
23 'Draining the City', 4; 'Hermes', *Evening News* (Sydney), 27 September 1902, 7.
24 'A Modern Hercules', *Western Mail* (Perth), 9 July 1902, 47.
25 'Sandow in Australia', *Sydney Morning Herald*, 15 July 1902, 7; 'Sandow Outrivalled', *World's News* (Sydney), 12 July 1902, 3.
26 Caroline Daley, 'The Strongman of Eugenics, Eugen Sandow', *Australian* (2002). *Historical Studies*, 33: 120, 236, 240.
27 'Draining the City', 4.
28 Clark, *Christopher Brennan*, 55, 70–1.
29 Paul Greenhalgh, 'The Style and the Age', in Paul Greenhalgh (ed.), *Art Nouveau 1890–1914*, 22.
30 Michael Gibson, *Symbolism* (Köln: Taschen, 2006), 31.
31 Gabriele Fahr-Becker, *Art Nouveau* (Potsdam: h.f.ullman publishing, 2010), 15.
32 Clark, *Christopher Brennan*, 70.
33 *Lone Hand*, 2 December 1907, 220; Martha Rutledge and Norman Cowper, 'McCrae, Hugh Raymond (1876–1958)', *Australian Dictionary of Biography*, National Centre of Biography, Australian National University, https://adb.anu.edu.au/biography/mccrae-hugh-raymond-7327/text12713, published first in hardcopy 1986 (accessed 14 August 2021).
34 *Lone Hand*, 1 August 1907, 448, 463. Frank Bongiorno, 'Bernard O'Dowd's Socialism', *Labour History*, No. 77 November 1999, 97–116.
35 Mimmocchi, *Australian Symbolism*, 25–6, 33.
36 Ibid., 110; 'Society of Artists Exhibition', *Daily Telegraph*, 2 October 1897, 10.
37 Radford, *Art Nouveau in Australia*, 18–22.
38 Mimmocchi, *Australian Symbolism*, 14–15, 90–2, 100, 105; Clark, *Christopher Brennan*, 83.
39 'Symbolism and the Stage', *Truth* (Sydney), 4 May 1902, 8.
40 'Symbolism in Nineteenth Century Literature', 87.
41 Clark, *Christopher Brennan*, 151.
42 Chisholm and Quinn, *The Verse of Christopher Brennan*, 66.

43 Clark, *Christopher Brennan*, 80–1, 108–9, 150–1.
44 Christopher Brennan, *Prose-Verse-Poster-Algebraic-Symbolico-Riddle Musicopoematographoscope; & Pocketmusicopoematographoscope* (Sydney: Hale and Iremonger, 1981).
45 Katherine E. Barnes 'With a Smile Barely Wrinkling the Surface: Christopher Brennan's Large *Musicopoematographoscope* and Mallarmé's *Un Coup de dés*', *Dix-Neuf*, 9, no. 1 (2007): 44. doi: 10.1179/147873107790725679.
46 Sturm, *Christopher Brennan*, xv.
47 Chisholm and Quinn, *The Verse of Christopher Brennan*, 169.
48 Ibid., 73.
49 Ibid., 52.
50 Edward Lucie-Smith, *Symbolist Art* (London: Thames and Hudson, 2001), 54–8.
51 'Stéphane Mallarmé', 312.
52 Sturm, *Christopher Brennan*, 436–7.
53 Elizabeth McCombie, 'Introduction', in Stéphane Mallarmé (ed.), *Collected Poems and Other Verse* (Oxford: Oxford University Press, 2006), xxv–xxvi.
54 'Another Australian Poet', *Freeman's Journal*, 14 August 1897, 18; Clark, 108.
55 Mimmocchi, *Australian Symbolism*, 111; Clark, *Christopher Brennan*, 146.
56 Clark, *Christopher Brennan*, 161–2.
57 Sturm, *Christopher Brennan*, 430.
58 *Australian Magazine*, 1, no. 2, 29 April 1899, 84–5, 93. State Library of New South Wales; Stephen Escritt, *Art Nouveau*, 115–24; Anke von Heyl, *Art Nouveau* (Königswinter: Tandem Verlag 2009), 167–9.
59 *Australian Magazine*, April 1899, 122–3.
60 'A New Literary Venture', *Illawarra Mercury*, 5 April 1899, 2; 'The Australian Magazine', *Daily Telegraph*, 22 August 1899, 3.
61 Vane Lindesay, 'Souter, David Henry (1862–1935)', *Australian Dictionary of Biography*, National Centre of Biography, Australian National University, http://adb.anu.edu.au/biography/souter-david-henry-8589/text14997, published first in hardcopy 1990 (accessed 1 May 2020).
62 'The University and Australian Literature', Chisholm and Quinn, *The Prose of Christopher Brennan*, 220.
63 Clark, *Christopher Brennan*, 181.
64 Chisholm and Quinn, *The Verse of Christopher Brennan*, 151.
65 Ibid., 165; Sturm, 'The Structure of Brennan's *The Wanderer*', 115–17.
66 Said, *On Late Style*, 24.
67 Chisholm and Quinn, *The Verse of Christopher Brennan*, 161; Peter Eisenman, 'Lateness: A Critique of the Metaphysics of Presence', *Thresholds*, 33, no. 11 (2007): 13.
68 Sturm, *Christopher Brennan*, 428.

69 Clark, *Christopher Brennan*, 185.
70 'Symbolism in Nineteenth Century Literature', 48–9; hereafter references to the lectures cited as Brennan, *Prose*.
71 Brennan, *Prose*, 53, 55; Charles Baudelaire, 'Correspondences', in *Flowers of Evil* (Oxford: Oxford University Press, 1998), 19. For a discussion of correspondences and 'moods' in Brennan's Symbolism lectures, see Katherine Barnes, 'Christopher Brennan and the Religion of Symbolism', in Rayment and Levon Byrne (eds), *Seeking the Centre*.
72 Brennan, *Prose*, 56, 60–1.
73 Lionel Lambourne, *The Aesthetic Movement* (London: Phaidon Press, 2011), 202–3.
74 Brennan, *Prose*, 63.
75 'To-day', *Sydney Morning Herald*, 15 June 1904, 9.
76 'News Summaries', *SMH*, 16 June 1904, 4.
77 'Symbolism in Literature', *Australian Star*, 16 June 1904, 2.
78 'Symbolism in Literature', *Daily Telegraph*, 16 June 1904, 7.
79 Brennan, *Prose*, 69–70; Max Nordau, *Degeneration* (1892; first English edition: London: William Heineman, 1895), 100.
80 Brennan, *Prose*, 74–6; Friedrich Nietzsche, *Twilight of the Idols* (Oxford: Oxford University Press, 1998), 8.
81 Brennan, *Prose*, 80–1.
82 Roe, *Nine Australian Progressives*, 1–3, 16.
83 Brennan, *Prose*, 83–4, 87.
84 Saler (ed.), *The Fin de Siècle World*, 3.
85 Lucie-Smith, *Symbolist Art*, 33–4; Gibson, *Symbolism*, 24.
86 Katherine Barnes, 'Christopher Brennan and the Religion of Symbolism', 113–14.
87 Brennan, *Prose*, 91, 105.
88 Ibid., 113–15.
89 Brennan, *Prose*, 108–9; Leo Damrosch, *Eternity's Sunrise, the Imaginative World of William Blake* (New Haven: Yale University Press, 2015), 155–7; William Vaughan, *William Blake* (London: Tate Publishing, 1999), 36.
90 Brennan, *Prose*, 97.
91 Buhagiar, 'The Erotic Secret Heart of Christopher Brennan's *Poems 1913*', 117.
92 'Poetic Literature', *Australian Star*, 30 June 1904, 2.
93 Christopher Brennan, 'Notes on German Literature, Symbolism, etc'. Sydney, Undated. Fisher Rare Books, University of Sydney Library.
94 Brennan, 'Notes on German Literature'; Edwin Ellis and W. B. Yeats, *The Works of William Blake: Poetic, Symbolic and Critical* (London: Bernard Quatrich 1893); see also George Bornstein, 'Yeats and Romanticism', in Majorie Howes and John Kelly (eds), *The Cambridge Companion to W. B. Yeats* (Cambridge: Cambridge University Press, 2007), 24–6.

95 Brennan, *Prose*, 105; W. B. Yeats, *Selected Poetry* (London: Pan Books, 1982), 33. For the importance of Yeats for Brennan and in particular *The Wind among the Reeds*, see Mary A. Merewether, 'Brennan and Yeats: An Historical Survey', *Southerly*, 37, no. 4 (1977): 398–9.

96 Brennan's 'Notes on German literature' pages are unnumbered. The Blake section was inscribed next to index pages at the back of the volume; the Yeats section begins on a blank page next to p. 149 of the Catalogue, and those adjacent page numbers are included in the citations below to provide some guidance.

97 Brennan, 'Notes on German Literature', 142.

98 Ibid., 138–9.

99 Ibid., 141.

100 Ibid., 91–2.

101 Ibid., 143–4.

102 Ibid., 135–6.

103 Ibid., 46–73; Peter Watson, *The Germans* (London: Simon and Schuster, 2010), 95–122.

104 Brennan, 'Notes on German Literature', 120–30; 'University Extension Lecture', *Australian Star*, 19 July 1904, 3.

105 Brennan, *Prose*, 136, 142–3.

106 Ibid., 153–5.

107 Ibid., 164–5.

108 Dorothy Green, *The Music of Love* (Melbourne: Penguin, 1984), 105.

109 Brennan, *Prose*, 67.

110 Clark, *Christopher Brennan*, 198–199; Ken Stewart, 'Stevens, Bertram William (Bert) (1872–1922)', *Australian Dictionary of Biography*, National Centre of Biography, Australian National University, http://adb.anu.edu.au/biography/stevens-bertram-william-bert-8651/text15127, published first in hardcopy 1990, accessed online 13 May 2020.

111 Brennan, *Prose*, 87.

112 Comment by Brennan in *Poems*, page unnumbered; Clark, *Christopher Brennan*.

113 'Some Books', *Lone Hand*, 1 April 1915, 334–5.

114 Barnes, *The Higher Self in Christopher Brennan's Poems*, 2–3.

115 Brady, 'The Wanderer on the Way to the Self', 252–3; Brennan, *Verse*, 165.

116 'The University and Australian Literature', Brennan, *Prose*, 224.

117 Ron Chernow, *The House of Morgan* (New York: Grove Press, 1990); Alice Teichova, 'A Legacy of *Fin de Siècle* Capitalism: The Giant Company', in Mikulas Teich and Roy Porter (eds), *Fin de Siècle and Its Legacy* (Cambridge: Cambridge University Press, 1990).

118 'THE WAR', *SMH*, 30 June 1904, 5, and 14 July 1904, 7.

119 Brennan, *Prose*, 68.

Chapter 4

1. 'Miss Goldstein at Prahran', *Argus*, 14 November 1903, 16.
2. 'Miss Vida Goldstein', *Advertiser* (Adelaide), 23 September 1903, 7.
3. 'The Coming Elections', *Argus*, 22 September 1903, 6.
4. Roe, 'Leading the World? 1901–1914'.
5. 'Women in Politics', *Advertiser*, 22 September 1903, 4.
6. Janette M. Bomford, *That Dangerous and Persuasive Woman, Vida Goldstein* (Carlton: Melbourne University Press, 1993), 10; C. R. Badger, 'Strong, Charles (1844–1942)', *Australian Dictionary of Biography*, National Centre of Biography, Australian National University, https://adb.anu.edu.au/biography/strong-charles-4658/text7697, published first in hardcopy 1976 (accessed 22 January 2021).
7. Bomford, *That Dangerous and Persuasive Woman*, 49–50; for Christian Science in Australia in the period, see Jill Roe, 'Testimonies from the Field: The Coming of Christian Science to Australia, c.1890–1910', *The Journal of Religious History*, 22, no. 3 (1998): 304–19.
8. 'Miss Vida Goldstein', *Table Talk*, 26 March 1903, 14; see also Jacqueline Kent, *Vida: A Woman for Our Time* (North Sydney: Penguin Random House Australia, 2020).
9. 'The International Woman Suffrage Conference', AWS, 10 April 1902, 164.
10. Hearn, 'Originally French but Afterwards Cosmopolitan', 375.
11. Ledger, 'The New Woman and Feminist Fictions', 154.
12. Showalter, *Sexual Anarchy*, 38.
13. Roberts, *Maybanke Anderson*, 134–6; Allen, *Rose Scott, Vision and Revision in Feminism*, 172–3, 198–201; Marian Quartly, 'Defending "The Purity of Home Life" against Socialism: The Founding Years of the Australian Women's National League', *Australian Journal of Politics and History*, 50, no. 2 (2004): 178–93.
14. Bomford, *That Dangerous and Persuasive Woman*, 19.
15. 'Our New Duties, and How to Fulfil Them', *Australian Woman's Sphere* (AWS), 10 June 1902, 176.
16. 'Town Talk', *Geelong Advertiser*, 14 September 1900, 2.
17. 'Miss Vida Goldstein', 7; 'American Prison Management', *Age*, 7 April 1903, 6.
18. 'A Bond of Union', *Advertiser*, 23 September 1903, 4.
19. 'Miss Vida Goldstein', 7.
20. Raelene Frances, 'Gender, Working Life and Federation', in Mark Hearn and Greg Patmore (eds), *Working the Nation, Working Life and Federation, 1890–1914* (Sydney: Pluto Press 2001), 38–9.
21. 'Sweating Women Teachers', *Advertiser*, 23 September 1903, 4.
22. 'National Council of Women', *Advertiser*, 23 September 1903, 7.
23. 'The World Moves', AWS, December 1900, 32.

24 Ibid., February 1901, 47.
25 Ibid., November 1900, 24.
26 'Abolishing War' *Advertiser*, 23 September 1903, 5.
27 'A Flag of Peace', *Advertiser*, 24 September 1903, 6. Philipp Blom, *The Vertigo Years, Change and Culture in the West, 1900–1914* (London: Phoenix Books, 2009), 196.
28 'Miss Vida Goldstein', 7.
29 'Comments', AWS, 10 October 1902, 209. For Goldstein's American visit, see also Lake, *Progressive New World*, ch. 5.
30 'The International Woman Suffrage Conference', 164; 'Miss Vida Goldstein', *Sydney Morning Herald*, 18 August 1902, 5.
31 Lake, *Progressive New World*, 3–5.
32 'Miss Vida Goldstein's Lecture Entertainment', *Table Talk*, 23 October 1902, 15.
33 'Miss Vida Goldstein', *Table Talk*, 30 October 1902, 6.
34 Peter Fritzsche, *Stranded in the Present* (Cambridge: Harvard University Press, 2004), 166–8.
35 'The Women's Federal Political Association', AWS, 10 September 1902, 343.
36 'Miss Goldstein's Candidature', AWS, 10 September 1902, 344.
37 'Miss Goldstein's Campaign', AWS, 10 October 1903, 357.
38 'The Senate Election', *Portland Guardian*, 14 October 1903, 3.
39 'Miss Vida Goldstein', *Ovens and Murray Advertiser* (Beechworth), 5 December 1903, 7.
40 West, *Fin de Siècle*, 96–7.
41 'Comment', AWS, 10 November 1903, 365.
42 AWS, 8 April 1903, 290.
43 'Miss Vida Goldstein', *Sydney Morning Herald*, 17 October 1903 11.
44 'Veni! Vida! Vici!' *Sunday Times* (Sydney), 9 August 1903, 3.
45 'The New Woman', 1.
46 Hearn, 'Originally French but Afterwards Cosmopolitan', 375.
47 Rowbotham, *Dreamers of a New Day*, 24–5.
48 'The Senate Election. Manifesto.' AWS, 10 October 1903, 360.
49 John Rickard, *H. B. Higgins, The Rebel as Judge* (Sydney: Allen and Unwin, 1984), 132–8.
50 'The Senate Election. Manifesto', AWS, 10 October 1903, 360.
51 Marilyn Lake, 'On Being a White Man: Australia, circa 1900', in Hsu-Ming Teo and Richard White (eds), *Cultural History in Australia* (Kensington: UNSW Press 2003), 98–112.
52 'The Woman's Rights Question'. *Bairnsdale Advertiser*, 21 November 1903, 3.
53 'Women in Politics', *Argus*, 14 October 1903, 6.
54 West, *Fin de Siècle*, 35.

55 'The Federal Elections', *Age*, 20 October 1903, 5.
56 'Miss Vida Goldstein', *Benalla Standard*, 1 December 1903, 2.
57 'The Senate Election', 3.
58 Rickard, *H. B. Higgins, The Rebel as Judge*, 137–8.
59 Sally Ledger, 'The New Woman and the Crisis of Victorianism', in Ledger and McCracken (eds), *Cultural Politics at the fin de siècle*, 38–41.
60 'Comment', *AWS*, 19 October 1902, 211.
61 Chandler, '*Fin de Siècle* Industrial Transformation', 28–9.
62 'The New Organisation', *AWS*, 10 December 1902, 238.
63 'Miss Goldstein at Prahran', *Argus*, 16.
64 Assmann, 'Transformations of the Modern Time Regime', 42–5.
65 Marshall, *The Cambridge Companion to the Fin de Siècle*, 4–5.
66 'Miss Goldstein's Candidature', *AWS*, 15 January 1904, 392–4.
67 'Present Position of candidates', *Age*, 18 December 1903, 5.
68 'The Women's Vote', *Age*, 17 December 1903, 5.
69 'Miss Vida Goldstein', *Australian Star*, 5 October 1904, 2.
70 Editorial, *Age*, 17 December 1903, 4.
71 'Views of Miss Goldstein', *Bendigo Advertiser*, 19 April 1901, 3.
72 'Defeated, but Still Victorious', *Woman Voter*, 3 June 1913, 1; 'Kooyong Election' *Woman Voter*, 22 September 1914, 1.
73 'Women's Political Association', *Woman Voter*, 10 June 1913, 4.
74 'More Sex Equality', *Punch*, 28 April 1910, 5.
75 'Kooyong Election', *Woman Voter*, 6 May 1913, 4.
76 'Australian Women's National League', *Age*, 7 March 1913, 7.
77 'Kooyong', *Age*, 16 May 1913, 10.
78 'Equal Pay for Equal Work', *Woman Voter*, 11 July 1912, 1.
79 Mark Hearn, 'Securing the Man: Narratives of Gender and Nation in the Verdicts of Henry Bournes Higgins', *Australian Historical Studies*, 127 (2006): 1–24.

Chapter 5

1 'Mr. Deakin's Condition', *Brisbane Courier*, 8 July 1907, 5; 'Personal', *Argus*, 8 July 1907, 7.
2 'About People', *Age*, 5 July 1907, 7.
3 Ibid., 6 July 1907, 13.
4 Ibid., 8 July 1907, 6.
5 'Mr. Deakin's Illness', *Argus*, 10 July 1907, 7.
6 *The Bhagavad Gita* (London: Penguin, 2008), 53.
7 'Mr. Deakin's Return to Melbourne', *Age*, 26 June, 7.

8 Alfred Deakin, *Diary*, 1907, Item 2/27, Alfred Deakin Papers, MS1540, Diaries Series 2, 1884–1916, National Library of Australia. Hereafter '*Deakin Diary*, 1907'.
9 'H.M.S. Powerful', *Age*, 29 June 1907, 8; 'About People', *Age*, 6 July 1907, 13.
10 Martha Rutledge, 'Fox, Sir Frank Ignatius (1874–1960)', Australian Dictionary of Biography, National Centre of Biography, Australian National University, https://adb.anu.edu.au/biography/fox-sir-frank-ignatius-6229/text10717, published first in hardcopy 1981 (accessed 28 January 2021).
11 La Nauze, *Alfred Deakin, A Biography*, 419–20.
12 'Federal Labor Caucus', *Age*, 3 July 1907, 7.
13 9, 16 and 17 April, *Deakin Diary*, 1907.
14 Patrick Joyce, *The Rule of Freedom* (London: Verso, 2003) 4.
15 'Australia's Prime Minister', *Townsville Daily Bulletin*, 23 August 1907, 4.
16 Eric Shiraev, 'Psychology and Psychiatry', in Michael Saler (ed.), *The Fin de Siècle World* (London: Routledge 2015), 477–8.
17 Killen, 'The Second Industrial Revolution', 46.
18 Editorial, *Age*, 25 June 1907, 4.
19 'Colonial Office. The Times Supports Mr Deakin', *Register* (Adelaide), Monday 26 August 1907, 5.
20 Greg Melleuish, 'Australian Liberalism', in J. R. Nethercote (ed.), *Liberalism and the Australian Federation* (Sydney: Federation Press, 2001), 34–5.
21 'Australia's Prime Minister', 4.
22 Mark Hearn, 'Compelled by the Circumstance of Our Time and Situation: Alfred Deakin's 1907 Defence Statement as Narrative of *Fin de Siècle* Acceleration', *History Australia*, 13, no. 4 (2016): 508–24. http://dx.doi.org/10.1080/14490854.2016.1249270.
23 John Jervis, 'The Modernity of the *Fin de Siècle*', 59.
24 Brett, *The Enigmatic Mr. Deakin*, 5.
25 Alfred Deakin Papers, MS1540, National Library of Australia.
26 Mark Hearn, 'A Transnational Imagination: Alfred Deakin's Reading Lists', in Desley Deacon, Penny Russell and Angela Woollacott (eds), *Transnational Ties: Australian Lives in the World* (Canberra: ANU E-Press, 2008).
27 'Series 3. Notebooks and general manuscripts, 1873-1917' MS1540 Deakin Papers, NLA.
28 Alfred Deakin, *Federated Australia, Selections from Letters to the Morning Post, 1900-1910*, John La Nauze (ed.) (Melbourne: Melbourne University Press, 1968), viii; La Nauze, *Alfred Deakin, A Biography*, 352.
29 'The Prime Minister at Home', *Lone Hand*, 2 September 1907, 501.
30 'List of Deakin's Books, Before Distribution', MS1540/4/692-721 Alfred Deakin Papers, NLA. La Nauze, *Alfred Deakin, A Biography*, 259–60.

31 Michael Saler, 'Introduction', 4–5.
32 The exactly one hundred books Deakin read in 1907 are listed in Alfred Deakin, *Diary*, 1907, Item 2/27, NLA.
33 Robert D. Richardson, *William James, In the Maelstrom of American Modernism* (New York: Houghton Mifflin, 2006), 485.
34 Roe, *Nine Australian Progressives*, 17–19; Hearn, 'A Transnational Imagination', 204, 207–8.
35 John La Nauze and Elizabeth Nurser (eds), *Walter Murdoch and Alfred Deakin on Books and Men, Letters and Comments 1900–1918* (Melbourne: Melbourne University Press, 1974), 31.
36 La Nauze, *Alfred Deakin, A Biography*, 90.
37 Remy de Gourmont, *Selected Writings* (Ann Arbor: University of Michigan Press, 1966), 179–181.
38 7 April, 21–22, 24 May, *Deakin Diary*, 1907; Margaret Macmillan, *Peacemakers* (London: John Murray, 2002), 37; Christopher Clark, *The Sleepwalkers, How Europe Went to War in 1914* (London: Penguin, 2013), 217; Sue Rowe, *In Montmartre, Picasso, Matisse and Modernism in Paris, 1900-1910* (London: Penguin 2014), 123.
39 Bogumila Zongollowicz, 'Wroblewski, Charles Adam Marie (1855–1936)', *Australian Dictionary of Biography*, National Centre of Biography, Australian National University, https://adb.anu.edu.au/biography/wroblewski-charles-adam-marie-13258/text4731 (accessed 30 November 2021); 'Alliance Française de Melbourne', https://stkildamelbourne.com.au/alliance-francaise-de-melbourne/ (accessed 30 November 2021).
40 'Marcel Crivelli', *The French Australian Dictionary of Biography*, https://www.isfar.org.au/bio/crivelli-marcel-1859-1948/ (accessed 30 November 2021).
41 'Fair Australian Women', *The Red Funnel*, 1 December 1906, 453–6, 492–6; *Henslowe's Annual* (Sydney: Henslowe Publishing Syndicate, 1903), 15, 38, 40–7.
42 Sylvia Lawson, 'Archibald, Jules François (1856–1919)', *Australian Dictionary of Biography*, National Centre of Biography, Australian National University, https://adb.anu.edu.au/biography/archibald-jules-francois-2896/text4155 (accessed 31 July 2021).
43 D. H. Souter, 'The Skirt Dancer', *Lone Hand*, 1 June 1907, 218; Stephen Escritt, *Art Nouveau* (London: Phaidon Press, 2000), 101–2.
44 *Lone Hand*, 1 May 1907, xxi.
45 La Nauze, *Alfred Deakin, A Biography*, 422.
46 'French Literature Today', *Lone Hand*, 1 May 1907, 42; 'Literary Life in Paris', *Lone Hand*, 1 June 1907, 140.
47 'The Paris Poor', *Lone Hand*, 1 July 1907, xlii.
48 'The Clerical Crisis in France', *Lone Hand*, 1 October 1907, 662; Vincent Cronin, *Paris on the Eve, 1900-1914* (London: Collins 1989), 203.

49 Emile Faguet, *L'Anticléricalisme* (Paris: Société Française D'imprimerie Et De Librairie, 1906), 2. https://www.gutenberg.org/files/42624/42624-h/42624-h.htm (accessed 10 August 2021).
50 Irving, *To Constitute a Nation*, 165-8.
51 Ruth Harris, *The Man on Devil's Island, Alfred Dreyfus and the Affair That Divided France* (London: Penguin, 2011), 218-23.
52 Faguet, *L'Anticléricalisme*, 326.
53 Harris, *The Man on Devil's Island*, 63-6.
54 Faguet, *L'Anticléricalisme*, 328.
55 Robert Gildea, *Children of the Revolution, The French 1799-1914* (London: Penguin, 2009), 421-31.
56 *Commonwealth Parliamentary Debates* (*CPD*), 13 December 1907, 7509.
57 Michael Newtown, 'Introduction', Joseph Conrad, *The Secret Agent* (London: Penguin 2007), xxi-xxii, 246.
58 'The Underground Man', *The Academy* (London), 69, no. 1750 (18 November 1905): 1202.
59 Javier Ortiz, 'Bernard Shaw's Ibsenisms', *Revista Alicantina de Estudios Ingleses*, 1 (1994): 151-8.
60 5 September, *Deakin Diary*, 1907.
61 Martha Banta, 'Men, Women, and the American Way', in Jonathan Freedman (ed.), *The Cambridge Companion to Henry James* (Cambridge: Cambridge University Press, 1998), 24, 28-9.
62 Mark Hearn, 'Industrial Defence against the Whole World: Deakinite New Protection as Narrative of Global Modernity', *Journal of Australian Studies*, 42, no. 3 (2018): 343-56, DOI:10.1080/14443058.2018.1485723.
63 'News of the Day', *Age*, 11 March 1907, 6.
64 Showalter, *Sexual Anarchy*, 48.
65 Hope Christiansen, 'Son(s) and Lovers: The Child as Narrative Linchpin in Marcelle Tinayre's *La Rebelle*', *Symposium: A Quarterly Journal in Modern Literatures*, 67, no. 3 (2013): 157-67. doi: 10.1080/00397709.2013.820055.
66 Gabay, *The Mystic Life of Alfred Deakin*, 82; La Nauze, *Alfred Deakin, A Biography*, 61-4; 'Mrs. Annie Besant', *Herald* (Melbourne), 24 June 1908, 3.
67 Gary Lachman, 'New Age *Fin de Siècle*', in Michael Saler (ed.), *The Fin de Siècle World*, 617.
68 William James, *Some Varieties of Religious Experience* (London Penguin, 1985), 64.
69 Jay and Neve, *1900: A Fin de Siècle Reader*, 113.
70 Richardson, *William James*, 261-2.
71 Saler, 'Introduction', 5.
72 Badger, 'Strong, Charles (1844-1942)' (accessed 10 February 2021).
73 'Clues' Notebook Vol. V 13 & 21 July 1907, MS1540/3/1/296-299 NLA.

74 Inscribed on a page for notes for the forthcoming February 1908. *Deakin Diary* 1907.
75 'The Prime Minister at Home', 501.
76 Editorial, *Times* (London), 17 May 1907, 5; for Milner, Adam Hochschild, *To End All Wars* (London: Macmillan, 2011), 22.
77 Editorial, *Argus*, 24 September 1907, 4; see also 'The Melbourne Welcome', *Age*, 26 June 1907, 7; 'Mr. Deakin Honoured', *Barrier Miner*, 8 July 1907, 2.
78 'The Prime Minister's Engagements', *Age*, 26 June 1907, 8.
79 'Mr. Deakin', *Herald* (Melbourne), 17 June 1907, 5.
80 Killen, 'The Second Industrial Revolution', 48–9.
81 La Nauze, *Alfred Deakin, A Biography*, 423.
82 'Federal Cabinet', *Sydney Morning Herald*, 31 July 1907, 9.
83 'Personal Element in Federal Politics', *Mercury* (Hobart) 2 September 1907, 4.
84 'Federal Politics', *West Australian*, 30 July 1907, 5.
85 'Federal Cabinet Mystery', 5.
86 'The Federal Cabinet', *Age*, 31 July 1907, 7.
87 'The Prime Minister', *Age*, 31 July 1907, 7.
88 'Federal Cabinet Mystery', *Register* (Adelaide), 30 July 1907, 5.
89 'Personal', *Brisbane Courier*, 20 August 1907, 7.
90 'Mr Deakin at Bundaberg', *Brisbane Courier*, 22 August 1907, 4; 'Mr Deakin at Bundaberg', *Brisbane Courier*, 23 August 1907, 4; 'Mr. Deakin's Health', *Examiner* (Launceston), Monday 26 August 1907, 5; 'Enquiry from Mr. Deakin', *Register* (Adelaide), 23 August 1907, 6.
91 'Personal Items', *Bulletin*, 31 October 1907, 18.
92 'Prime Minister's Visit', *Townsville Daily Bulletin*, 2 September 1907, 4, 5; 'Mr. Deakin's Health', *Examiner* (Launceston), 26 August 1907, 5.
93 L. F. Fitzhardinge, *William Morris Hughes: A Political Biography* (Sydney: Angus and Robertson, 1964), 191.
94 5, 17, 20–4 September; 3, 6–9, 13 October, *Deakin Diary* 1907.
95 'Personal', *Sydney Morning Herald*, 24 September 1907, 6.
96 'The Federal Letter' *Examiner* (Launceston), 24 September 1907, 5.
97 'The Prime Minister at Home', *Lone Hand*, 2 September 1907, 501.
98 'Deakin and the Spooks', *Truth* (Brisbane), 20 October 1907, 6.
99 'The Federal Outlook', *Sydney Morning Herald*, 25 September 1907, 8.
100 'The Federal Letter', 5.
101 'Political Uncertainty', in La Nauze, *Federated Australia*, 206.
102 'The Australian Navy', *Sydney Morning Herald*, 14 October 1907, 6.
103 'Federal Campaign', *Sydney Morning Herald*, 30 October 1903 7; for Deakin's attitude to the Indigenous, see *CPD*, 12 September 1901, 4805.
104 Laura Tabili, 'Race and Ethnicity' in Michael Saler (ed.), *The Fin de Siècle World*, 518–20.

105 Lake, 'On Being a White Man', 101.
106 *CPD*, 12 September 1901, 4804.
107 'Labour Conference and Compulsory Military Training', *The Call*, Australian National Defence League, August 1908, 21.
108 *CPD*, 13 December 1907, 7509–10.
109 Roy Hattersley, *The Edwardians* (London: Little, Brown, 2004), 91–2.
110 'Universal Military Training', *Times* (London), 17 May 1907, 4.
111 Ross Foreman, 'Empire', in Gail Marshall (ed.), *The Cambridge Companion to the Fin de Siecle*, 91–2; Walker, *Anxious Nation*.
112 'The Quarter' and 'Before and After Universal Service', *The Call*, November 1907, 2, 10.
113 The diary entries tally with the numbered sequence in the 1907 reading list – nos. 32, 34, 38 respectively. *Deakin Diary*, 1907.
114 Leo Tolstoy, *War and Peace* (London: Penguin, 2007), 837; Adam Zamoyski, *1812, Napoleon's Fatal March on Moscow* (London: Harper Perennial, 2005), 287.
115 Lachman, 'New Age *Fin de Siècle*', 621.
116 Laurie L. Patton, 'Introduction', in *The Bhagavad Gita* (London: Penguin 2008), vii–viii.
117 Taylor, *Annie Besant*, 278; La Nauze, *Alfred Deakin, A Biography*, 68.
118 Patton, 'Introduction', ix.
119 'Mr. Deakin. A Character Sketch', *Herald* (Melbourne), 17 June 1907, 5.
120 'The Prime Minister at Home', 503.
121 David Kahan, 'The Pathway to Reality', https://www.giffordlectures.org/lectures/pathway-reality (accessed 5 February 2021).
122 Brett, *The Enigmatic Mr. Deakin*, 350.
123 Imperial Conference April–May 1907 Minutes of Proceedings, printed 17 July 1907. Parliamentary Papers, Commonwealth of Australia Session 1907–8, Vol. III Reports of Conferences, 322, 396–8.
124 *Deakin Diary*, 20 April 1907.
125 'The Territorial Army. Mr. Haldane's Memorandum', *Times* (London), 9 April 1907, 5.
126 Clark, *The Sleepwalkers*, 166–7, 201–3; Niall Ferguson, *The Pity of War* (London: Penguin 1999), 102.
127 'Return of the Prime Minister', *Sydney Morning Herald*, 26 September 1907, 8.
128 Alfred Deakin, *Diary*, 1907, Alfred Deakin Papers, MS1540 Item 2/27-s152 Diaries Series 2, 1884–1916, National Library of Australia. https://nla.gov.au:443/tarkine/nla.obj-225823233.
129 Editorial, *Argus*, 14 December 1907, 18.
130 'Exclusion of Asiatics', *Sydney Morning Herald*, 14 December 1907, 13.
131 Osterhammel and Petersson, *Globalization, A Short History*, 81, 84.
132 Hearn, 'Industrial Defence', 344.

133 *CPD*, 13 December 1907, 7472.
134 Ibid., 7511–12, 7528.
135 Ibid., 7508.
136 'Race Suicide', *Sydney Morning Herald*, 12 August 1907, 7.
137 'The Polar Expedition' and 'An appeal to Australia', both *Sydney Morning Herald*, 14 December 1907, 13.
138 *CPD*, 13 December 1907, 7491.
139 'Mr. Deakin. A Character Sketch', *Herald* (Melbourne), 17 June 1907, 5.
140 La Nauze, *Alfred Deakin, A Biography*, 405.
141 *CPD*, 13 December 1907, 7463.
142 Ibid., 7472.
143 Ibid., 7510, 7527, 7528.
144 Ibid., 7491.
145 Ibid., 7535.
146 Ibid., 7509–10.
147 Ibid., 7525, 7534–5.
148 La Nauze, *Alfred Deakin, A Biography*, 514.
149 'The Colonial Premiers at Portsmouth', *Times* (London), 4 May 1907, 16.
150 *CPD*, 13 December 1907, 7511, 7524.

Chapter 6

1 'Black Genius', *Sun* (Sydney), 12 July 1914, 1.
2 'An Ingenious Aboriginal', *Advertiser* (Adelaide), 12 April 1907, 4.
3 Philip Jones, 'Unaipon, David (1872–1967)', *Australian Dictionary of Biography*, National Centre of Biography, Australian National University, http://adb.anu.edu.au/biography/unaipon-david-8898/text15631 (accessed 3 November 2018).
4 Ronald M. Berndt, *A World That Was: The Yaraldi of the Murray River and the Lakes, South Australia* (Melbourne: Melbourne University Press, 1993), 19; see also 'Aboriginal People of South Australia: Ngarrindjeri', State Library of South Australia, https://guides.slsa.sa.gov.au/c.php?g=410294&p=2795401 (accessed 10 March 2021).
5 Berndt, *A World That Was*, 294; see also 'Aboriginal Mission in South Australia: Point McLeay', https://guides.slsa.sa.gov.au/Aboriginal_Missions/PointMcLeay (accessed 19 February 2021).
6 Robert Foster and Amanda Nettlebeck, *Out of the Silence, The History and Memory of South Australia's Frontier Wars* (Kent Town: Wakefield Press, 2012), 104.
7 'Incorrigible Aborigines', *Register* (Adelaide), 18 September 1906, 4.

8   Mark Hearn, 'Cultivating an Australian Sentiment: John Christian Watson's Narrative of White Nationalism', *National Identities*, 9, no. 4 (2007): 360-1. DOI: 10.1080/14608940701737375.
9   *Sydney Mail*, cover illustration, 5 April 1911.
10 D. H. Souter, 'The Growth of Culture in Australia', *Lone Hand*, 1 May 1908, 111.
11 'Australia Felix', 117-20.
12 'Black Trackers', *Lone Hand*, 1 April 1908, 665.
13 'An Ingenious Aboriginal', 4.
14 'An Aboriginal Genius', *Daily Herald* (Adelaide), 1 June 1914, 9.
15 Helge Kragh, 'The New Physics', in Michael Saler (ed.), *The Fin de Siècle World* (London: Routledge 2015), 441.
16 Ledger and Luckhurst, *The Fin de Siècle: A Reader*, 221-2.
17 Konishi, 'First Nations Scholars, Settler Colonial Studies, and Indigenous History', 293.
18 'An Aboriginal Genius', 9.
19 Philip Jones, 'Unaipon, David (1872-1967)', *Australian Dictionary of Biography*.
20 'Intelligence of Australian Aborigines', *Register* (Adelaide), 9 July 1907, 6.
21 'Country Intelligence', *Southern Argus* (Port Elliott SA), 8 July 1909 3.
22 'Thy Touch Still Has Its Ancient Power', *Methodist*, 23 September 1911, 11.
23 Karen Trimmer, Graeme Gower and Graeme Lock, 'Reinventing Another Unaipon: Indigenous Science Leaders for the Future', *The Australian Journal of Indigenous Education*, 47, no. 2 (2017): 216-25. doi: 10.1017/jie.2017.14.
24 Alexander, 'Following David Unaipon's Footsteps'.
25 'Black Genius', 1.
26 'Australian Aboriginal Inventor', *Richmond River Herald* (NSW), 12 February 1915, 8.
27 'Black Genius', 1.
28 'Perpetual Motion Seekers', *Evening Journal* (Adelaide), 20 June 1903, 4.
29 'Perpetual Motion "Solved" Again', *Evening Journal* (Adelaide), 25 April 1903, 1.
30 'Gravitation and Repulsion', *Advertiser* (Adelaide), 21 January 1901, 4.
31 Kragh, 'The New Physics', 443-4.
32 Erwin N. Hiebert, 'The Transformation of Physics', in Mikulas Teich and Roy Porter (eds), *Fin de Siècle and Its Legacy* (Cambridge: Cambridge University Press), 245.
33 'Photographing the Invisible', *Register* (Adelaide), 30 November 1907, 8.
34 Alison Holland, *Breaking the Silence, Aboriginal Defenders and the Settler State, 1905-1939* (Melbourne: Melbourne University Press, 2019), 94.
35 Russell McGregor, *Imagined Destinies, Aboriginal Australians and the Doomed Race Theory, 1880-1939* (Melbourne: Melbourne University Press, 1997), 65-6, 69.
36 'An Aboriginal Genius', 9.

37 'News from Eden', *Express and Telegraph* (Adelaide), 28 July 1906, 4; For Basedow's Lemuria claims, see 'The Australian Aborigine', *Advertiser* (Adelaide), 22 July 1914, 18; 'Lost Continent of Lemuria', *Mail* (Adelaide), 19 April 1919, 2.
38 'Where Was Eden', *South Eastern Times*, 4 June 1909, 6; Nicholas Ruddick, 'The Fantastic Fiction of the *Fin de Siècle*', in Gail Marshall (ed.), *The Cambridge Companion to the Fin de Siècle*, 204; Roe, *Beyond Belief*, 76–9.
39 'An Aboriginal Genius', 9.
40 'Australian Aborigines, Laws, Customs and Traditions', *Ballarat Star*, 3 July 1914, 7.
41 McGregor, *Imagined Destinies*, 49.
42 Ibid., 53, 54–5, 58.
43 Karl Pearson, 'National Life: From the Standpoint of Science' (1901), in Jay and Neve, *1900: A Fin de Siècle Reader*, 38.
44 'The Aborigines', *Advertiser* (Adelaide), 12 September 1914, 14.
45 'Presbyterian Guild', *Geelong Advertiser*, 7 October 1914, 6.
46 Burrow, *The Crisis of Reason*, 46.
47 'Social', *Malvern News*, 15 August 1914, 2.
48 'Reflections in Christ Church', *Daylesford Advocate*, 31 July 1915, 3.
49 Ledger and Luckhurst, *The Fin de Siècle: A Reader in Cultural History*, 221–2; see also Burrow, *The Crisis of Reason*, 96–7; Edwin Ray Lankester, *Degeneration: A Chapter in Darwinism*, in Jay and Neve (eds), *1900: A Fin de Siècle Reader*, 15.
50 Vincent Lloyd, 'Christianity' in Michael Saler (ed.) *The Fin de Siècle World*, 577.
51 Burrow, *The Crisis of Reason*, 64.
52 'Reflections in Christ Church', 3.
53 Joyce, *The Rule of Freedom*, 102.
54 Maria Nugent, 'Aboriginal People and Their Children', in Michelle Hetherington (ed.), *Glorious Days, Australia 1913* (Canberra: National Museum of Australia Press, 2013), 89.
55 Irving, *To Constitute a Nation*, 112.
56 McGregor, *Imagined Destinies*, 69.
57 'Aborigines', *Register* (Adelaide), 24 December 1906, 4; G. H. Knibbs, *Official Year Book of the Commonwealth of Australia, 1901-1907* (Melbourne: Commonwealth Bureau of Census and Statistics, 1908), 148.
58 'A Dying Race', *Daily Herald*, 7 February 1913, 8.
59 Ibid., *Advertiser*, 19 July 1913, 6.
60 Ibid., *Daily Herald*, 7 February 1913, 8.
61 Paul Sendziuk and Robert Foster, *A History of South Australia* (Cambridge: Cambridge University Press, 2018), 102.
62 'Among the Natives', *Daily Herald*, 20 May 1911, 3.
63 *Progress Report of Aborigines Royal Commission, including Minutes of Evidence* (Adelaide: South Australian Government Printer 1913), 32–4, 37.

64 'Point McLeay Mission Station (1859-1974)', https://www.findandconnect.gov.au/ref/sa/biogs/SE01329b.htm (accessed 3 March 2021).
65 Progress Report of Aborigines Royal Commission, viii–ix.
66 Michel Foucault, 'Different Spaces', in Michel Foucault (ed.), *Aesthetics, Essential Works*, Vol. 2 (London: Penguin 2000), 177–8.
67 Joyce, *The Rule of Freedom*, 222.
68 'Rail and River Excursion', *Advertiser* (Adelaide), 22 December 1909, 2.
69 'Fifty Years at Point McLeay', *Advertiser* (Adelaide), 14 May 1909, 11.
70 Foucault, 'Different Spaces', 182.
71 'Aborigines for Tasmania', *Evening Journal* (Adelaide), 2 February 1910, 1.
72 Lyndall Ryan, *Tasmanian Aborigines: A History since 1803* (Sydney: Allen & Unwin, 2012, 270).
73 'The Hobart Carnival', *Mercury* (Hobart), 21 February 1910, 5.
74 Foucault, 'Different Spaces', 184.
75 'The Hobart Carnival', *Mercury* (Hobart), 21 February 1910, 5.
76 Murray Johnson and Ian McFarlane, *Van Dieman's Land, An Aboriginal History* (Sydney: UNSW Press, 2015), 36.
77 'The Hobart Carnival', *Mercury* (Hobart), 1 March 1910, 5.
78 James Cook, *The Journals* (London: Penguin Books, 2003), 446–7; Ryan, *Tasmanian Aborigines*, 40.
79 'The Hobart Carnival', *Mercury* (Hobart), 3 March 1910, 5.
80 Tabili, 'Race and Ethnicity', 518.
81 'The Aborigines at Richmond', *Mercury* (Hobart), 3 March 1910, 2.
82 'Church Notes', *Advertiser* (Adelaide), 19 August 1911, 22.
83 'Reflections in Christ Church', *Daylesford Advocate*, 31 July 1915, 3.
84 'Familiar Fallacies Refuted', *Daylesford Advocate*, 29 July 1915, 3.
85 'Black Genius', 1.

Chapter 7

1 Family correspondence, Dwyer papers ML MSS 290, box 2, State Library of New South Wales.
2 1906 list of Central Methodist Mission office bearers. *Our Weekly Greeting*, journal of the Sydney Central Methodist Mission, 15 September 1906, SLNSW.
3 John Dwyer, 'The Public Schools and Religion', November 1913, Dwyer papers ML MSS 2184/3; Minutes of the Social Democratic Federation, 10 October 1907, Dwyer papers ML MSS 2184/8 Item 6.
4 John Dwyer, 'Family History of John Dwyer from About 1770-1775', *c.* 1912, Dwyer papers ML MSS 290 box 1, 6.

5. Dwyer papers, ML MSS 2184 and ML MSS 290, SLNSW. An extensive range of material deposited by Dwyer is also scattered under various subject headings in the SLNSW Collection.
6. John Dwyer, 'The Book of Notes and Observations on the Occult Subjects', 1897, Dwyer papers, ML MSS 2184/3, item 1, 33.
7. West, *Fin de Siècle*, 104.
8. Roe, *Beyond Belief*, 18, 20.
9. Colin Haydon, 'I Love My King and My Country, but a Roman Catholic I Hate': Anti-Catholicism, Xenophobia and National Identity in Eighteenth-Century England', in Tony Claydon and Ian McBride (eds), *Protestantism and National Identity, Britain and Ireland, c.1650-c.1850* (Cambridge: Cambridge University Press 1998), 52.
10. Mark Hearn, 'John Dwyer's London Stories', *Labour History*, 109 (2015): 25–40.
11. 'Family History of John Dwyer', 2.
12. Ibid., 21.
13. Lilian Lewis Shiman, *Crusade against Drink in Victorian England* (London: Macmillan 1988); Dwyer to Grand Chief Templar (NSW), IOGT, 4 March 1890, general correspondence, Dwyer papers, ML MSS290.
14. Hearn, 'A Wild Awakening', 153–71.
15. 'Babylon the Great', anon., Dwyer papers ML MSS 2184/1.
16. Dwyer papers, ML MSS 2184/3 'Occult Writings'. For Praed's interest in spiritualism, see Patricia Clarke, *Rosa! Rosa! A Life of Rosa Praed, Novelist and Spiritualist* (Carlton: Melbourne University Press), 1999; Kay Ferres, 'Rosa Praed and Spiritualism', *Australian Cultural History*, 23 (2004): 7–23.
17. Roe, *Beyond Belief*, xii.
18. Taylor, *Annie Besant*, 224.
19. Dwyer papers, ML MSS 2184/3 'Occult Writings'.
20. 'Karma and Reincarnation', *Theosophical Society in Australasia, Tracts*, SLNSW. All the pamphlets in this bound volume are stamped 'John Dwyer'.
21. Dwyer papers, ML MSS 2184/3 'Occult Writings'.
22. 'Winged Seed', *Theosophical Society in Australasia, Tracts*. Dwyer deposit in SLNSW.
23. Taylor, *Annie Besant*, 227–9.
24. West, *Fin de Siècle*, 115–16.
25. 'Family History of John Dwyer', p. 1; John Dwyer, Seamen's Discharge Certificates, re service on SS *Monowai*; all items in Dwyer papers ML MSS 290 box 1.
26. 'Family History of John Dwyer', 17.
27. Annie Dwyer to John Dwyer, 17 July 1893, 'family correspondence', Dwyer papers ML MSS 290 box 2.
28. Annie Dwyer to John Dwyer, undated, 'family correspondence'.

29 Ellen Ross, 'Labour and Love: Rediscovering London's Working Class Mothers, 1870-1918', in Jane Lewis (ed.), *Labour and Love, Women's Experience of Home and Family, 1850-1940* (London: Basil Blackwell, 1986), 74–85.
30 Annie Dwyer to John Dwyer, 3 August 1893, 'family correspondence'.
31 Ibid., 8 December 1893, 'family correspondence'.
32 Ibid., 23 December 1893, 'family correspondence'.
33 Ibid., 3 August 1893, 'family correspondence'.
34 Ibid., 17 July 1893 'family correspondence'.
35 Ibid., 17 July 1893, 'family correspondence'.
36 Ibid., 23 December 1893, 'family correspondence'.
37 *Australian Star*, 13 June 1894.
38 'Tommy Dodd and Company', *Evening News*, 14 June 1894, 5.
39 'The Libel on Mr. Slattery, M.P.', *Daily Telegraph*, 14 June 1894, 6.
40 Annie Dwyer to John Dwyer, 24 July 1894. Dwyer papers ML MSS 290.
41 Ibid., 15 July.
42 Ibid., 24 July.
43 Ibid., 2 December.
44 Ibid., 15 and 17 July, 29 August.
45 Ibid., 24 July, 29 August and 12 October.
46 Ibid., 24 July.
47 Ibid., 15 and 24 July, 31 August.
48 Annie Dwyer to John Dwyer, 12 October.
49 Lizzie Dwyer to John Dwyer, 29 August and 12 October.
50 Minutes of the 1st Annual Convention of the Theosophical Society in Australasia, 11 December 1895, 10, pamphlet stamped 'John Dwyer', Theosophical Society in Australasia, Tracts, 212/T. Mitchell Collection, SLNSW. Dwyer is also listed as a Lodge member in the Isis Lodge charter, issued 16 December 1897. Dwyer papers, ML MSS 290.
51 'The Anarchist', a collection of manuscript notes, printed matter, cartoons and two Active Service Brigade leaflets, 1896–7. C497 SLNSW.
52 Hearn, 'Struggle amongst Strangers', 155, 179.
53 Dwyer, 'The Book of Notes and Observations', 3–4, 62, 65–6.
54 John Dwyer, 'The Book of Notes and Observations on the Occult Subjects', Dwyer papers, ML MSS 2184/3, item 1, 2.
55 Burrow, *The Crisis of Reason*, 92.
56 Henry Maudsley, *Pathology of Mind* (extract) in Jay and Neve, *1900: A Fin de siècle Reader*, 8. For Draper, see Peter Gay, *The Cultivation of Hatred* (London: Fontana Press, 1995), 38.
57 Cherry Gilchrist, *Theosophy, The Wisdom of the Ages* (New York: HarperCollins 1996) 3.
58 John Dwyer, 'What Is a State?' notes *c.* 1895 in ML MSS 2183/3, item 3, p. 1.

59 John Dwyer, *Diary*, 1903-4, 1914, Dwyer papers ML MSS 290.
60 Appeal for 'John Dwyer's Shelter for the Relief of the Temporarily Necessitous', March 1903, Dwyer papers ML MSS 2184/7.
61 Elizabeth Dwyer to John Dwyer, 31 January 1906, Dwyer papers family correspondence ML MSS 290.
62 'Family History of John Dwyer', c. 1912, Dwyer papers MSS 290.
63 'Note re birthdays'; clipping from the *Sun*, 14 August 1910, Dwyer papers ML MSS 290.
64 Timm Dwyer to John Dwyer, October 1910, Dwyer papers family correspondence ML MSS 290.
65 Daniel Dwyer to John Dwyer from Harden, c. 1910, Dwyer papers family correspondence ML MSS 290.
66 Reverend P. J. Stephen, 'Among the Evangelists', in *Evangelism and Social Regeneration*, 24th anniversary souvenir booklet, Sydney Central Methodist Mission, 1908, 9. SLNSW.
67 Sydney Central Methodist Mission Annual report for 1907, 41 SLNSW. For the mission's activities, see also Richard Broome, *Treasure in Earthen Vessels, Protestant Christianity in New South Wales, 1900-1914*, (St Lucia: University of Queensland Press, 1980), 42–3.
68 Reverend P. J. Stephen, 'Among the Evangelists'.
69 Daniel Dwyer to John Dwyer, 30 September 1908, family correspondence ML MSS 290.
70 Broome, *Treasure in Earthen Vessels*, 46–8.
71 Daniel Dwyer to John Dwyer from Harden, c. 1910, Dwyer papers family correspondence ML MSS 290.
72 'Family History of John Dwyer', c. 1912, Dwyer papers ML MSS 290.
73 Gault to Dwyer, 4 November 1913, Dwyer papers family correspondence ML MSS 290.
74 F. B. Smith, *The Retreat of Tuberculosis, 1850-1950* (London: Croom Helm 1988), 97; Arthur Gault, 'The Present Position of the Sanatorium Treatment in Australasia', in *Transactions of the Australasian Medical Congress*, Adelaide September 1905, South Australian Government Printer 1905, 33. SLNSW.
75 J. S. C. Elkington, 'Tuberculosis and Australia', *Lone Hand*, 1 May 1909, 90.
76 John Powles, 'Keeping the Doctor Away', *Making a Life, A People's History of Australia since 1788* (Melbourne: McPhee Gribble/Penguin, 1988), 75.
77 *Commonwealth Department of Trade and Customs, Report on Tuberculosis*, 1916, 15, SLNSW.
78 F. S. V. Zlotowski, 'Tuberculosis, Its History, Causation and the Means to be Employed to Prevent Its Spread', in *Sanitary Inspectors Association of New South Wales, Official Report of Lectures and Proceedings of the First Annual Conference, 1912*, 71. SLNSW.

79 M. McIntyre Sinclair, 'The Prognosis of Pulmonary Tuberculosis', in *Transactions of the Australasian Medical Congress*, Adelaide September 1905, South Australian Government Printer 1905, 38.
80 Marius Turda, 'Biology and Eugenics', in Michael Saler (ed.) *The Fin de Siècle World*, 456–60; Mark Hearn, 'Great Progress and Evolution': The 1911 Australasian Medical Congress and *Fin de Siècle* Nation Building in Australia', *Journal of the Royal Australian Historical Society*, 103, Part 1 (2017): 61–79.
81 'Presidential Address', *Sydney Morning Herald*, 19 September 1911, 5; Hearn, 'Great Progress and Evolution', 71–3.
82 'Local Government', *Sydney Morning Herald*, 12 March 1914, 7.
83 Dr W. G. Armstrong, 'Powers and Duties of Sanitary Inspectors', in *Sanitary Inspectors Association of New South Wales, Official Report of Lectures and Proceedings of the first annual conference, 1912*, 71, 34–5. SLNSW.
84 Telegram to John Dwyer, 21 September 1908; Daniel Dwyer to John Dwyer, 30 September 1908, Dwyer papers family correspondence ML MSS 290.
85 Ibid.; Annie Dwyer to John Dwyer, September 1908, ibid.
86 Robin Walker, 'The Struggle against Pulmonary Tuberculosis in Australia, 1788-1950', *Historical Studies*, 20 (1983): 449.
87 'Amy B' to Annie Dwyer, 18 February 1914, 'family correspondence'.
88 Annie Dwyer to John Dwyer, 21 February 1914, 'family correspondence'.
89 Ibid., 25, 26 and 27 February 1914, 'family correspondence'.
90 Ibid., 25 February 1914, 'family correspondence'.
91 Dwyer papers, ML MSS 290.
92 Daniel Dwyer to John Dwyer, 14 January 1914, 'family correspondence'.
93 'Consumption, the State Health Policy', *Sydney Morning Herald*, 1 May 1914, 7; Bede Nairn, 'Flowers, Fred (1864–1928)', *Australian Dictionary of Biography*, National Centre of Biography, Australian National University, https://adb.anu.edu.au/biography/flowers-fred-6198/text10651 (accessed 12 February 2021).
94 John Dwyer to Lomas, 19 February 1914, 'family correspondence'.
95 Official notice from the Waterfall Sanatorium, Hospital and Asylum for the Infirm, New South Wales, to John Dwyer, 6 March 1914, 'family correspondence'.
96 Daniel Dwyer to John Dwyer, 'family correspondence'.
97 'Fighting Consumption', *Daily Telegraph*, 25 June 1914, 6; clipping in ML MSS 290.
98 Death certificate for Daniel John Dwyer, 18 June 1916, NSW Registrar of Births, Deaths and Marriages; 'Family History of John Dwyer', p. 15.
99 F. B. Smith, *The Retreat of Tuberculosis, 1850-1950*, 47–9, ch. 3.
100 *Commonwealth Department of Trade and Customs, Report on Tuberculosis*, 1916, 9, 153.
101 *National Association for the Prevention and Cure of Consumption, First Annual Report, 1914*, SLNSW.

102 Gault, 'The Present Position of the Sanatorium Treatment in Australasia', 33; *Commonwealth Department of Trade and Customs, Report on Tuberculosis*, 1916, 27–8.
103 *Commonwealth Department of Trade and Customs, Report on Tuberculosis*, 1916, 8; Robin Walker, 'The Struggle against Pulmonary Tuberculosis in Australia, 1788-1950', 452.
104 *Commonwealth Department of Trade and Customs, Report on Tuberculosis*, 1916, 4–5.
105 Ibid., 1916, 19.
106 Daniel Dwyer to John Dwyer from Wingham, *c.* 1910, 'family correspondence'.
107 *Diary*, 10 May 1914, Dwyer papers ML MSS 290.
108 West, *Fin de Siècle*, 104.
109 Ledger and Luckhurst, *The Fin de Siècle: A Reader*, 221–2.

Conclusion

1 Hoff, *Charles Conder*, 103; Barry Pearce, 'Between Worlds: Conder in Australia', in Galbally and Pearce (eds), *Charles Conder* (Sydney: Art Gallery of New South Wales, 2003), 26.
2 'The National Gallery of Australia Acquires a Lost Icon of Australian Art', 29 June 2006 https://nga.gov.au/aboutus/press/ConderAquisition.cfm (accessed 23 July 2021).
3 John Rothenstein, *Life and Death of Conder* (London: J.M. Dent and Sons, 1938), 30.
4 Holbrook Jackson, *The Eighteen Nineties* (London: The Cresset Library, 1988), 331–2.
5 'CONDER COMES HOME AGAIN', *Home*, 1 August 1927, 54. SLNSW.
6 William Moore, *The Story of Australian Art*, Vol. 1 (Sydney: Angus and Robertson Ltd., 1934), xix–xx.
7 Rothenstein, *Life and Death of Conder*, xviii.
8 Merlin Holland and Rupert Hart-Davis, *The Complete Letters of Oscar Wilde* (London: Fourth Estate, 2000), 1060; Ann Galbally, 'Charles Conder: A *Fin de Siècle* Enigma', in Galbally and Pearce (ed.), *Charles Conder* (Sydney: Art Gallery of New South Wales, 2003), 43.
9 Hayden White, 'The Burden of History', in Hayden White (ed.), *Tropics of Discourse, Essays in Cultural Criticism* (Baltimore: Johns Hopkins University Press 1985), 50.
10 'Australian Poetry', *Sydney Morning Herald*, 30 November 1918, 8.
11 John Jervis, 'The Modernity of the *Fin de Siècle*', 73.
12 Melleuish, *Cultural Liberalism in Australia*, 47–8.
13 'Dr. Mannix', *Sydney Morning Herald*, 7 December 1917, 8.

14 Joan Beaumont, *Broken Nation, Australians in the Great War* (Sydney: Allen & Unwin, 2013), 235.
15 Pam McLean, 'War and Australian Society', in Joan Beaumont (ed.), *Australia's War, 1914–1918* (Sydney: Allen and Unwin, 1995), 82–3.
16 'Anti-Conscription', *Mercury* (Hobart), 10 December 1917, 3.
17 'Women's Peace Delegation to Europe', *Woman Voter*, 1 May 1919, 2.
18 'The Bachelor Woman', *Weekly Times* (Melbourne), 24 June 1922, 54.
19 Bomford, *That Dangerous and Persuasive Woman*, 206.
20 'Women's Viewpoint', *Argus*, 22 August 1949, 6.
21 'Remember Pioneers', *Argus*, 23 August 1949, 2.
22 La Nauze, *Alfred Deakin, A Biography*, 637.
23 Editorial, *Age*, 8 October 1919, 8.
24 Editorial, *Argus*, 8 October 1919, 14.
25 La Nauze, *Alfred Deakin, A Biography*, 625.
26 Paul Strangio, 'Who Were Australia's Best Prime Ministers? We Asked the Experts', *The Conversation*, 2 August 2021. https://theconversation.com/who-were-australias-best-prime-ministers-we-asked-the-experts-165302 (accessed 2 August 2021). See also Bob Birrell, *Federation: The Secret Story* (Sydney: Duffy & Snellgrove, 2001); Alan Fenna, 'Putting the Australian Settlement in Perspective', *Labour History* 102 (May 2012): 99–118; Ian Marsh, 'The Federation Decade', in J. R. Nethercote (ed.), *Liberalism and the Australian Federation* (Sydney: Federation Press, 2001), 69–97; Roe, 'Leading the World? 1901–1914'; Sawer, *The Ethical State?*.
27 Beaumont, *Broken Nation*, 44–6.
28 Mark Hearn, 'Citizen Dwyer', in Hearn & Patmore (eds), *Working the Nation* (Sydney: Pluto Press, 2001), 264–81.
29 'Holman Joins Wade', *Australian Worker*, 16 November 1916, 22.
30 Hearn, 'Rose Summerfield's Gospel of Discontent', 79; Souter, *A Peculiar People*, 229–31.
31 'Death of Rose Summerfield' *Worker* (Brisbane), 3 August 1922, 18.
32 Death certificate for Annie Matilda Dwyer, 14 June 1954, NSW Registrar of Births, Deaths and Marriages.
33 Death certificate for John Dwyer, 1 February 1934, NSW Registrar of Births, Deaths and Marriages.
34 John Dwyer, 'The Book of Notes and Observations on the Occult Subjects', 1897, Dwyer Papers, ML MSS 2184/3, item 1, pp. 40–1.
35 'Australian Verse', *Sydney Morning Herald*, 6 March 1915, 8.
36 Clark, *Christopher Brennan*, 250–70.
37 'Obituary', *Sydney Morning Herald*, 6 October 1932, 10.
38 'C. J. Brennan', *Sydney Morning Herald*, 15 October 1932, 9.

39 'Chris Brennan Dead', *Catholic Press*, 13 October 1932, 17.
40 'The Late Christopher John Brennan', *Advocate* (Melbourne), 13 October 1932, 5.
41 Hilary M. Carey, 'The Land of Byamee: K. Langloh Parker, David Unaipon, and Popular Aboriginality in the Assimilation Era', *The Journal of Religious History*, 22, no. 2 (1998): 200–18.
42 'A Black "Wolsely"', *Worker* (Brisbane), 30 July 1914, 13.
43 Unaipon, *Legendary Tales of the Australian Aborigines*, xii.
44 Jeanine Leane, 'Biography: David Unaipon', *Australian Quarterly*, 86, no. 1 (January–March 2015): 28–30, 36.
45 https://banknotes.rba.gov.au/australias-banknotes/people-on-the-banknotes/david-unaipon/ (accessed 15 March 2021).
46 Lawson, *A Camp-Fire Yarn*, 39.
47 Lawson, *A Fantasy of Man*, 615.
48 'Henry Lawson's War Songs', *Freeman's Journal*, 16 September 1915, 9.
49 Roderick, *Henry Lawson*, 393–4.
50 'Henry Lawson. Death Announced', *Sydney Morning Herald*, 4 September 1922, 8.
51 'Henry Lawson', *Sydney Morning Herald*, 29 July 1931, 10.
52 'Mr. Lang to Move', *Sydney Morning Herald*, 29 July 1931, 10; 'Sydney Domain Demonstration', *Australian Worker*, 29 July 1931, 7.
53 'Henry Lawson', *Sydney Morning Herald*, 29 July 1931, 10.

Bibliography

Note: Please see the Endnotes for details of primary sources cited.

John Alexander, 'Following David Unaipon's Footsteps', *Journal of Australian Studies*, 21 (1997): 54–55, 22–29. DOI: 10.1080/14443059709387333.

Judith Allen, *Rose Scott, Vision and Revision in Feminism*, Melbourne: Oxford University Press, 1994.

Aleida Assmann, 'Transformations of the Modern Time Regime', in Berber Bevernage and Chris Lorenz (eds), *Breaking Up Time: Negotiating the Borders between Present, Past and Future*, Göttingen: Vandenhoeck & Ruprecht, 2013.

Alan Atkinson, *The Europeans in Australia, Vol. 3: Nation*, Sydney: NewSouth Publishing, 2014.

Katherine Barnes, *The Higher Self in Christopher Brennan's Poems*, Leiden and Boston: Brill, 2006.

Alison Bashford and Catie Gilchrist, 'The Colonial History of the 1905 Aliens Act', *The Journal of Imperial and Commonwealth History*, 40, no. 3 (2012): 423, 427. DOI:10.1080/03086534.2012.712380

Christopher Bayly, *The Birth of the Modern World, 1780–1914*, Oxford: Blackwell Publishing, 2004.

Joan Beaumont, *Broken Nation, Australians in the Great War*, Sydney: Allen & Unwin, 2013.

Matthew Beaumont, 'Socialism and Occultism at the *Fin de Siècle*: Elective Affinities', *Victorian Review*, 36, no. 1 (Spring 2010): 217–232.

James Belich, *Replenishing the Earth: The Settler Revolution and the Rise of the Angloworld*, Oxford: Oxford University Press, 2009.

Melissa Bellanta, 'Rethinking the 1890s', in Alison Bashford and Stuart Macintyre (eds), *The Cambridge History of Australia*, vol.1, Melbourne: Cambridge University Press, 2013.

Alexis Bergantz, *French Connection: Australia's Cosmopolitan Ambitions*, Sydney: NewSouth Publishing, 2021.

Ronald M. Berndt, *A World That Was: The Yaraldi of the Murray River and the Lakes, South Australia*, Melbourne: Melbourne University Press, 1993.

Bob Birrell, *Federation: The Secret Story*, Sydney: Duffy & Snellgrove, 2001.

Philipp Blom, *The Vertigo Years, Change and Culture in the West, 1900–1914*, London: Phoenix Books, 2009.

Janette M. Bomford, *That Dangerous and Persuasive Woman, Vida Goldstein*, Carlton: Melbourne University Press, 1993.
Frank Bongiorno, 'Bernard O'Dowd's Socialism', *Labour History*, 77 (1999): 97–116.
Frank Bongiorno, 'A Short History of New Thought in Australia, 1890–1914', *Australian Cultural History*, 23 (2004): 25–42.
Judith Brett, *The Enigmatic Mr. Deakin*, Melbourne: Text Publishing, 2017.
Asa Briggs and Daniel Snowman (eds), *Fins de Siècle: How Centuries End, 1400–2000*, New Haven: Yale University Press, 1996.
Richard Broome, *Treasure in Earthen Vessels, Protestant Christianity in New South Wales, 1900–1914*, St Lucia: University of Queensland Press, 1980.
Verity Burgmann, *In Our Time, Socialism and the Rise of Labor, 1885–1905*, Sydney: George Allen & Unwin, 1985.
Robyn Burrows and Alan Barton, *Henry Lawson, A Stranger on the Darling*, Sydney: Angus and Robertson, 1996.
J. W. Burrow, *The Crisis of Reason: European Thought, 1848–1914*, New Haven: Yale University Press, 2000.
Leon Cantrell (ed.), *Bards, Bohemians, & Bookmen*, St Lucia: University of Queensland Press, 1976.
Leon Cantrell (ed.), *Writing of the Eighteen Nineties*, St Lucia: University of Queensland Press, 1977.
Hilary M. Carey, 'The Land of Byamee: K. Langloh Parker, David Unaipon, and Popular Aboriginality in the Assimilation Era', *The Journal of Religious History*, 22, no. 2 (1998): 200–218.
J. Edward Chamberlin and Sander L. Gilman (eds), *Degeneration, the Dark Side of Progress*, New York: Columbia University Press, 1985.
Ron Chernow, *The House of Morgan*, New York: Grove Press, 1990.
A. R. Chisholm and J. J. Quinn, *The Prose of Christopher Brennan*, Sydney: Angus and Robertson, 1960.
A. R. Chisholm and J. J. Quinn, *The Verse of Christopher Brennan*, Sydney: Angus and Robertson, 1960).
Axel Clark, *Christopher Brennan, a Critical Biography*, Melbourne: Melbourne University Press, 1980.
Christopher Clark, *The Sleepwalkers, How Europe Went to War in 1914*, London: Penguin, 2013.
Jane Clark and Bridget Whitelaw, *Golden Summers, Heidelberg and Beyond*, Melbourne: International Cultural Corporation of Australia Ltd., 1985.
Patricia Clarke, *Rosa! Rosa! A Life of Rosa Praed, Novelist and Spiritualist*, Carlton: Melbourne University Press.
William Coleman (ed.), *Only in Australia, The History, Politics, and Economics of Australian Exceptionalism*, Melbourne: Oxford University Press, 2016.
Vincent Cronin, *Paris on the Eve, 1900–1914*, London: Collins, 1989.

Caroline Daley, 'The Strongman of Eugenics, Eugen Sandow', *Australian Historical Studies*, 33 (2002): 120.
Jessica M. Dandona, *Nature and the Nation in Fin-de-Siècle France, The Art of Emile Gallé and the Ecole de Nancy*, London: Routledge, 2017.
Graeme Davison, 'Sydney and the Bush: An Urban Context for the Australian Legend', *Australian Historical Studies*, 18, no. 71 (1978): 191–209.
Alfred Deakin, *Federated Australia, Selections from Letters to the Morning Post, 1900–1910*, edited by John La Nauze, Melbourne: Melbourne University Press, 1968.
John Docker, *The Nervous Nineties: Australian Cultural Life in the 1890s*, Melbourne: Oxford University Press, 1991.
Paul Eggert, *Biography of a Book, Henry Lawson's While the Billy Boils*, Sydney: Sydney University Press, 2013.
Peter Eisenman, 'Lateness: A Critique of the Metaphysics of Presence', *Thresholds*, 33 (2007).
T. S. Eliot, *Four Quartets*, London: Faber and Faber, 2001.
Stephen Escritt, *Art Nouveau*, London: Phaidon Press, 2000.
Gabriele Fahr-Becker, *Art Nouveau*, Potsdam: h.f.ullman publishing, 2010.
Kay Ferres, 'Rosa Praed and Spiritualism', *Australian Cultural History*, 23 (2004): 7–23.
L. F. Fitzhardinge, *William Morris Hughes: A Political Biography*, Sydney: Angus and Robertson, 1964.
Robert Foster and Amanda Nettlebeck, *Out of the Silence, the History and Memory of South Australia's Frontier Wars*, Kent Town: Wakefield Press, 2012.
R. F. Foster, *Vivid Faces, The Revolutionary Generation in Ireland, 1890–1923*, London: Penguin, 2015.
Jonathan Freedman (ed.), *The Cambridge Companion to Henry James*, Cambridge: Cambridge University Press, 1998.
Peter Fritzsche, *Stranded in the Present*, Cambridge: Harvard University Press, 2004.
Michel Foucault, *Aesthetics, Essential Works*, Vol. 2, London: Penguin, 2000.
Al Gabay, *The Mystic Life of Alfred Deakin*, Melbourne: Cambridge University Press, 1992.
Ann Galbally, *Charles Conder, the Last Bohemian*, Melbourne: Melbourne University Publishing, 2002.
Ann Galbally and Barry Pearce, *Charles Conder*, Sydney: Art Gallery of New South Wales, 2003.
Peter Gay, *The Cultivation of Hatred*, London: Fontana Press, 1995.
Michael Gibson, *Symbolism*, Köln: Taschen, 2006.
Robert Gildea, *Children of the Revolution, The French 1799–1914*, London: Penguin, 2009.
Paul Greenhalgh, ed., *Art Nouveau 1890–1914*, London: V&A Publications, 2000.
Patricia Grimshaw, Marilyn Lake, Ann McGrath and Marian Quartly, *Creating a Nation*, Melbourne: Penguin Books, 1996.

Ruth Harris, *The Man on Devil's Island, Alfred Dreyfus and the Affair that Divided France*, London: Penguin, 2011.

Roy Hattersley, *The Edwardians*, London: Little, Brown, 2004.

Mark Hearn and Harry Knowles, *One Big Union, a History of the Australian Workers Union, 1886–1994*, Melbourne: Cambridge University Press, 1996.

Mark Hearn and Greg Patmore (eds), *Working the Nation, Working Life and Federation, 1890–1914*, Sydney: Pluto Press, 2001.

Mark Hearn, 'A Wild Awakening: The 1893 Banking Crisis and the Theatrical Narratives of the Castlereagh Street Radicals', *Labour History*, 85 (2003): 153–172.

Mark Hearn, 'Rose Summerfield's Gospel of Discontent: A Narrative of Radical Identity in Late Nineteenth Century Australia', *Labour History*, 87 (2004): 65–82.

Mark Hearn, 'Securing the Man: Narratives of Gender and Nation in the Verdicts of Henry Bournes Higgins', *Australian Historical Studies*, 127 (2006): 1–24.

Mark Hearn, 'Cultivating an Australian Sentiment: John Christian Watson's Narrative of White Nationalism', *National Identities*, 9, no. 4 (2007). doi: 10.1080/14608940701737375.

Mark Hearn, 'A Transnational Imagination: Alfred Deakin's Reading Lists', in Desley Deacon, Penny Russell and Angela Woollacott (eds), *Transnational Ties: Australian Lives in the World*, 197–211, Canberra: ANU E-Press, 2008.

Mark Hearn, 'Struggle Amongst Strangers: The Anarchist Andrews in *Fin de Siècle* Sydney', *Journal of Australian Colonial History*, 1 (2012): 14.

Mark Hearn, 'John Dwyer's London Stories', *Labour History*, 109 (2015): 25–40.

Mark Hearn, 'Compelled by the Circumstance of Our Time and Situation: Alfred Deakin's 1907 Defence Statement as Narrative of *Fin de Siècle* Acceleration', *History Australia*, 13, no. 4 (2016): 508–524. http://dx.doi.org/10.1080/14490854.2016.1249270

Mark Hearn, 'The Spirit of Inquiry and Unrest Is Everywhere: John Dwyer's *Fin de Siècle* Narrative of Transformation', *Journal of Australian Colonial History*, 18 (2016): 139–160.

Mark Hearn, '"Great Progress and Evolution": The 1911 Australasian Medical Congress and *Fin de Siècle* Nation Building in Australia', *Journal of the Royal Australian Historical Society*, 103, Part 1 (2017): 61–79.

Mark Hearn, 'Industrial Defence against the Whole World: Deakinite New Protection as Narrative of Global Modernity', *Journal of Australian Studies*, 42, no. 3 (2018): 343–356, DOI:10.1080/14443058.2018.1485723

Mark Hearn, 'Originally French but Afterwards Cosmopolitan: Australians Interpret the *Fin de Siècle*', *Journal of Australian Studies*, 43, no. 3 (2019): 365–380. DOI:10.1080/14443058.2019.1643391

Mark Hearn, 'Restoring Order in "The Present Scare": The Bridge Street Affray in *Fin de Siècle* Sydney', *Journal of the Royal Australian Historical Society*, 107, Part 1 (2021): 52–74.

Michelle Hetherington (ed.), *Glorious Days, Australia 1913*, Canberra: National Museum of Australia Press, 2013.

Eric Hobsbawm, *The Age of Empire*, London: Abacus Books, 2002.
Ursula Hoff, *Charles Conder*, Melbourne: Landsdowne Press, 1972.
Alison Holland, *Breaking the Silence, Aboriginal Defenders and the Settler State, 1905–1939*, Melbourne: Melbourne University Press, 2019.
Merlin Holland and Rupert Hart-Davis, *The Complete Letters of Oscar Wilde*, London: Fourth Estate, 2000.
Rachel Holmes, *Eleanor Marx*, London: Bloomsbury, 2015.
Helen Irving, *To Constitute a Nation, A Cultural History of Australia's Constitution*, Cambridge: Cambridge University Press, 1997.
Holbrook Jackson, *The Eighteen Nineties*, London: The Cresset Library, 1988.
Mike Jay and Michael Neve, *1900: A Fin de Siècle Reader*, Harmondsworth: Penguin Books, 1999.
Murray Johnson and Ian McFarlane, *Van Dieman's Land, An Aboriginal History*, Sydney: UNSW Press, 2015.
Patrick Joyce, *Democratic Subjects, the Self and the Social in Nineteenth Century England*, Cambridge: Cambridge University Press, 1994.
Patrick Joyce, *The Rule of Freedom*, London: Verso, 2003.
Jacqueline Kent, *Vida: A Woman for Our Time*, North Sydney: Penguin Random House Australia, 2020.
Stephen Kern, *The Culture of Time and Space 1880–1918*, Cambridge, MA: Harvard University Press, 1983.
Wallace Kirsop, 'Christopher Brennan's Reading', *Southerly*, 68, no. 3 (Autumn 2008): 229–243.
Shino Konishi, 'First Nations Scholars, Settler Colonial Studies, and Indigenous History', *Australian Historical Studies*, 50, no. 3 (2019): 285–304, DOI:10.1080/1031461X.2019.162030.
Reinhart Koselleck, *The Practice of Conceptual History*, Stanford: Stanford University Press, 2002.
Reinhart Koselleck, *Sediments of Time: On Possible Histories*, Sean Franzel, and Stefan-Ludwig Hoffmann (eds), Stanford: Stanford University Press, 2018.
Lionel Lambourne, *The Aesthetic Movement*, London: Phaidon Press, 2011.
Marilyn Lake, 'The Politics of Respectability: Identifying the Masculinist Context', *Historical Studies*, 22, no. 86 (1986): 116–131.
Marilyn Lake, 'On Being a White Man: Australia, Circa 1900', in Hsu-Ming Teo and Richard White (eds), *Cultural History in Australia*, 98–112, Kensington: UNSW Press, 2003.
Marilyn Lake and Henry Reynolds, *Drawing the Global Colour Line, White Men's Countries and the Question of Racial Equality*, Melbourne: Melbourne University Press, 2008.
Marilyn Lake, *Progressive New World, How Settler Colonialism and Transpacific Exchange Shaped American Reform*, Cambridge, MA: Harvard University Press, 2019.

John La Nauze, *Alfred Deakin, a Biography*, Melbourne: Melbourne University Press, 1965.

Henry Lawson, *Letters 1890–1922*, Colin Roderick (ed.), Sydney: Angus and Robertson Ltd., 1970.

Henry Lawson, *Autobiographical and Other Writings, 1887–1922*, Colin Roderick (ed.), Sydney: Angus and Robertson Ltd., 1972.

Henry Lawson, *A Camp-Fire Yarn, Complete Works 1885–1900*, Dingley: Redwood Editions, 2000.

Henry Lawson, *A Fantasy of Man, Complete Works 1901–1922*, Dingley: Redwood Editions, 2000.

Henry Lawson, *While the Billy Boils, the Original Newspaper Versions*, Paul Eggert (ed.), Sydney: Sydney University Press, 2013.

Jeanine Leane, 'Biography: David Unaipon', *Australian Quarterly*, 86, no. 1 (January–March 2015): 28–30.

Sally Ledger and Scott McCracken (eds), *Cultural Politics at the Fin de Siècle*, Cambridge: Cambridge University Press, 1995.

Sally Ledger and Roger Luckhurst, *The Fin de Siècle: A Reader in Cultural History*, Oxford: Oxford University Press, 2000.

Christopher Lee, *City Bushman, Henry Lawson and the Australian Imagination*, Fremantle: Curtin University Books, 2004.

Edward Lucie-Smith, *Symbolist Art*, London: Thames and Hudson, 2001.

Laura Marcus, Michèle Mendelssohn, and Kirsten E. Shepherd-Barr (eds), *Late Victorian into Modern*, Oxford: Oxford University Press, 2016.

Susan Magarey, Sue Rowley, and Susan Sheridan (eds), *Debutante Nation: Feminism Contests the 1890s*, St Leonards: Allen & Unwin, 1993.

Susan Margarey, *Passions of the First Wave Feminists*, Kensington: University of New South Wales Press, 2001.

Gail Marshall, ed., *The Cambridge Companion to the Fin de Siècle*, Cambridge: Cambridge University Press, 2007.

Brian Matthews, *Louisa*, Melbourne: McPhee Gribble, 1987.

Russell McGregor, *Imagined Destinies, Aboriginal Australians and the Doomed Race Theory, 1880–1939*, Melbourne: Melbourne University Press, 1997.

Ian McLean, *Why Australia Prospered*, Princeton: Princeton University Press, 2013.

Pam McLean, 'War and Australian Society', in Joan Beaumont (ed.), *Australia's War, 1914–1918*, Sydney: Allen and Unwin, 1995.

Greg Melleuish, *Cultural Liberalism in Australia*, Cambridge: Cambridge University Press, 1995.

Greg Melleuish, 'The Master and the Disciples: A. R. Chisholm, Randolph Hughes and Carl Kaeppel on Christopher Brennan', *Journal of Australian Studies*, 32, no. 1 (March 2008): 103–114.

Denise Mimmocchi, *Australian Symbolism: Art of Dreams*, Sydney: Art Gallery of NSW, 2012.

J. R. Nethercote (ed.), *Liberalism and the Australian Federation*, Sydney: Federation Press, 2001.

Richard Nile (ed.), *The Australian Legend and Its Discontents*, St Lucia: Queensland University Press, 2000.

Maria Nugent, 'Aboriginal People and Their Children', in Michelle Hetherington (ed.), *Glorious Days, Australia 1913*, Canberra: National Museum of Australia Press, 1913.

Deaglan Ó Donghaile, *Oscar Wilde and the Radical Politics of the Fin De Siècle*, Edinburgh: Edinburgh University Press, 2020.

Jürgen Osterhammel and Nick P. Petersson, *Globalization, a Short History*, Princeton: Princeton University Press, 2005.

Jürgen Osterhammel, *The Transformation of the World, a Global History of the Nineteenth Century*, Princeton: Princeton University Press, 2014.

Vance Palmer, *The Legend of the Nineties*, Carlton: Melbourne University Press, 1954.

Matthew Potolsky, 'Fin de Siècle', *Victorian Literature and Culture*, 46, no. 3–4 (2018): 697–700. DOI: https://doi.org/10.1017/S1060150318000591.

Marian Quartly, 'Defending "the Purity of Home Life" against Socialism: The Founding Years of the Australian Women's National League', *Australian Journal of Politics and History*, 50, no. 2 (2004): 178–193.

Ron Radford, *Art Nouveau in Australia*, Canberra: Australia Council and Art Gallery Directors Council, 1980.

Robert D. Richardson, *William James, In the Maelstrom of American Modernism*, New York: Houghton Mifflin, 2006.

John Rickard, *H. B. Higgins, The Rebel as Judge*, Sydney: Allen and Unwin, 1984.

Jan Roberts, *Maybanke Anderson, Sex, Suffrage and Social Reform*, Sydney: Ruskin Rowe Press, 1997.

Colin Roderick, *Henry Lawson, A Life*, Sydney: Angus and Robertson, 1991.

Jill Roe (ed.), *Social Policy in Australia*, Sydney: Cassell Australia, 1976.

Jill Roe, *Beyond Belief: Theosophy in Australia, 1879–1939*, Kensington: University of New South Wales Press, 1986.

Jill Roe, 'Testimonies from the Field: The Coming of Christian Science to Australia, c.1890–1910', *The Journal of Religious History*, 22, no. 3 (1998): 304–319.

Michael Roe, *Nine Australian Progressives: Vitalism in Bourgeois Social Thought, 1890–1960*, St Lucia: University of Queensland Press, 1984.

John Rothenstein, *Life and Death of Conder*, London: J.M. Dent and Sons, 1938.

Sheila Rowbotham, *Edward Carpenter, A Life of Liberty and Love*, London: Verso, 2008.

Sheila Rowbotham, *Dreamers of a New Day, Women Who Invented the Twentieth Century*, London: Verso, 2011.

Sheila Rowbotham, *Rebel Crossings, New Women, Free Lovers, and Radicals in Britain and the United States*, London: Verso, 2016.

Tim Rowse, 'Indigenous Heterogeneity', *Australian Historical Studies*, 45, no. 3 (2014): 297–310. DOI: 10.1080/1031461X.2014.946523.

Lyndall Ryan, *Tasmanian Aborigines: A History since 1803*, Sydney: Allen & Unwin, 2012.
Edward Said, *On Late Style*, London: Bloomsbury, 2006.
Michael Saler (ed.), *The Fin de Siècle World*, London: Routledge, 2015.
Marian Sawer, *The Ethical State? Social Liberalism in Australia*, Melbourne: Melbourne University Press, 2003.
Bruce Scates, *A New Australia: Citizenship, Radicalism and the First Republic*, Melbourne: Cambridge University Press, 1997.
Kay Schaffer, *Women and the Bush, Forces of Desire in the Australian Cultural Tradition*, Melbourne: Cambridge University Press, 1988.
Carl Schorske, *Fin de Siècle Vienna*, New York: Vintage Books, 1981.
Paul Sendziuk and Robert Foster, *A History of South Australia*, Cambridge: Cambridge University Press, 2018.
Elaine Showalter, *Sexual Anarchy: Gender and Culture at the Fin de Siècle*, London: Virago, 1992.
Bernard Smith (ed.), *Documents on Art and Taste in Australia, 1770–1914*, Melbourne: Oxford University Press, 1990.
F. B. Smith, *The Retreat of Tuberculosis, 1850–1950*, London: Croom Helm, 1988.
Gavin Souter, *A Peculiar People, The Australians in Paraguay*, Sydney: Sydney University Press, 1981.
Ken Stewart (ed.), *The 1890s, Australian Literature and Literary Culture*, St Lucia: University of Queensland Press, 1996.
Anne Taylor, *Annie Besant*, Oxford: Oxford University Press, 1992.
Terry Sturm (ed.), *Christopher Brennan*, St Lucia: University of Queensland Press, 1984.
R. J. Solomon, (ed.)., *The Richest Lode: Broken Hill 1883–1988*, Sydney: Hale & Iremonger, 1988.
Mikulas Teich and Roy Porter (eds), *Fin de Siècle and Its Legacy*, Cambridge: Cambridge University Press, 1990.
Karen Trimmer, Graeme Gower and Graeme Lock, 'Reinventing Another Unaipon: Indigenous Science Leaders for the Future', *The Australian Journal of Indigenous Education*, 47, no. 2 (2017): 216–225 DOI: 10.1017/jie.2017.14
David Unaipon, *Legendary Tales of the Australian Aborigines*, Stephen Muecke and Adam Shoemaker (eds), Melbourne: Miegunyah Press, 2001.
David Walker, *Anxious Nation: Australia and the Rise of Asia, 1850–1939*, St Lucia: University of Queensland Press, 1999.
R. B. Walker, *The Newspaper Press in New South Wales, 1803–1920*, Sydney: Sydney University Press, 1976.
R. B. Walker 'The Struggle against Pulmonary Tuberculosis in Australia, 1788–1950', *Historical Studies*, 20 (1983): 439–461.
Russel Ward, *The Australian Legend*, Melbourne: Oxford University Press, 1978.

Richard Waterhouse, *The Vision Splendid, A Social and Cultural History of Rural Australia*, Fremantle: Curtin University Books, 2005.
Shearer West, *Fin de Siècle: Art and Society in an Age of Uncertainty*, London: Bloomsbury, 1993.
Hayden White, *Tropics of Discourse, Essays in Cultural Criticism*, Baltimore: Johns Hopkins University Press, 1985.
Michael Wilding, *Studies in Classic Australian Fiction*, Sydney: Sydney Studies, 1997.

Index

Aborigines 12, 16, 39–40, 125, 135–54
   and Commonwealth and state
      law 146–7
acceleration 3–4, 8, 13, 17, 22–4, 42, 60,
      107, 122, 133, 179
Active Service Brigade 158, 162, 164,
      165
Afghan Cameleers 28, 29
Aliens Act (Britain) 6
Amalgamated Shearer's Union 24
anarchism 2, 36, 38, 163, 164
Andrews, John Arthur 38, 163, 164
Anthony, Susan B. 92
Archibald, J. F. 17, 26, 116
Art Nouveau 2, 69, 73, 77, 116, 137
Asquith, Herbert 129
Assmann, Aleida 102
Atlantis 143, 164
Australasian Secular Association 44
Australian Church 88, 121
Australian Labor Party 50, 59, 99, 103,
      104, 106, 122, 126, 137, 173, 178,
      181
Australian Magazine 69, 72–3
Australian National Defence
      League 127, 128
Australian Socialist League 43, 45, 54
Australian Town and Country Journal 23
Australian Women's National League 89,
      105–6
Australian Woman's Sphere 90, 91
Australian Workers' Union 25, 32
   and Women's Division 50

Barrier Miner 55
Basedow, Herbert 142–3
Bates, Daisy 144
Baudelaire, Charles 67, 68, 76, 83
Bayly, Christopher 4, 7
Beale report into patent medicines
      131–2
Belich, James 24
Bellamy, Edward 37

Bergson, Henri 114
Besant, Annie 5, 54–5, 120, 158
Bhagavad Gita 109, 128–9, 133
Blake, William 67, 76, 79–81
Blavatsky, Helena Petrovna 120, 159–60
Bomford, Janette 89
Boomerang 18
Bourke 10, 16, 23, 28–9
   Dunlop Pastoral Station 23
   E. Rich & Co. 22–3
   Petrolia Boring Company 23
   Toorale Pastoral Station 22, 23, 30
Bradlaugh, Charles 158
Brady, Veronica 84
Brennan, Christopher 1, 2, 6, 11, 12, 14,
      63–86, 178, 179, 183
   and 'the Absolute' 65
   and Casuals Club 83
   Chant of Doom 178, 183
   and education 65–6
   'Musicopoematographoscope' 71, 72
   Poems 66, 83–4, 183
   and Romanticism 79
   and Stéphane Mallarmé 71–2
   and Symbolism 68–70
   'Symbolism in Nineteenth Century
      Literature' lectures 11, 67, 70,
      75–82
   Towards the Source: XXI Poems 70
   'The Wanderer' 11, 64–5, 75
Brereton, John Le Gay 72
Bulletin 17, 19, 25–7, 35, 40, 72, 74,
      123–4, 184
Bunny, Rupert 69
Burrow, John 145

Caesar's Column 36, 37
Caffyn, Katherine Mannington 45
   The Yellow Aster 45–6
Campbell-Bannerman, Henry 112, 129
Carnegie, Andrew 37
Carnot, Sadi 38
Carpenter, Edward 3

Catholicism   31, 65, 67, 117, 118, 157, 158, 179
Clark, Axel   82
Clemenceau, Georges   115
Combes, Emile   117
Commonwealth Franchise Act. *See* women's suffrage
compulsory military training   6, 127
Conder, Charles   3, 9, 20, 46, 70, 177–8
  Hot Wind   9, 20–1, 46, 177
  Mirage   9, 21, 70
  While Daylight Lingers   3, 9, 10, 21
Conrad, Joseph   118
conscription (First World War)   179
Cook, James   153
Crivelli, Marcel   109, 110, 116
Cutcliffe Hyne, C. J.   143

Daley, Victor   69
Dandona, Jessica M.   3
Darwinism   1, 12, 13, 138, 139, 145, 165, 174, 175
Deakin, Alfred   1, 4, 6, 8, 12, 13, 109–34, 179–81
  and defence policy   125–8, 130, 132–3
  and federation (Australia)   6, 113
  and French influence   114–15
  and Greater Britain   6
  and Imperial Conference   111–12, 129
  and liberalism   111, 113, 115, 120, 129
  and nervous breakdown   12, 109–10, 122–5
  and New Protection   130–1
  as Prime Minister   110, 112, 122–3, 132
  and race   6, 125–7
  and reading   114
  and religion and spiritualism   120–1, 128–9
  and self-reflection   113, 132
defence policy   112–13, 118, 126–31, 133
degeneration   8, 11, 34, 38, 68, 77, 128, 138, 145, 165, 175
de Gourmont, Remy   115
de L'Isle Adam, Villiers   68, 81
Desmond, Arthur   38, 163
Dibbs, George   37, 158
Dodd, Tommy   162, 164

Donnelly, Ignatius   37
Doomed Race Theory   144
Draper, John   165
Dreyfus Affair   118
Dwyer, Annie   1, 158, 160–1, 175, 182
  and boarding house management   163–4
  and care of Daniel Dwyer   171–2
Dwyer, Daniel   155–7, 161, 167, 168, 170, 171, 174–5, 182
  and Central Methodist Mission   168–9
  and tuberculosis   171–5
Dwyer, Elizabeth   157, 160, 161, 163, 164, 166–8
Dwyer, Henry   157, 160, 161, 166–8
Dwyer, John   1, 8, 13, 14, 55, 155–75, 181–3
  and Active Service Brigade   158–9, 165
  and Christianity   156–8
  and Darwinism   165
  and family life   160–2, 165–6, 173, 175
  and life in London   157–8
  and Theosophy and the Occult   157, 159–60, 162, 164
  and unemployment activism   162, 164, 181–2
Dwyer, Kate   89
Dwyer, Timm Stephen   157, 166–8, 173

Edgeworth David, T. W.   132
Eliot, T. S.   14
equal pay for women   26, 47, 106
eugenics   2, 12, 144–5, 170–1

Faguet, Emile   115, 117–18, 124
Fin de Siècle, definition and characteristics   1, 42, 47, 67
  Australia and global *fin de siècle*   5–8
  biographical research   3–4, 9
  historiography   5
Fisher, Andrew   133
Flowers, Fred   173
Forrest, John   110, 122–3
Foster, R. F.   3
Fox, Frank   110, 116
France, cultural influence in Australia   2, 114, 116

freedom of contract   24
Free Trade Party   101, 103, 106, 110, 112
Fritzsche, Peter   94
Fuller, Loïe   77, 116

Gallé, Emile   3
Gallipoli landing   184
Galton, Francis   13, 138, 171
Gauguin, Paul   71
Gault, Arthur   170, 174
General Labourers' Union   29, 30, 53–4
globalization   6, 7, 14, 17, 25, 59, 101, 130
Golding, Anne   89
Golding, Belle   89
Goldstein, Vida   1, 6, 8, 11, 14, 87–108, 179–80
   and Christian Science   88, 180
   and equal pay for women   91, 98, 106
   and family life   88
   and International Woman Suffrage Conference   92–3
   and National Council of Women   90, 92
   and New Woman   89, 95–7
   and 1903 Senate Campaign   94–104
   and 1910 Senate Campaign   104–5
   and party politics   99–102
   and penal reform   90
   and political activism and social reform   89–91
   and tariff protection   98
   and White Australia   98–100
Gonne, Maud   120
Gordon, Jim   30, 35, 40
Green, Dorothy   82–3

Haeckel, Ernst   146
Hague Peace Conferences   92
Haldane, Richard   128–30
Heidelberg School   9, 21
Henry, Emile   38
Henry Lawson Memorial   185–6
Hermes   64–7, 74
Hermetic Order of the Golden Dawn   120
Heterotopia   149, 151
Higgins, Henry Bournes   98, 100, 106
Hobart Carnival   151
Holmes, Rachel   3

Howitt, A. W.   144
Hughes, William Morris   124, 179, 185
Hummer   25, 29, 37, 43, 52
Huxley, T. H.   13, 139, 145, 165
Huysmans, Joris-Karl   68

Ibsen, Henrik   45, 47, 119
Immigration Restriction Act   6, 60, 98, 101, 126, 133, 146
Imperial Conference (1907)   109–13, 129
imperial federation   6, 112–13, 122
Independent Order of Good Templars   54, 158
industrial arbitration   98, 106, 112
industrial disputes   24, 33
   Broken Hill strike   24, 37
   Homestead strike (USA)   37
industrial modernity   2, 4, 7, 17, 37, 122
industrial revolution. *See* second industrial revolution
International Council of Women   92
International Women's Peace Congress   180
International Woman Suffrage Conference   92
Irvine, William   132
Irving, Helen   146

Jackson, Holbrook   177
James, Henry   119
James, William   78, 114, 120
Japan-Russo War   85, 113
Jervis, John   7–8, 113
Joyce, Patrick   9

Killen, Andreas   8, 24, 111
Koselleck, Reinhart   3
Kropinyerie, Matthew   148, 150

labour movement   24–6, 100, 101
labour press   24–6, 43, 52
Lambert, George   185
Lane, William   10, 18, 32, 57–8
Lankester, Edwin Ray   13, 138, 145
Lawson, Henry   1, 4, 8–10, 13–42, 44, 74, 163, 184–6
   and 'Australian Legend'   21–2
   'Baldy Thompson'   26
   and Bourke   29–30, 40–1

'The Bush Undertaker' 9, 19, 39–40
'The Cant and Dirt of Labor
   Literature' 32
'The Drover's Wife' 19
'In a Dry Season' 27
'The Dying Anarchist' 38–9
and early career 18
'Faces in the Street' 18
'Hungerford' 40
'In a Wet Season' 40–1
and labour movement 26, 32
'The Leader of the Future' 36–7
'Mitchell: a Character Sketch', 'Mitchell
   Doesn't Believe in the Sack' 35–6
My Army, O, My Army! 184, 185
and non-fiction sketches 26
'On the Edge of a Plain' 20
'The Shearers' 22
Short Stories in Verse and Prose 25
'A Song of the Republic' 18
'Stragglers' 26, 33–5
and Toorale Pastoral Station 22, 30
'The Union Buries its Dead' 31–2, 39
While the Billy Boils 25, 41
Lawson, Louisa 18, 45
   Dawn 43, 45
Leadbeater, Charles 120
Ledger, Sally 13, 100, 138, 145
Lemuria 142, 143, 164
Liberalism 2, 4, 89, 99, 111, 112, 118, 146
Liberal Party 105
Liberal Protectionist Party 103, 105, 106, 110, 116, 120
Lindsay, Norman 2–3, 126, 128
Lloyd George, David 129
Lombroso, Cesare Lombroso 55
Lone Hand 2–3, 26, 69, 110, 114, 116, 117, 125, 137
Long, Sydney 69, 72, 73
Luckhurst, Roger 13, 138, 145
Lyne, William 122–3, 125

MacCallum, Mungo 75, 77
McCrae, Hugh 69
MacDonald, J. Ramsay 6
McGregor, Russell 144
Mackennal, Bertram 69
Maeterlinck, Maurice 115

Mallarmé, Stéphane 6, 67, 71–2, 76, 82, 83
Manet, Édouard 71
Mannix, Daniel 179
Marconi, Guglielmo 5, 142, 165
Margarey, Susan 45
Marshall, Gail 11, 103
Marx, Eleanor 3, 45
mateship 21, 22, 26, 32
Maudsley, Henry 165
Melleuish, Greg 67
Mercer, Edward 119, 121
Methodism 155, 158, 167, 168, 182–3
Mill, John Stuart 91
Milner, Alfred 122
Moore, William 177
Moréas, Jean 68
Morgan, John Pierpont 85
Morris, William 59, 61
Munch, Edvard 71
Murdoch, Walter 115

National Council of Women 90, 92
Naval Review 1907 134
Neurasthenia 111, 124
New Australia 10, 57
New Physics 138, 141–2
New Protection 119, 130–2
New Woman 2, 3, 8–9, 11, 43, 46–7, 55–6, 61–2, 89, 97, 119–20
Ngarrindjeri 136
   and Hobart Carnival 151–3
   and Point McLeay Mission 148–9
Nietzsche, Friedrich 78
Nordau, Max 8, 37, 38, 77
'Novalis' (Friedrich von Hardenberg) 68, 76, 79
Nuenonne Clan 153

occult 13, 120, 143, 156–7, 159, 165
Ó Donghaile, Deaglan 3
O'Dowd, Bernard 69
O'Reilly, Dowell 72
Osterhammel, Jürgen 17

pastoral industry 22–3, 29–30
Pastoralists' Union 24
Pearson, Karl 144, 171
Piper, Leonora 120

Pockley, Frank Antill 170–1
Poincaré, Raymond 115
Point McLeay Mission (Raukkan) 136, 147–50
Porter, Roy 4
Praed, Rosa Campbell 159
protectionism 6, 98, 101, 112, 119, 125, 129–32. *See also* New Protection

race 6, 28–9, 51–2, 61, 98–100, 116, 125–6, 130, 137, 144–7, 154, 165
Ravachol 37–8
Reid, George 48, 68, 101, 110, 163
religion 12, 65, 67, 88, 118, 120, 121, 135–6, 153–4, 157–8, 167
Rhodes, Cecil 68
Roberts, Lord Frederick 127
Roberts, Tom 9, 70
Roe, Jill 157
romanticism 67, 68, 79
Roosevelt, Theodore 89, 119
Ross, Ellen 160
Rothenstein, John 178
Rowbotham, Sheila 3, 8, 54, 97
Rowse, Tim 12
Ruskin, John 91
Ryan, Lyndall 151

Said, Edward 11, 75
Sandow, Eugene 68
Schreiner, Olive 119
science 13, 138
Scott, Rose 48, 89
second industrial revolution 2, 7, 16–17, 22, 42, 101, 106–7, 111
Seeley, John 6
Shackleton, Ernest 132
Shaw, George Bernard 45, 119
Shiel, Matthew Phipps 127
Sinclair, McIntyre 170
Slattery, Thomas 158, 162
social Darwinism. *See* Darwinism
Social Democratic Federation (Australia) 57
Social Democratic Federation (Britain) 55, 158
socialism 13, 32, 44, 45, 49, 54, 55, 57, 104, 106, 119, 160
Souter, David Henry 69, 72–4, 116, 137
South, William Garnet 147, 149, 151

Spearritt, Katie 44
Spencer, Herbert 13, 138, 165
Spencer, Walter Baldwin 144
spiritualism 12, 13, 120, 121, 157, 184
Stephens, A. G. 73, 75
Stevens, Bertram 83, 84
Streeton, Arthur 9, 70
Strong, Charles 88, 121
Summerfield, Rose (Rose Cadogan from 1899) 1, 4, 8, 10, 11, 13, 43–62, 182
  and Bourke 49–52
  and early life and social activism 44
  and Independent Order of Good Templars 54
  and Jack Cadogan 59–60
  and labour press 52
  and 'Master and Man' address 44, 50–1, 57
  and New Australia 57–60
  and New Woman 46–7, 55–6, 60–2
  and race 51–2
  and Womanhood Suffrage League (NSW) 48, 54
Sydney Mail 23, 28–9
Symbolism 2, 11, 21, 67–9, 71–2, 115, 116

Taplin, George 148, 150
Tarde, Gabriel 118
Tasmania 151–3
Teich, Mikulas 4
temperance 43, 44, 54, 55, 57, 94, 157, 158, 167
Theosophy 5, 13, 55, 120, 157, 159–60, 164
Thomson, William (Lord Kelvin) 7
Tinayre, Marcel 119–20
Tolstoy, Leo 47, 128
Toulouse-Lautrec, Henri de 177
Truganini 152
Truth 70, 125
tuberculosis 170–1, 174
Tyson, James 31

Unaipon, David 1, 7, 8, 12–14, 135–54, 184
  and Christianity 135–6, 153–4
  and evolutionary theory 145–6
  and Herbert Basedow 142–3
  and Hobart Carnival 151–3

as Indigenous Spokesperson 145–6
and inventions 139–41
and *Legendary Tales of the Australian Aborigines* 12, 184
and 1913 Royal Commission on Aborigines 147–9
and Point McLeay Mission 135–6, 150
and science 138
and spiritualism 143–4

Verlaine, Paul 71
Victorian Women's Federation 101
Vitalism 78, 114
von Arnim, Elizabeth 120

Waite, Arthur 120
Waterfall sanatorium 172–3
Watson, John Christian 110, 126, 137
Webb, Beatrice 97
West, Shearer 8, 14, 95
Whistler, James McNeill 71
White, Hayden 178
White Australia. *See* Immigration Restriction Act; race

Wilde, Oscar 3, 46, 81, 177, 178
Wolstenholme, Maybanke 48, 49, 89
Womanhood Suffrage League (NSW) 48
  Commonwealth Franchise Act 87–8
Woman Voter 104, 180
Women's Christian Temperance Union 94, 103
Women's equality 47–9, 61–2, 88–91
Women's Federal Political Association 94, 104
Women's Liberal League 89
Women's Peace Army 180
Women's Political and Educational League 89
Women's Progressive Association 89
Women's Suffrage 88–9, 94
  and Commonwealth Franchise Act 87–88
Worker [Brisbane] 182, 184
Worker [Sydney] 25, 36, 38, 43, 48, 49, 52, 56–9

Yeats, William Butler 77, 81, 84, 120

www.ingramcontent.com/pod-product-compliance
Lightning Source LLC
Chambersburg PA
CBHW062144300426
44115CB00012BA/2033